POWER TO WIN

Power to Win

The **Living Wage Movement** in Aotearoa New Zealand

LYNDY McINTYRE

OTAGO UNIVERSITY PRESS
Te Whare Tā o Te Wānanga o Ōtākou

For Rebecca Nyakuong Kuach and all courageous workers who stand up and tell their stories to build power to win the living wage.

Contents

Preface	Ko Te Awa Kairangi tōku awa	7
Chapter 1	The idea: 2011	13
Chapter 2	At the grassroots: 2012	35
Chapter 3	Building blocks: 2013	53
Chapter 4	The game changer: 2013	73
Chapter 5	Trailblazing: 2014	93
Chapter 6	Organising everywhere: 2015	107
Chapter 7	People vs Institution: 2015	121
Chapter 8	The power of assembly: 2016	133
Chapter 9	Lives transformed: 2017	151
Chapter 10	New beginnings: 2018	169
Chapter 11	No permanent friends, no permanent enemies: 2019	185
Chapter 12	Mā te wā: 2020 and on	207
Postscript	February 2024	232
Appendix	Comparison between New Zealand living wage and minimum wage, 2012–23	235
Timeline		236
Acronyms		240
Interviews		241
Notes		242
Acknowledgements		250
Index		252

Preface

Ko Te Awa Kairangi tōku awa

Beside Te Awa Kairangi Hutt River, and just north of Pōmare, is the entrance to Stokes Valley, where I spent the first 13 years of my life. My friends at Stokes Valley School came from a wide range of families. In Kamahi Street, by the bus barns and the top shops, lived a ship's captain, a dentist and a dustman. After school, we played at each other's homes. Some were flasher than others, but they were all comfy, warm and dry. We shared meals together. We went to the flicks at the Bug House on Saturday afternoon down on Main Road, past the fire station and the butcher's shop. To my young eyes, it looked as if everyone had enough; as if all families did things together. In my Stokes Valley world, where the mums stayed at home and every dad had a job, it seemed as if everyone could afford the fare, the sports gear or the movie ticket.

How different my old home is now. The Hutt Valley is a place of huge disparity, with extreme wealth and poverty. I took a drive up Stokes Valley recently. The streets are worn out and beaten up, and the valley is home to the families of low-paid workers who must weigh up what the family can do without.

Lemo Lemo lives with his wife on Stokes Valley Road, not far from Kamahi Street. He's 62 and works two jobs to pay the bills and to support his extended family. Although their flat is small and basic and doesn't feel the sun until late in the day, the rent is $400 a week. Lemo is a long way from his village, Safotu, on the Sāmoan island of Savai'i. Stokes Valley is home now, but with a full-time labouring job on road works plus a cleaning job for four hours, five nights a week, Lemo scarcely sees it. He rises at 5am and travels to Wellington in company transport for his labouring job. After being dropped home at the end of the day, he drives himself back to the city to clean at Victoria University before arriving home again after 11.30pm. Life is 'work, home, work, home, work'. When he's 65, he says, he'll 'carry on'.

The fifties and sixties were a time of plentiful housing, near-zero unemployment and wages families could live on. In the Hutt Valley, car factories offered a bonus to staff who could get others to work with them for more than three months. Staff were bused in from other areas. Jobs were plentiful, and even the lowest-paid positions attracted allowances and penal rates for evening and weekend work.

Somewhere in the past 50 years, between my life in the valley and today, Aotearoa went from being one of the most equal countries in the OECD to one with pronounced inequality of incomes and wealth.[1] We see the results all around us.

Every evening, thousands of cleaners like Lemo Lemo leave their homes to clean through the night in the city. In Wellington, they come from outlying suburbs like Stokes Valley, Cannons Creek and Naenae. This invisible army travels by public transport when they can and by car if they can't; if that car breaks down on the way to work and there is no credit on their cellphone to ring the boss, they risk getting the sack.

They leave their families behind in cold substandard rentals with empty cupboards and piles of unpaid bills. Those who are parents may have crossed paths briefly with their partner to hand over the care of their children, or the kids are home alone. Most, but not all, of these cleaners are women. They are very likely to be Māori, Pacific or a new migrant.

In 1990 I started working as an organiser for the Northern Hotel and Hospital Workers Union, which, through amalgamations with other unions, became first the Service Workers Union of Aotearoa, then the Service and Food Workers Union, and later the union E tū. Our union's membership included three of the lowest-paid jobs in Aotearoa: cleaners, security guards and caregivers. In 2011 I returned to the Service and Food Workers Union as media officer and magazine editor, and met hundreds of low-paid workers with the same stories. I went into their homes and saw the reality of the working poor: families huddled under rugs in houses without heating, their couches threadbare, their fridges empty.

Union members had already been campaigning for years to change this. One of these, cleaner and union delegate Jaine Ikurere, after some 20 years of cleaning the prime minister's office was still working two jobs and putting in 50 hours a week to make ends meet. In October 2011 she and other parliamentary cleaners hosted a lunch for politicians, at which they told their stories. On the table in front of them they placed a meagre pile of groceries, the typical contents of a weekly shopping basket for a cleaner on

PREFACE

In October 2011, Parliament's cleaners invited politicians to hear their stories of life on low pay. Photo: SFWU archives

Parliamentary cleaner Mareta Sinoti outside her workplace, February 2013.
Photo courtesy of NZ Herald archive

the minimum wage. For Jaine, a pay rise would allow her to buy food, heat her home and buy birthday presents for her grandchildren.[2]

In May 2013 I visited cleaner Mareta Sinoti's house in Cannons Creek to prepare for an interview for the television current affairs programme, *Campbell Live*. The film crew wanted to follow Mareta and other cleaners as they worked through the night at Parliament. Mareta had two teenage sons, and her husband was unwell and unable to work. Mareta worked two jobs to support the family. Before her shift at Parliament, she cleaned the High Court in Molesworth Street, across the road from the Beehive, then, at midnight, after an hour's unpaid break, she joined other cleaners at the seat of power. They worked for the minimum wage with no extra pay to acknowledge the inhospitable hours.

In the cleaners' homes I heard story after story of working long hours to feed the family. At every visit I asked our members, 'What is your dream?' The answer was always the same: a better life for their children. In Mareta's house there was little furniture, but the walls were covered in family photos along with certificates and other evidence that the children were doing all right at school. Mareta wanted to buy rugby boots and other sports gear and pay for school trips: 'All the things we need to give our kids an equal chance.' Long hours and poverty-level income could not realise this dream; workers routinely missed parent-teacher appointments, and their children missed out on class trips and lunches.

Nearly five years later these cleaners finally won the pay rise they had campaigned for. On 18 December 2017, around 20 leaders from faith groups, community organisations and unions gathered at Parliament to hear the Speaker of the House announce that parliamentary cleaners had been awarded the living wage – a pay rise of around 30 percent.

The outcome was the legacy of the hundreds of cleaners who had campaigned tirelessly. It came too late for Jaine Ikurere, and Mareta Sinoti, her children now grown, was by this time cleaning the National Library across the road from Parliament, but it was their legacy too. For the cleaners who came after them, the increase was transformative. At Parliament in December 2017, E tū member and cleaner Eseta Ailaoa told workers and supporters that at last she'd be able to save money to take her children on a holiday.

The community leaders who gathered at Parliament in December 2017 were celebrating a victory for Living Wage Movement Aotearoa NZ. This is the story of that movement.

PREFACE

Author's note

Power to Win tells the story of the Living Wage Movement in Aotearoa. It is a story that I lived as I travelled throughout the country and joined grassroots networks and actions from Bluff to Auckland and beyond as a leader, an activist and a supporter. I was present at many, but not all, of the events recounted in this book, including the original 2011 event at Parliament that highlighted the impact of low pay on the lives of parliamentary cleaners.

These stories changed the way we talk about wages in Aotearoa; they changed the lives of thousands of workers and their families; and they changed the social justice activism of organisations. Here are the brave moments I have witnessed of workers telling their stories. Here are the battles I've fought with others and the exhilaration we have shared together.

The history of the Living Wage Movement would fill many books: we are a story-telling movement, a story-telling culture. This is my personal story of Living Wage Movement Aotearoa NZ.

A note on sources

From 2020 I conducted over 40 interviews for this book, mainly face to face, but also by Zoom, telephone and email. Many of the workers' stories are taken from speeches written for living wage events and delegations. Those of Emma and Peniata Endermann, Kelly Belcher and Ika Hiko are from a *Campbell Live* Television New Zealand series broadcast in May 2012. Some were part of a photo exhibition highlighting issues of low pay for refugee background workers. Others shared their stories with media and in union publications.

CHAPTER 1

The idea: 2011

'I've got an idea.'
JOHN RYALL, Service and Food Workers Union

The problem of poverty pay

Why are cleaners' wages so low in New Zealand? It hasn't always been this way. Before 1991, cleaners were paid well above the minimum wage. There were penal rates for night and weekend work, living costs were lower and housing was more affordable. Union membership sat at around 50 percent. It was a world of national awards and an arbitration court where, in the mid-1980s, commercial cleaners won a pay increase of nearly 30 percent.

It wasn't all rosy before 1991. From the late 1970s, inflation was on the rise and unemployment was increasing. But while inflation reduced the value of real wages, most New Zealand workers in the private sector were guaranteed the pay and conditions of union-negotiated national awards. Under state service pay-setting arrangements, unions and the State Services Commission or its health equivalent would negotiate. To give their agreements effect, the relevant ministers issued 'determinations'. Union negotiations with employers in the private and public sectors were backed by an arbitration system, and workers enjoyed a raft of legal protections.

Cocooned in over 100 years of national employment agreements, unions were slow to appreciate that changes which began to occur in the 1980s would eventually blow this protectionist system away. The National government's introduction of voluntary unionism in 1983, although quickly reversed when a Labour government returned to power, was a shot over the bow. Another warning was the dismantling of compulsory arbitration in 1984. But it was the removal of tariffs, the corporatisation of public services and the market-driven economic policies of the late 1980s that left the structure of worker protections in a vulnerable state.

Into this environment, on 15 May 1991, a bomb was dropped on New Zealand's industrial landscape. The newly elected National government pushed through a radical new industrial relations law, the Employment Contracts Act 1991 (ECA). The Act opened up wage bargaining to enable employers to bypass unions and impose lower pay and conditions on individuals and groups of workers. Although union leaders were aware of what was to come with a change of government, the union movement lacked the unity or power to oppose National's plan to liberalise employment law in favour of employers, and was ill-equipped to organise opposition.

After the passage of the ECA, cleaners' pay rates spiralled downwards. Penal rates disappeared and the other protections offered by union membership and collective bargaining were swept away. Contractors had always dominated the commercial cleaning sector, albeit regulated by a national award. Now they spread rapidly into schools and hospitals as a wave of outsourcing swept across the industry. The contract-for-services model favoured the lowest bidders and encouraged many to shave as much as possible off their wages bill. A cleaner could lose their job every time a contract changed hands, and many did. For most, the new 'normal' meant permanent financial insecurity. The story was the same for other low-paid workers. Union membership plummeted to around 12 percent of the private sector workforce.

The advent of the ECA led to many amalgamations of New Zealand unions. The day before the Act became law on 15 May 1991, five of the regionally based Hotel and Hospital Workers unions amalgamated with four regional cleaners unions to become the Service Workers Union of Aotearoa (SWU). In 1997 the SWU amalgamated with the United Food and Beverage Workers Union to become the Service and Food Workers Union (SFWU). From the 1990s, the SWU and then the SFWU searched for ways to win back power and decent wages for members. The search would span 20 years.

The SWU was one of the first unions to prepare for change by embracing a new union organising model in the early 1990s. This contrasted with the existing servicing model, which was all about paid union officials looking after their members with little involvement of the members themselves. The organising model focused on member activism, supporting union members who were leaders in their workplaces and prioritising the recruitment of new members by others who were already part of the union. But while activism and member engagement grew with the adoption of the organising model, pay rates did not.

Another of the union's responses to the ECA was to campaign for job security for vulnerable workers whose incomes depended on their contractor winning a tender. SFWU's 'transfer of undertakings' campaign sought to win job protection rights for vulnerable workers such as cleaners, hospital orderlies and catering and laundry workers as they transferred from one contractor to the next and from one employer to the next. The campaign, launched in 1998, was led by Annie Newman, who would later lead the Living Wage Movement. Six years later, a Labour government passed an amendment to the Employment Relations Act 2000, the labour law that replaced the ECA, embedding these protections for vulnerable workers. 'Part 6A' made a difference to job security, but did not address low pay.

After a new Labour government was elected in 1999, SFWU and other unions sought political support to reverse the impact of the ECA and return bargaining power to low-paid workers. But the changes that did eventuate were insufficient to return to unions the power to achieve large wage increases in bargaining. In 2008, cleaning contractors and the Labour government agreed on a set of standards to guide the tendering process via an agreement between the government, the SFWU, Property Council New Zealand and the Building Service Contractors of New Zealand.[1] The agreement supported collective bargaining and excluded companies that paid less than accepted industry-level wage rates. These rates were already so low, however, that the impact of this agreement was minuscule.

After the advent of the ECA, the union ramped up industrial action. SFWU members participated regularly in stop-works, pickets and strikes. In the aged care sector, where collective bargaining was barely making a dent in wage rates, caregivers took strike action in an attempt to force employers to pass on increases provided by the government funding agencies. In this the strikes were successful, but pay rates remained stubbornly low.

No matter how hard SFWU members organised and took action, they simply did not have the necessary power to win decent pay and conditions. It was time for the union to find a different way to shift poverty pay rates. SFWU leadership decided to look to the community to build that power.

Searching for solutions

John Ryall, national secretary of SFWU, was a long-time community activist. His roots went back to the early 1970s when he was involved with the Young

Christian Students movement. In his time the movement grew to around a thousand secondary school students in the Wellington region. After leaving school, John trained as a journalist and then headed to Victoria University of Wellington, where he was employed part time by the Catholic Education Office to maintain the organising efforts of the Young Christian Students and spread social justice values on campus. He was also editor of the university's student magazine, *Salient*. Politically, John was involved in organised opposition to apartheid by Halt All Racist Tours (HART), and actively opposed the Vietnam War and the visits of nuclear-powered or -armed ships. 'These movements were wider than just our small groups,' he recalls. 'With HART and the anti-apartheid movement, effort was made to involve churches and local community organisations. We went to those organisations and talked about linking their values to those of the anti-apartheid movement.'

In university holidays, John worked in car plants in the Hutt Valley. In 1976 he started working full time at New Zealand Motor Corporation in Petone where he found the union ineffective and inactive. He wasn't alone in wanting to shake things up. With delegates from other local motor plants, including Robert Reid and Peter Cranney, and supported by Wellington Trades Council president Pat Kelly, the young activist visited Hutt Valley worksites to organise opposition to the Robert Muldoon-led National government and its agenda of a wage freeze and tax cuts for the wealthy.

John learnt union activism at the plant, and in 1982 he took an organising job in the Wellington office of the Hotel and Hospital Workers Union. Here he found a different workforce, in fast food and hospitals, with no culture of direct action – insecure groups of workers who could be replaced easily. Many hospital workers were employed by contractors: 'Every time a contract changed, we had to organise support from their communities, their local church ministers and priests, and do whatever we could to make sure these workers were taken over by the new employer with no loss of terms and conditions.'

John Ryall was elected national secretary of the SFWU in 2005. After 30 years of union involvement, he understood the impact of poverty pay rates. Always passionate about finding solutions, he was more interested in finding a way to improve workers' lives than in his own position and power.

One strategy adopted by the union was to take legal cases to test the law and find ways to lift members' incomes. The union's first successful legal challenge was known as the 'sleepover case'. Workers who stayed overnight in premises where they were employed to care for people with disabilities received less than the minimum wage; the successful case delivered full pay for these workers. Another taken by SFWU to address the low pay of members was an equal pay case for rest-home workers, widely known as the 'Kristine Bartlett case' after the SFWU member it was taken for. The argument that caregivers in rest homes were underpaid because they were predominantly women was successful, and Kristine went on to become New Zealander of the Year and was awarded a Companion of the New Zealand Order of Merit for services to equal pay advocacy. Peter Cranney, John's comrade from the motor plants, was now an employment lawyer, and the pair were the driving force behind these cases, which lifted the incomes of over 60,000 care and support workers.

Along with other unions, the SFWU was committed to a political strategy of pushing politicians to improve employment law for the lowest paid. But any law changes rested with the government of the day, and those wheels turned very slowly. John had given up putting pressure on contractors, who were themselves pawns in the race-to-the-bottom tendering system. 'We were looking to achieve things for workers who had no direct power to influence the companies and organisations who funded the contracts that provided their work,' he recalls. 'Although the workers themselves had no links to the source of funding for contracts, often other citizens, church-goers and community organisations did have those links.'

A new kind of campaign

In 1990 I was employed in my first union job as an organiser for the Northern Hotel and Hospital Workers Union, and from 1993 I worked for various unions in New Zealand and briefly in Australia. In the early eighties I had been a compositor on printing sites and a Printers Union delegate at a range of newspapers, and had witnessed collective power on the job: when the typesetters and compositors downed tools on deadline day in support of our co-worker taking time off to pick up her daughter from school, we won. My years as a young mother in the Aro Valley had also taught me the power of collective action: when Aro Valley mothers campaigned for a new hall for our preschool, the hall was built. Community action united diverse groups around common ground; united communities and united workers had power.

In 2011 I took up a media and communications role with SFWU. Our strategy was to put our efforts into giving members a voice to tell the stories that exposed the reality of lives on low pay, and to build broad community support to change that reality.

Petone was SFWU's Wellington base. John Ryall and I were early starters and would begin the day by discussing ideas over coffee. One morning, John spoke the words he said so often: 'I've got an idea.' He had been thinking about the biggest issue facing SFWU's members. No matter how hard they worked to win pay rises, how staunch they were, how well they organised on the job, they always came out with pitifully small increases that kept them in poverty wages. John described a new kind of campaign that he and his wife, Muriel Tunoho, had encountered in London five years earlier.

Like John, Muriel had roots as a community activist. With Tainui and Raukawa affiliations, she was from a whānau of six children; her mother was from a family of 18. Muriel's values were influenced by her early home life in Petone. 'My life was located in the whānau,' she recalls. 'The values of aroha and manaakitanga were very strong. There was always a pot of kai on the stove. We always had visitors and cousins or aunties staying.' Her father worked at Odlins timber mill on the Petone foreshore. There were plenty of jobs, although not all were well paid. The family lived in a house provided by the company but it wasn't flash, and every year Muriel's mother papered the walls to keep out the southerly that blew across the harbour. But while living standards were low, their values of whānau and looking out for others were strong.

Muriel was the only one of her siblings to leave school with a qualification: one subject in school certificate. She remembers her parents' pride: 'I felt like I'd won the lottery.' Muriel's mother was on a mission to find her a good job, and after a stint in a jeans factory, Muriel became a teller at the Bank of New Zealand and went on to be a pay clerk at the local council.

Activism in opposition to the 1981 Springbok tour of New Zealand brought John Ryall and Muriel Tunoho together. Their son Anaru was born in 1988 and Taneora a few years later. They were a union family, and Muriel recalls taking a very young Taneora to an SFWU picket line at Romanos Pizzas in Lower Hutt. Joining the local mothers' group opened Muriel's eyes to her own community, and when a coordinator's role came up at a community house she took it on. Muriel was active in the Community Services

Union (CSU), which later became part of SFWU, and she organised a collective agreement for workers employed in community houses.

Muriel's experience of unions began to intersect with her te ao Māori values. She worked with union organiser Bella Pardoe (Rongowhakaata; Ngāti Porou), who was passionate about organising Māori union members. Bella had also grown up in a large whānau, in a small and predominantly Māori community outside Gisborne. Some years later, as an NZEI Te Riu Roa (New Zealand Educational Institute) advocate, she would become a leader in the Living Wage Movement in her community in Porirua.

In 2006 Muriel accompanied John on a trip to the United Kingdom. John had a grant from the Industrial Relations Foundation to look at tendering in Britain's public hospitals, a follow-up to a study he'd done 20 years earlier. In London they stayed with a couple who worked for the public sector union, UNISON. Their host, Michael Walker, introduced them to Deborah Littman, a Canadian woman employed as a community organiser by UNISON. She worked with organisations that had an interest in workers' issues but were outside the union, including one group called London Citizens Workers Centre (LCWC), an organisation funded by churches, unions and local authorities to support migrant workers to stand up for their rights.

Deborah had been involved in campaigning for a living wage since 2001, initially with the East London Communities Organisation (TELCO). Like SFWU in Aotearoa, TELCO was looking for ways to address the low pay that plagued its communities. Its campaigns were aimed at winning a wage that meant more than just survival, one that meant workers and their families could live in dignity and participate in society. The TELCO living wage campaigns were initially in East London hospitals, where UNISON had members, and in the financial centres of Canary Wharf and the central city, where low-paid cleaners were not part of any union.

TELCO became a chapter of the community alliance London Citizens, which brought together churches, mosques, synagogues, schools, student groups, unions and other grassroots organisations from across London. 'We needed an entity workers could join to bring them into London Citizens and allow us to deal with employers on their behalf while we found an appropriate union to take them on,' explains Deborah. 'So we set up the London Citizens Workers Centre.' LCWC helped workers to document their stories and challenge employers in hospitality, finance and other non-union sectors.

The Transport and General Workers Union and UNISON were supporting London Citizens to organise workers. Deborah invited John and Muriel to a meeting at the Transport and General Workers Union to see the work LCWC was doing. Neil Jamieson, the London Citizens convenor, opened the gathering of around 30 people. Then young organisers from migrant communities, mostly from Eastern Europe, South America and the Philippines, took over and supported groups of migrant workers to tell their stories. These were marginalised workers that unions weren't reaching: cleaners, hotel housekeeping staff and others employed by contractors and subcontractors. People spoke of their campaigns, which were all about organising around working lives. They told stories of racism and exploitation, of having their wages cut and of cleaning contractors changing. A chorus of different languages followed as workers rehearsed a role play in preparation for ambushing their employers to demand payment of unpaid wages. They were planning an action at the Hilton London Metropole Hotel, where LCWC was campaigning for migrant housekeeping workers employed through agencies. The workers had tried to engage with hotel management over the housekeeping workers' pay and conditions, but management refused to meet. The workers devised a plan. They would assemble outside the hotel then go in one at a time and ask to see the manager. If the receptionist said the manager wasn't available, they would sit down and occupy the foyer. 'The Transport and General Workers Union had a long history of militant unionism, but the union seemed irrelevant to what was happening at the meeting,' John recalls. 'It was the community group that was organising the action.'

John was struck by the enthusiasm of these people – so keen on organising and with an energy not often found in the union movement – to carry out actions with workers who were some of the hardest to organise. 'In New Zealand we were struggling to organise cleaners and weren't even trying with housekeeping workers in hotels. I thought, there's something we need to look into further and get on board with.' Deborah describes the meeting as chaotic: 'a busy, crazy meeting because everything had to be translated back and forth'. She apologised to John and Muriel – who assured her that it was the best meeting they had attended in their time in London. So began a relationship that would continue over the years; Deborah and John began to correspond regularly, and Deborah updated him on developments in the living wage movement in London.

By this time Muriel was a community health worker at Hutt Union and Community Health Service, working closely with patients and their communities. 'To turn up at that hall and see the richness of cultural diversity ... it had a different feel. It wasn't a meeting dominated by union officials, but it had a clear kaupapa. Both of my worlds – of working in the community and being a union leader – came together.'

Time for change

The activist couple from Aotearoa New Zealand came home impressed with the outcomes of the London living wage campaigns. These included pay hikes for contract cleaners at Barclays Bank and a commitment from the mayor of London, Ken Livingstone, to adopt the living wage for the council's workforce, won at a public election forum at which London Citizens assembled nearly 2000 people from 60 of their member organisations. For London's lowest-paid workers, these wins demonstrated the success of building an alliance between faith groups, unions and community organisations.

London Citizens was part of a national organisation called Citizens UK, which in turn was part of the global movement the Industrial Areas Foundation (IAF), founded in Chicago by Saul Alinsky in 1940. The IAF's approach was to establish relationships between diverse communities and to build grassroots networks of faith and community organisations committed to creating local capacity and leadership for citizen-led action to achieve change.

From 2001, TELCO and London Citizens won big pay rises for workers through living wage campaigns directed at London's powerful finance sector, the Greater London Authority (GLA) and the workforce of the London Olympics. Over 10 years, Deborah Littman held leadership roles in many of these campaigns. After Mayor Ken Livingstone agreed to adopt the living wage at the Greater London Authority, Deborah worked with council staff on the implementation. 'At first they dragged their feet. It was a complex situation with multiple subcontractors. We were able to teach GLA how to get through implementation.' Deborah went on to spend over six years working for the IAF as lead organiser for Vancouver Metro Alliance. In time her experience with the living wage movement in the UK would prove invaluable to the New Zealand movement.

On his return to Aotearoa John Ryall wrote a report on the UK trip for the Industrial Relations Foundation. He highlighted the London meeting with Deborah and the possibilities he had taken away from it. He recalls:

> I was looking for legislative protections for workers, but what struck me was that there are other forms of leverage we can use. It was about how you give workers the ability to exercise collective power. This didn't rely on a union, although the union was there to support it. It relied on a wider group of people who, because of their influence in their communities, probably had more power than the union.

Inspired by the meeting and the success of London Citizens, John began to develop a vision for something similar in Aotearoa. SFWU would reach out to the community to build power together in a new campaign based around winning the living wage. Neither SFWU nor the collective union movement had a monopoly on caring about poverty and inequality; thousands of New Zealanders in faith groups and community organisations shared that concern. Union members themselves belonged to these groups, and in many cases their church and community were a greater part of their lives than the union. Surely working together could create the power to win.

With their backgrounds in community activism, this idea came naturally to John and Muriel. But for many in New Zealand's trade union movement, this was a very different approach and would challenge the sole focus on union power as the solution to workers' problems. A shift to an activist model that included partnership with community groups as well as the union would take commitment, courage and leadership. Getting it off the ground would require funding and a leader.

In 2005 SFWU had established a victory fund to enable the union to create campaigns to make a difference to members' lives and increase membership and influence. Over the next few years, the fund supported the union's organising work in aged care, schools, hospitals and community services: recruiting members and leaders and empowering workers to unite around campaigns to lift their pay and conditions.

John Ryall knew there was potential for a wider campaign that could unite the union, of which around two-thirds of members were low paid, their wages funded by organisations that were not their direct employer. In 2011 he put forward a proposal to the SFWU national executive to use the victory fund to set up a living wage campaign.[2]

Andrea Rushton was part of the union's senior leadership team and familiar with the living wage concept. She had also met Deborah Littman and attended one of London Citizens' assemblies: 'Deborah gave me quite a bit of the history of it, so I came into the meeting having experienced all that.' Andrea says John had an extraordinary ability to promote a new idea:

> He met with each of us and talked about the next big thing that was really going to make a difference to members on low wages. He planted the seed. His report contained something each of us had said and so we were already locked into it. I thought, you cunning bugger!

The SFWU executive backed the campaign, and John swiftly produced a paper called 'Campaigning for a Living Wage in 2012'.[3] It drew on a strategy borrowed from Australian trade unionist and Liquor, Hospitality and Miscellaneous Union (LHMU or 'Missos') leader Michael Crosby, who described the two parts of a campaign as the 'air war' and the 'ground war'. The air war was the public section that explained what a living wage is, how it is measured, what it means economically and the importance of allies: other unions, faith groups, media, social commentators, politicians, funders of services. The ground war covered the organisation of activities. 'We need more activists and more members,' John wrote. 'We need an involved membership, who have decided they cannot sit back and be victims but will step up to be part of the solution through the union.'[4] There would be a campaign team, but all the union's staff needed a clear understanding of the campaign so that they could explain its aims and objectives to anyone who asked.

In February 2012 SFWU employed Annie Newman as campaign director, tasked with leading the living wage campaign in partnership with the community. In 1986 Annie was waiting tables at a Wellington restaurant. Although the eighties was a time of compulsory unionism, in reality many workers in casualised sectors such as hospitality were not unionised. There she saw the powerlessness and exploitation of the hospitality workforce, and in that year became a delegate in the Hotel and Hospital Workers Union (HHWU). At the union's women's conference she met dedicated unionists fighting for low-paid hospitality workers and decided to get on board. In 1990 Annie joined the staff at the Wellington office of the HHWU as an educator, and by 1999 she was an Auckland-based assistant regional secretary of SFWU. She left to join the Department of Labour as a mediator in the years of the Helen Clark-led Labour government, when such a role promised to be part of progressive change for workers. In 2011, with a National government in place, the prospects of progressive industrial changes were grim. Annie told her union comrade John Ryall that she wanted to return to SFWU. John responded: 'I'm thinking of doing a living wage campaign. Would you be interested? If it is as good as the transfer of undertakings campaign, that would be great.'

Annie replied: 'It will be better.'

Up and running

Annie began to build the living wage campaign based on the principles adopted by London Citizens and on SFWU's history of working with allies in the community. Auckland-based SFWU staff members Jen Natoli and Fala Haulangi were allocated to work full time on the campaign. They were confident and experienced organisers.

Fala was deeply involved in the Tuvaluan and wider Pacific community. Born in Tuvalu, she was raised in Nauru and studied in Fiji. Her family came to Aotearoa in 1989 where her first job was picking strawberries. Within a couple of weeks she was 'having a go' at the boss because 'he was exploiting my people'. One of Fala's cousins was a cleaner at Television New Zealand, and Fala started cleaning there while studying at Auckland University of Technology (AUT). On the job she met the SFWU organiser, Sarah Helm. 'She came around talking to cleaners, as union organisers do,' recalls Fala. Sarah invited her to attend delegate training; there was a vacancy for a union organiser, and Fala got the job.

Keen to get the living wage campaign up and running, Annie didn't muck around. On 17 February 2012 around a dozen SFWU staff and member leaders, including myself, gathered for a planning day at Kōkiri Marae in the Hutt Valley. We considered options for developing the campaign, including a name and branding. In line with similar campaigns around the world, the living wage definition was agreed as 'a wage that allows workers and their families to not only survive but to participate in society'.

The meeting was full of hope for real change. We aimed to tap into the sense of fairness in New Zealand and seek support to redefine wages as the income necessary to lead a decent life. From the start, there was an expectation that this campaign would have wide public appeal. On a whiteboard we brainstormed what success would look like. Jen Natoli suggested it would be making the front page of the *NZ Herald* – and interestingly, that wasn't too far away. The new campaign would mobilise members, unionists and political and community allies in a coalition aimed at ending poverty pay rates.

Our goals were ambitious and wide reaching: to reduce poverty in New Zealand, raise awareness of broader factors such as housing and health, win a significant lift in wages for low-paid workers, change the lives of SFWU members and deliver membership growth for the union. What set this campaign apart was the goal to build long-term, sustainable community links and create a wider political movement. We planned to mobilise the union's members and delegates, to build a coalition of community groups committed to addressing poverty and inequality, and to mount a high-profile media campaign to win widespread support. Andrea Rushton was part of this group and already enthusiastic about the campaign: 'We really started drilling down and saying: how do we build this bigger, more significant alliance to move forward? And then it just started to build. The planning day was the impetus needed to get started.'

Work began on branding that would appeal to union members and staff, community partners, other unions and the media. Muriel Tunoho, now an elected leader in SFWU, recollects there was a strong desire for an appropriate logo with 'an indigenous flavour that grounded us here in Aotearoa'. The final design included a koru, the Māori symbol of new life, growth and strength. 'The koru depicted a new beginning, something quite significant that we were to launch,' Muriel recalls. 'We were putting our name to a movement that had the potential to transform not only workers' lives but also our society as we knew it.' With its identity confirmed, the new movement was ready to emerge.

In March 2012 Annie Newman ran a workshop on the living wage campaign with SFWU's national management team. On the agenda was a brainstorm of industrial targets within the union's membership. Work was also underway to identify partners – other unions, faith groups and community organisations with a shared concern about poverty and inequality and the capacity to mobilise people. The focus was on finding common ground and seeking commitment from like-minded organisations to a simple but powerful statement:

> A living wage is the income necessary to provide workers and their families with the basic necessities of life. A living wage will enable workers to live with dignity and to participate as active citizens in society. We call upon the government, employers and society as a whole to strive for a living

wage for all households as a necessary and important step in the reduction of poverty in New Zealand.

'We started having conversations with our community leaders about the living wage,' Fala Haulangi recalls. In the first few months of 2012, groups came together in Tāmaki Makaurau Auckland and Te Whanganui-a-Tara Wellington to talk, and plans for a national campaign launch in Auckland were soon underway. Before the launch, more than 50 organisations signed up in support of the statement, including Justice and Peace Commission Catholic Diocese of Auckland, Auckland Action Against Poverty, New Zealand Sikh Women's Association, Wesley Community Action, Working Women's Resource Centre, St Matthew-in-the-City, Congregational Christian Church of Samoa and a long list of unions. Their diversity shows the reach of the movement at this early stage.

While working on building a community alliance, Annie Newman also focused on her union role: to embed a new way of organising that was rooted in alliance building and community partnership. She had been employed to establish a campaign to solve persistent poverty wages among SFWU's members. She described the union's vision in an early project brief.[5] Top of the campaign goals were 'to win a significant lift in wages for identified groups of low-paid workers so they can provide for their basic needs and participate as active citizens in society'; and 'to grow the size of the SFWU in numbers, political power and influence'. Benefits to the union included 'new ways of generating sustainable membership' and 'a strong and invigorated activist base'.

There were clear community goals too: 'to build an enduring network of unions, churches, and community organisations around the values that underpin the living wage campaign, and to gain political commitment to an industrial, social and economic platform that will deliver a living wage'. As the campaign shifted quickly towards becoming a social movement, the union became increasingly committed to this new way of organising.

I was part of the SFWU campaign organising team alongside Jen Natoli and Fala Haulangi. Jen's focus was on the union members and Fala's was on building community partnerships. My own role was to coordinate the media to ensure that stories of members and their families were at the heart of our communication.

An industrial target was identified: Auckland University of Technology. A large number of low-paid unionised cleaners worked on the site, the vice-chancellor appeared supportive, and the Tertiary Education Union (TEU) and SFWU were keen. A political strategy was underway. Meetings had taken place with Auckland MPs and broad support was secured from New Zealand First, the Labour Party and the Green Party. A meeting with Auckland Council local board representatives confirmed an approach based on finding champion board members, public meetings and regular engagement.

Inside SFWU, we delivered education about the new campaign to delegates, members and staff; outside the union, we made contact with over 100 organisations, and meetings took place with faith groups, community organisations and unions in Auckland and Wellington. Those meetings were bearing fruit. The number of organisations signing on to the living wage statement was growing, and the new supporters were keen to explore how to work together.

The idea goes public

The living wage campaign was launched on 23 May 2012 at St Stephen's Presbyterian Church in Ponsonby, Auckland. Sometime beforehand, the organisers got wind of a rumour that the Labour Party was about to launch their own living wage campaign. The party appeared intent on capturing the brand. Annie jumped on the phone to Darien Fenton, a Labour MP and former SFWU national secretary, and the Labour Party backed off. The last thing the movement needed was to hitch our wagon to a political party.

On the day of the launch, an SFWU media release signalled 'the beginning of a new community movement, with a goal to end poverty wages and achieve a living wage for all workers'. There was standing room only in the modest church hall. The launch was reminiscent of an electrifying gospel meeting. The MC, Reverend Mua Strickson-Pua, also known as the Rapping Reverend, was dynamite. Dressed in a dog collar, lavalava and trainers, he leapt about with his microphone. When he invited Reverend Uesifili Unasa to join him for a foot-stamping version of *She Works Hard for the Money*, the Donna Summer anthem to low-paid female workers, everyone took to their feet, dancing and singing, and the room resounded with clapping and cheering.

Andrea Rushton was one of the organisers. She remembers an event that created excitement but also 'a bit of nervousness because we were still kind of strangers for a lot of people in the room. That event helped us move

New Zealand Council of Trade Unions president Helen Kelly launches the Living Wage Movement in Auckland, 23 May 2012. Photo: Simon Oosterman Beckers

forward in terms of "this is amazing, this is not just about unions". I was nervous but really uplifted by the experience.'

The speakers represented the three streams that became the backbone of the Living Wage Movement: faith, community and union. There was Darryl Evans from a budget support service in Ōtara, Auckland University chaplain Reverend Uesifili Unasa, Reverend Margaret Mayman, John Ryall and SFWU president Barbara Wyeth. Sitting in the front row, surrounded by low-paid workers, was the New Zealand Council of Trade Unions Te Kauae Kaimahi (NZCTU) president Helen Kelly, who officially launched the campaign with a powerful endorsement of the movement.

There was a great deal to achieve and the bar was high. The minimum wage was $13.50, compared to $15.51 in Australia (the equivalent of NZ$20 at that time). John Ryall had no doubt that this was going to change. 'We're here today because we care about poverty and inequality in Aotearoa New Zealand,' he told those assembled at the hall:

> We're here to launch a new and exciting movement for change. The SFWU represents many workers living on or just above the minimum wage. Many workers on these incomes work 60 to 70 hours a week to make ends meet. The living wage must enable workers to live a decent life and to avoid the chronic stress of poverty.

Service and Food Workers Union national secretary John Ryall at the launch of the Living Wage Movement. Photo: Simon Oosterman Beckers

He told the hall the union had looked overseas and seen how successful living wage campaigns had lifted low pay in the UK, US and Canada. 'But we knew we couldn't do it on our own. When I look at the people here today, I know we will succeed in our goal of addressing poverty through lifting low wages.'

Barbara Wyeth, a cook at North Shore Hospital in Auckland, introduced herself as a worker, a unionist, a mother and a grandmother who had been in low-paid jobs all her working life. 'I've struggled and I've seen many, many workers who are struggling to get by, working long hours just to put food on the table, and living with the stress of low pay,' she said. 'Our children and grandchildren should be able to participate in activities that children do without feeling the pressure and stress of their parents having to work 24/7.'

At the conclusion of the formalities, community leaders were invited to come forward and sign up to support the movement. Community organisations, faith groups and unions lined up to put their signatures on a giant poster of the living wage statement. Then we pushed the chairs aside and shared food from a laden table. The atmosphere was celebratory.

Media interest was high. Some of Auckland's lowest-paid workers were in the hall ready to tell their stories. Despite frequently published commentary at the time – that workers, particularly low-paid 'unskilled' workers, were *lucky* to have jobs – the media was receptive because the launch centred around the real stories of workers and their families, painting a picture of what life was like for thousands of New Zealanders.

In the days before the launch, Emma Endermann, Kelly Belcher and Ika Hiko, all SFWU members and minimum-wage cleaners, featured on the current affairs television programme *Campbell Live*. Film crews had visited the workers' homes to uncover the reality of life on the minimum wage in New Zealand's largest city. On the night of the launch, *Campbell Live* screened an interview with John Ryall about the proposed solution to poverty wages: the living wage.

Single mother Emma Endermann was supporting four children with her minimum-wage cleaning job. She worked 35 hours a week for $13.50 an hour. Her son, 16-year-old Peniata, was in his final year at college and cleaning every day after school to bring in extra money for the family. Peniata said he had no choice but to help his mother look after his younger siblings; his contribution helped to pay for school uniforms and stationery. To Emma, winning the living wage would mean she had time to help her children with their homework and eat a meal together in the evening as a family.[6]

Kelly Belcher was also a single mother, with two children aged five and seven. She worked 24 hours a week while studying to be a paramedic in order to provide a better life for her family. Although Kelly wanted to work, she said she would actually be $170 better off on a benefit. Her rent of $250 a week meant going without a car to take her children to school and travel to work. 'My kids get the raw end of the deal,' she said. 'I want to be able to live comfortably and reasonably. I want my kids to have a chance. But at the moment I can't get ahead.'[7]

Ika Hiko had two part-time cleaning jobs spread over 40 hours and seven days. Her husband worked full time as a storeman. Their five children were aged from three to nine. Although they had two incomes and their own home, it was still a strain to find money for necessities like the mortgage, power, rates and groceries. Despite their best efforts to save, the bills piled up. Ika said her kids wanted cereal but she couldn't afford it. 'Sometimes they say, "Mum, are we short of money?" I say, "Yes, we can't afford to buy that because we have to pay our mortgage. Because if we don't pay it, we don't have any house and we're going to sit on the road."' Ika didn't want an

'Rapping Reverend' Mua Strickson-Pua at the launch of the Living Wage Movement in Auckland, 23 May 2012. Photo: Simon Oosterman Beckers

extravagant lifestyle, 'just enough to pay off the mortgage. I want to work and look after my kids until they are old enough to look after themselves.'[8]

Fala Haulangi was skilled at identifying workers to share their stories. She empathised with what they had to say, especially as many were Pacific women cleaners, just as she had been. But it was more than that: Fala was able to gain the confidence of her members. She understood why stories were important and never shied away from asking members to speak out, because that was how campaigns were won. 'Sitting down with members and hearing their stories, which were the reality of low-paid work, was empowering and inspiring,' says Fala:

> I started to realise the power of telling the stories of our members.
> I remember when John Campbell went to Ika's house. He walked in and the kids were running around and the first thing he said was, 'How do you live in this house? It's so cold.' He opened the fridge and there was hardly anything there. That got him rarked up. I thought: John Campbell, welcome to the reality of our members.

These televised stories of low-paid workers took the living wage message into the New Zealand sitting rooms. Now it was time to reach out, grow and build community power.

Support was not unanimous in left-wing circles, however. Political commentator and columnist Chris Trotter was invited to the launch but did not attend. He outlined his reasons in a column published in the *Press* in February 2013, after the announcement of the first New Zealand living wage rate. 'When I first learned about the Living Wage Campaign I was dubious; not about its ultimate purpose – who can dispute the sorry state of New Zealand wage rates? No, what bothered me were the means which the promoters of the Living Wage were employing to achieve their objective.'

Trotter challenged what he viewed as the movement's reliance on the 'moral persuasion' of employers. He questioned the strategy, writing: 'Most perplexing of all about the Living Wage Campaign is its origin in the trade union movement. It is hard to think of a more glaring admission of defeat than launching a campaign whose success is ultimately dependent on melting the hearts of the employing class.' He concluded:

> The most effective instrument for securing a living wage for all workers is a large, strong and confident labour movement. It is not the pity and charity of the middle-class New Zealanders being targeted by the Living

Wage Campaign that low-paid workers need – it's their solidarity. The only melting of hearts I have ever witnessed is when people stand and struggle together – for justice.[9]

Trotter's analysis failed to understand the relationship of workers to their communities and the potential of uniting those communities around a common concern to end in-work poverty. The goal of the movement was not to persuade employers, although that is not a bad thing, and there are many employers whose stated commitment to social responsibility should logically include a commitment to the living wage. The goal was to build power to exert pressure on employers from a strong and united community movement. The solidarity of people standing together for wage justice was exactly the strategy of the Living Wage Movement, but it extended beyond traditional union silos into the communities where workers live.

The impact of the movement became evident in the wider community following the launch. On 16 June 2012 the Living Wage Movement joined Advance Pasifika, a march organised by Reverend Uesifili Unasa for a better future for Pacific people in Tāmaki Makaurau. Fala and I joined SFWU members as the march left Albert Park with the living wage banner flying high. The movement was becoming a familiar sight in the fight against poverty and inequality, and the living wage message was emblazoned on many banners on that march. Soon after, Auckland groups were invited to a West Auckland living wage community meeting, and another, to establish an Auckland network, was held on 5 July at the launch venue, the St Stephen's Presbyterian church hall.

The movement was up and running and raring to go.

CHAPTER 2

At the grassroots: 2012

'It was that sense of getting people excited about a different way of working. We were so frustrated with the standard ways of doing things. It felt like a union-driven thing, but we made an intentional decision to be a community, church, union, faith groups combination, swinging into that combined campaigning.'

PAUL BARBER, St Andrew's on The Terrace

Learning from London and New York

After the Auckland launch of the Living Wage Movement, Annie Newman travelled to London and New York, where she took the opportunity to hear about different models of community organising around the living wage. In London she visited the public sector union, UNISON, which had ongoing engagement with Citizens UK, London Citizens and the Living Wage Foundation, the latter set up to manage the annual identification of the UK living wage rate and increase the number of accredited Living Wage Employers. UNISON had over a million members, and many in the union were committed to community organising and campaigning for the living wage.

Annie got a picture of relationships that had become competitive around living wage campaigns in London.

> UNISON said they'd find out belatedly that London Citizens was campaigning for a living wage where they had members and the union didn't have time to go in and do the organising. From the Living Wage Foundation there was a sense of frustration that they couldn't get unions to engage. The foundation had people coming to them wanting to be part of a campaign for the living wage; it wanted to bring unions into the picture but the unions were too slow. In the end the foundation drove towards a living wage anyway, because they were not going to allow a union to get in the way of them winning. There were two stories, and probably the truth lies somewhere in the middle.

A meeting with Jane Holgate provided a different perspective. An academic with roots in the union movement, Jane had undertaken research on union engagement with communities. She was an activist and involved in Hackney Unites, a grassroots organisation in her own community. UK unions faced the same issues as those in Aotearoa, and with the growth of precarious work and the decline of union membership and power, new strategies were needed to organise workers. Jane advocated for unions to adopt a community organising approach, to rebuild the union movement by broadening its base to include organisations across civil society. This brought its own challenges. She spoke of the issues unions faced in building community alliances, including personality clashes between leaders, tensions between methodologies, and different levels of commitment to working cooperatively.

In New York Annie searched for connections to living wage campaigns, including following up an address she found on the internet. After climbing many stairs in an old building, she found a 'closed' notice on the door; neighbours said the organisation had ceased to exist long ago. She did meet with one organisation established within the Service Employees International Union, a sister union of SFWU. It had been set up to bring communities into the union's campaigns but was firmly controlled by the union – not the model of partnership the New Zealand movement was seeking.

Then Annie met with Mike Gecan, the executive director of United Power for Action and Justice, a Chicago-based affiliate of the IAF. She was joined by John Ryall and Muriel Tunoho, who were returning from an International Labour Organization meeting. Gecan explained that the IAF approach depended on a model of alliance where the rank and file – ordinary people from groups within the alliance – stepped into leadership roles and mobilised others in their own organisations. These grassroots alliances were capable of attracting large numbers of people to mass events or assemblies, which put pressure on politicians and other decision-makers to agree to the community's demands. The IAF principles were the foundation of US living wage campaigns. Leader training and mass turnout had been key to nearly 75 years of big wins across a range of issues, including the living wage, in cities throughout the United States.

Annie recognised that the IAF principles and approach were what the Living Wage Movement in Aotearoa was looking for. When she asked him why United Power for Action and Justice wasn't working with unions, Mike Gecan was frank. Union officials, he felt, were primarily interested in their own benefits:

I would challenge any union to get 2000 people into a hall to challenge public officials. But we can do that. Why? Because we organise leaders, and every leader has a group of people that they bring to that hall, and we have comprehensive organisation that makes it work. I've never seen a union do that.

'A little bit of me thought, that's just outrageous, what a terrible thing to say,' recalls Annie. 'But this was America, a different world from New Zealand, and he understood what worked and what didn't. The organisation was not anti-union and was actually starting to work with the teachers' union in the hope that IAF training would shift thinking about the power of community organising.'

Gecan explained that, in the US, the left was a small minority. Survey after survey showed a small percentage of the population on the left, or who were progressive, a huge proportion in the middle, and a very big conservative band. He said: 'You want to try and organise without any of that middle? If you can't bring that in, you are not going to win. The numbers are stacked against you.'

Annie says Gecan's ability to articulate 'the world as it is' didn't stop him having a vision for a future transformation of civil society, but he had a clear understanding of the real-world context. Some years later, when in New York for a conference about organising the fast-food workforce, she met Gecan again. 'It was a lesson to me, that he was practising the relational organising that was at the heart of IAF organising. He gave me the time and he gave New Zealand the opportunities. Without that we might not have built the movement we did here.'

The growth of networks

When Annie returned to New Zealand, the Auckland living wage network began to meet regularly. Thirty or 40 people would turn up, initially at the SFWU offices in Kingsland. 'We invited a whole lot of people along to start this conversation,' Andrea Rushton recalls. 'We couldn't hold all the meetings in a union office because we hadn't built a relationship, so we'd go to these freezing church halls. We were starting to reach out and develop relationships in a broader community.'

Network meetings were energetic with break-out groups and butcher's paper to pool ideas. The campaign had hit a nerve and people kept coming.

'We were supported early on by the Anglicans, whose loyalty and commitment never ceased … Jean Brookes, David Hall, Reverend Susan Adams and many more,' Annie recalls.

Susan Adams had arrived from England with her parents around 1950 and grew up in the now-affluent Auckland suburb of Parnell. 'In those days, the bottom of Parnell – where now it's all flash apartments – was pretty run down,' she recalls. 'It was a mixed population of Māori and Pākehā. One side of St Stephens Avenue was very rich and the other side was not so rich. We were immigrants. My father had a good job but we were living down among those who came mainly from Northland, many of them Ngāpuhi.' Susan found the inequality perplexing: 'I could never understand the disparity between those at the top of the hill and the poverty of those at the bottom. The inequality, the divide.'

Susan's family weren't churchgoers, but she attended services at the cathedral at the top of the hill. 'In later life I became a priest, determined always that, if the church had anything to say, it had to be change and hope for the most disadvantaged who struggled to live well in the city.'

After she was ordained Susan took on parish work at the Anglican church, St Matthew-in-the-City. She ran an education programme for the Methodist church based on a liberation model and social justice principles. She came across the Living Wage Movement when she was retiring, and turned up at a meeting. It was a bit tricky, since she came as an individual and the movement was looking for organisations, but she picked up an interim position with St Matthew-in-the-City, and the church became a key member of the Auckland network and hosted many living wage events. With a long history as Auckland's workers' church, St Matthew's was an ideal gathering place for a movement addressing in-work poverty.

Susan became part of an Auckland group within the faith stream of the Living Wage Movement that included Quakers, Catholics, Anglicans, Methodists and Presbyterians. It felt important for the faith groups to have their own space, to work within their own stream while supporting the wider organisation. The group organised faith-based forums and produced a pamphlet setting out the Christian argument for the living wage.

Unions were represented at Auckland network meetings, but it was mainly dedicated individuals, rather than union leaders, who ensured the support of their union. SFWU campaign leaders Fala Haulangi and Jen Natoli and the union's northern region director of organising Andrea

Rushton attended. Andrea worked hard to ensure SFWU staff were on board and found it an easy concept to explain:

> It could make a real difference in so many people's lives. It was something that was easy to excite people about. Most people came to the events and supported them. Then we had to start saying that we didn't want as many Service and Food Workers Union people there, because we didn't want to dominate it.

She says this was a deliberate decision because there was not a lot of trust between unions and community. 'For so long we'd told them what we wanted them to do rather than having a conversation about how we could change society together.'

Political parties were not invited to join the movement. The message was clear: this new organisation was non-party political. Annie says this was one of the most difficult messages: 'This meant holding separate meetings with political allies to discuss the concept and ensure that they understood. New Zealand is a small place and relationships matter.'

The early days were notable for the influential leaders who provided critical public profiles, such as Darryl Evans from the Māngere Budgeting Services Trust, operating as Māngere Budgeting and Family Support, who was vocal about food insecurity among the working poor. Another was Reverend Uesifili Unasa, a Methodist minister based at Auckland University's McLaurin Chapel and also a Pacific Peoples Advisory Panel representative to Auckland Council, who was passionate about elevating the role and influence of Pacific peoples in civil society. The challenge for the movement in the future would be to achieve the commitment of whole organisations, but these early leaders were critical to building a compelling narrative.

Wellington supporters were also starting to build a grassroots network. Meetings were held at St Andrew's on The Terrace, the Presbyterian church where Reverend Margaret Mayman was minister. I attended the first meeting along with Annie, John, Muriel, Dave Hanna from Wesley Community Action and Fiona Osten from Newtown Union Health Service. Margaret invited Paul Barber, a St Andrew's parishioner and policy advisor with the New Zealand Council of Christian Social Services. It was new and felt exciting.

A small group of interested faith leaders came to the second meeting in a pokey back room of St Andrew's. The room may have been small, but the passion and commitment was deep. I attended with John and Muriel.

Reverend Mayman welcomed us along with three Pacific supporters: SFWU organiser Mea'ole Keil; Reverend Ola Tofilau, minister of the Pacific Islanders' Presbyterian Church in Newtown; and Reverend Perema Leasi from the Pacific Islanders' Presbyterian Church in Cannons Creek, Porirua. Living Wage Wellington was starting to take shape.

St Andrew's was one of New Zealand's progressive churches, and Margaret Mayman was a leader in the campaign for marriage equality for same-sex couples. Reverend Ola Tofilau, a social conservative, opposed this campaign, while Reverend Perema Leasi, though traditional in his beliefs, was more open. But the differences in theological beliefs were put aside: the Living Wage Movement was a place where finding common ground was the focus. The common interest was in lifting the incomes of the working poor in New Zealand to a level where workers could lead decent lives and participate in society. That meant having time to go to church, to fulfil community obligations and to invest in their children's futures by spending family time together.

The early support from Pacific leaders was essential. Many Pacific families had migrated to New Zealand in search of better lives for their children, but Pacific churches were full of low-paid workers. Many church leaders were first-generation migrants who had arrived and found themselves in cleaning jobs. They knew only too well the impact of low pay. 'We thought, well, how's this going to work? But it's a good idea. We'll do what we can to support it,' Paul Barber recollects:

> It was that sense of getting people excited about a different way of working. We were so frustrated with the standard ways of doing things. The goal was really good. It felt like a union-driven thing, but we made an intentional decision to be a community, church, union, faith groups combination, swinging into that combined campaigning.

That second Wellington meeting supported the call for the living wage, and a bigger meeting was planned to develop the next steps. This took place at Epworth House behind the Wesley Methodist Church in Taranaki Street, and some 40 people packed the room. The meeting, chaired by John Ryall, agreed to follow Auckland's lead and hold a launch at the church in August. An organising group was set up that included Muriel Tunoho, Reverends Tofilau and Leasi, Sam Huggard from the National Distribution Union and me. Our aim was to fill the church, demonstrate publicly the power of community support for the living wage, and provide local lift-off for the campaign.

Lift-off in Te Whanganui-a-Tara

The launch in Te Whanganui-a-Tara Wellington took place on 30 August 2012 at the Wesley Methodist Church. The building was very large and we wondered how we would fill it, but nearly 300 workers and supporters came from across the Wellington region, including two busloads from Porirua, and the place was packed. Many were SFWU members and wore red living wage T-shirts.

The launch was attended by political party leaders, some of whom have long since left Parliament, including David Shearer from Labour, Hone Harawira from the Mana Party and Russel Norman from the Greens, along with a number of other members of parliament. Politicians were not invited to speak, however. The message was clear: listen to the voices of the community. Numerous local body politicians came too, including Wellington's mayor, Celia Wade-Brown. Her office had said that she was unavailable to attend, but I knew the mayor and years earlier had supported her campaign to win a council seat on the Alliance party ticket. A personal phone call to her had a positive result and she came. Mayor Wade-Brown was surprised to see her office cleaner, Angela Toa, in a living wage T-shirt. It was one of many moments at this event that cemented Wade-Brown's determination to have her council be the first in New Zealand to formally adopt the living wage.

The MC was Dr Jean Mitaera, a Pacific academic from Whitireia Polytechnic in Porirua. Speakers included a church minister, a health campaigner, a Pacific community leader and John Ryall. The most powerful speaker was Sosefina Masoe, an SFWU member and minimum-wage cleaner from Cannons Creek, Porirua.

Sosefina and her husband were both cleaners at the police college in Porirua and were supporting their youngest son in his final year of school and four grandchildren under five. Sosefina told the crowd, 'I start at 5am. I work during the week and the weekend too. I work for 12 hours on Sundays, even though I want to be with my family.' She explained that they cared for their grandchildren so that the children's parents could study to 'make a better life': 'My husband and I talk about how we could do something different, but we are stuck in cleaning jobs on low pay.'

I had accompanied a reporter from the *Dominion Post* to the couple's home the day before, and Sosefina's story, alongside a large photo of her with her grandchildren, was in the paper on the morning of the launch. The article told of how the couple struggled to get by on a near-minimum wage of $13.85 an hour. The Masoes weren't paid enough to feed their family and cover other living costs, and bills were mounting up. 'I want to move on but I can't,' said Sosefina. 'I have to stay in the job for my kids' sake, to get the money for them to survive. I'm struggling right now so they can get a better life.'[1]

Wellington journalist and inequality commentator Max Rashbrooke described the launch as a powerful lesson in the way that equal opportunities and equal incomes are linked, saying the highlight was Sosefina's speech. 'What's especially powerful about Sosefina's story,' he wrote, 'is that, even if some respondents to the *Dominion Post* story questioned whether there should be so many children in the family, and asked how much money was sent back to Sāmoa, in all other respects the Masoes are following the American – or even Kiwi – dream template. They are working incredibly hard – including 12-hour stints on Sundays – and have very few if any luxuries.' He concluded:

> If they earned a living wage, that money would, Sosefina said, go into paying for their children's education, or to basics, like better food so that their children and grandchildren won't get sick. The Masoes believe firmly in equality of opportunity, in trying to get ahead, in moving up the ladder – but those very opportunities are being severely impeded, to say the least, by an inequality of outcome, in this case, low pay. When people are earning less than enough to live well on, they can't take advantage of the opportunities that theoretically exist – not without an extraordinary, and probably damaging, sacrifice. So even if the only thing that you care about is creating more opportunities, you can't ignore the need for better, and fairer, pay.[2]

The launch ended with a rousing rendition of *We Shall Not Be Moved*, which came to be known as the 'living wage song'. Everyone was on their feet, stamping and clapping. I looked around the crowd. There was hope and power in that church.

Impressed by the presence of some 300 workers and community, faith and union leaders, and after posing for photos with her minimum-wage cleaner, Angela Toa, in her living wage T-shirt, Celia Wade-Brown declared her commitment to making Wellington City Council the first living wage council in New Zealand. She never wavered in that commitment, but it would take a determined and public campaign and six years of consistently demonstrating community support to get this vision over the line. By that time Wade-Brown was no longer mayor of Wellington, but her courage and determination set the wheels in motion.

Wade-Brown's early years in London shaped her life. She grew up in a council flat where tenants shared a bathroom and attended a mixed-race inner-city school where her friends were Jamaicans, Greeks and other migrants. Her family was a political melting pot, and there were frequent political arguments at family get-togethers. Wade-Brown initially opted for the Liberal Party. After leaving school she worked in Ghana as a laboratory assistant in a girls' school, where she saw real poverty. Back in the UK she studied philosophy, worked for IBM and trained as a teacher at the University of Warwick, 'a hotbed of politics at the time'. With itchy feet, and 'pissed off about the Thatcher re-election', Wade-Brown came to Aotearoa in 1983.

Her interest in environmental issues led her to a Greenpeace beach clean-up, which she wrote about in an article for the local community newspaper. When approached to stand for the Greens in the Wellington City Council elections, she agreed. Her first attempt was unsuccessful, but she was elected to the council as part of the Alliance in a by-election in 1994, campaigning under the banner 'Policies that Don't Cost the Earth'. The Green Party was one of five that made up the Alliance.

By 2012, and in her first term as mayor of Wellington, Celia Wade-Brown was ready to embrace the living wage concept. It matched her values of social justice and equity. Frustrated at the lack of support for transport issues around the council table, she sensed this was an opportunity to achieve consensus. But her political will and the support of the majority of councillors were not enough. It would also take the determination of Living Wage Wellington.

After the Wellington launch the network began to meet regularly. New leaders emerged quickly. One was Rebecca Matthews, a passionate activist who worked at the finance union, Finsec. Rebecca, who came from an authoritarian, working-class Auckland household, has been an activist for as long as she can remember. The first in her family to attend university, in the 1990s she embraced feminism and student activism and held various roles in student politics. She became active in the Alliance and headed to Wellington to work at Parliament before taking a job at the New Zealand

Union of Students' Associations. Rebecca also worked at the Association of University Staff of New Zealand (AUS) and in campaigning roles at Finsec, FIRST Union and NZEI Te Riu Roa. These jobs allowed her to lead an activist life around issues like abortion law reform and in the campaign for MMP (mixed member proportional), a new parliamentary electoral system more representative of voters' party preferences.

Rebecca came to union work in the post-ECA environment. 'A lot of people in the movement had experienced the "good old days" of compulsory unionism and awards and had lived through the experience of when unions were strong,' she recalls. 'I came in when the union movement was in decline. The old way of doing things didn't seem to be working, and sometimes unions replicated power structures of the industries they worked in.' The most insecure and lowest-paid workers, who brought in the lowest union dues, were often seen as too hard to organise. 'That's a hard fight you have in unions. In NZEI you had support staff or early childhood workers as opposed to principals, and within AUS the focus was on academic staff as opposed to general staff.' The concept of a living wage appealed to her as a way to get around the lack of power of low-paid workers and to build power in a different way.

Rebecca quickly became a regular at Living Wage Wellington meetings and a leader in the movement. With Celia Wade-Brown's declaration of intent and commitment to make Wellington City Council New Zealand's first living wage council, the network met and considered whether to take up the challenge of a campaign. The meeting broke into the three streams – faith, community and unions – to consider the move. The decision was not a foregone conclusion. Some felt it was too soon: the movement should grow first and bring in new organisations. Others saw it as a golden opportunity. Rebecca recalls, 'We recognised that this was a long-term building relationships thing and the movement had the opportunity to move to a quick win. So, there was concern. Are we ready? Is it too risky? Is it too much too soon? Are we up to the challenges?'

A consensus was reached: to commit to a campaign that would demonstrate the success of working in alliance to build community power and transform the lives of hundreds of low-paid council workers. But it wasn't going to happen overnight.

Building a national movement

Meanwhile, work was underway to establish a national body. A national transition management committee was set up with Margaret Mayman, Reverend Clay Nelson from Auckland's Unitarian Church and David Hall from the Anglican Diocese of Auckland's Social Justice Council as faith representatives; Agnes Granada from Migrant Action Trust, Rory McCourt from Victoria University of Wellington Students' Association (VUWSA) and Leonie Morris from Auckland Women's Centre represented the community stream; and John Ryall, Robert Reid from FIRST Union, Peter Conway from the NZCTU and Brenda Pilott, national secretary of the Public Service Association (PSA), represented the union stream. These early leaders were vital to the establishment of the new movement and an important support for Annie Newman's leadership role.

There was no blueprint for getting the movement started. 'I wanted to get some funding and to do that I needed to create an incorporated society,' Annie recalls. David Hall offered to help. David brought with him extensive experience in NGOs. After a career as an electrical engineer and manager, in 1993 he became executive director of the Leprosy Mission New Zealand, part of an international development agency in which he was involved in human rights and social justice issues in various countries including India and Ethiopia. He retired in 2009 but remained involved in social justice issues, particularly those concerning the growing inequality in New Zealand.

David and Annie set about pulling together a set of rules. Towards the end of the process David commented, 'This is not a campaign, it's a movement.' The rules were submitted to the Registrar of Incorporated Societies under the name 'Living Wage Movement'. The application was sent back with the word 'movement' replaced with 'campaign'. Annie and David resubmitted the application with its original wording and the movement was formally born.

'We set it up to have that balance of community, union and faith, and to be honest, it was unclear what the leadership would be,' Annie recalls. John Ryall and Brenda Pilott contributed knowledge and experience in governance. Peter Conway was the link between the movement and the NZCTU. His background in the private sector National Distribution Union meant he understood and sympathised with low-paid workers. Peter continued to support and contribute to the movement until he left the CTU not long before his death in June 2015.

In these early days we looked for support wherever we could find it. I called on my friend and neighbour Prue Hyman, an economist and former associate professor at Victoria University of Wellington. Prue began a literature review and contributed her expertise and knowledge to the economic argument in papers, research and in many forums as our 'secret weapon'.

Setting the rate

People within the movement felt it was time to come up with an actual living wage rate, saying we needed more than a statement about workers earning 'enough to participate in society'. John approached Charles Waldegrave from the Family Centre Social Policy Research Unit in Lower Hutt to take on the job of identifying a New Zealand rate. Waldegrave was well known and respected for his work identifying the poverty line through the New Zealand Poverty Measurement Project, which he helped to establish in 1992. This project developed the methodology, still in use today, to measure income poverty.

Waldegrave, a psychologist and Anglican priest, led the Family Centre Social Policy Research Unit. He was supported in the work of identifying the living wage rate by Dr Peter King, a senior research associate at the Family Centre until 2018. Both were acknowledged experts in their field. It was agreed that SFWU would identify workers and their families to participate in focus groups and provide funding for the research.

The methodology used to identify the New Zealand living wage rate was similar to that used around the world. Waldegrave and King used data from sources such as the University of Otago Department of Human Nutrition's annual 'Food Cost Survey' and Stats NZ's 'Household Economic Survey' average expenditure figure. The Ministry of Business, Innovation and Employment's (MBIE) average lower quartile national rent figures were used to estimate housing costs. Facilitated groups of low-paid workers were set up in Wellington and Auckland to discuss what their households required to sustain a higher standard of living than that associated with the poverty line.

All this information was used to identify a rate that fulfilled the living wage definition: 'The income necessary to provide workers and their families with the basic necessities of life. A living wage will enable workers to live in dignity and to participate in society.' Waldegrave was well aware that the second sentence – involving social participation – is what distinguishes the living wage from the poverty threshold. It embraces small but important things like being able to pay for a school trip, having a home computer, an occasional family meal out and being able to fulfil community responsibilities. Waldegrave would later reflect:

> New Zealand was one of the lowest wage-paying countries in the OECD when the Living Wage Movement began. The Ministry of Social Development's annual *Household Incomes in New Zealand* report consistently noted that 40 percent of children in poverty were from working families. There was a need for a realistic discussion about people in work being paid at least an adequate sum to meet their basic needs and to be able to participate modestly in society.

Targeting local democracy

As anticipation grew about the announcement of the living wage rate, regular network meetings took place in Auckland and Wellington. Driven by his commitment to Pacific people having a greater say and influence in their city, Reverend Uesifili Unasa suggested targeting the next local body elections in 2013. Local organisations had an investment in their councils and in fair wages for the workforce of their communities. At a meeting at Trades Hall, the Auckland network discussed the following year's local government election and agreed on a campaign to win support for Auckland Council to become a living wage council.

The network organised delegations to local boards. Annie Newman and Fala Haulangi led this process and ensured broad community representation in every delegation. In September and October 2012, representative groups appeared at nine Auckland local board meetings. Every delegation had a worker as a speaker and a group from each community. Although the living wage rate had not yet been identified, the delegations sought political support for the living wage in principle. Their presentations included information about the benefits to employers in terms of staff morale, recruitment and retention, absenteeism and productivity.

The network used Auckland Council's own long-term plan as a rationale for adopting the living wage:

> We will ensure that growth is inclusive and equitable, so that all Aucklanders participate in growing the economy and can enjoy its benefits.

> We need to earn more income, increase our skills, use our resources more effectively and make better use of our comparative advantages. This is especially important for Auckland, because prosperity and opportunity are unevenly distributed.[3]

It was time to make these words a reality for Auckland workers, starting with the council's own workforce. But to do that, a strong alliance of unions, faith groups and community organisations was necessary.

The three-way alliance

The central principle of the three-way alliance in the Living Wage Movement – the partnership of community organisations, unions and faith groups – is fundamental to the power-building strategy. Alone, unions lack the power to deliver the living wage to Aotearoa's lowest-paid workers. The organisations in the living wage alliance share a common concern about poverty wages and use their combined power to call on corporate businesses and institutions funded by public money to pay the living wage. It is through the work of this alliance that living wage campaigns are won.

Winning decent wages for members is a core goal for unions; achieving social justice and eradicating poverty form part of the scriptural teaching that unites many faith groups; and community organisations are often built on a desire to collectivise individuals – such as migrants and refugees or people concerned with environmental issues – and unite them around particular issues or identities. The living wage alliance unites around the common cause of lifting workers and their families from poverty. Differences on other issues are left intentionally at the door in a well-grounded principle of IAF organising.

From the beginning, this ensured a diverse alliance. Unions were quick to join the movement and most took up formal membership, including some with higher-paid members, such as the Association of Salaried Medical Specialists (the senior doctors' and dentists' union) and the Tertiary Education Union. TEU national secretary Sandra Grey explains why the union backed campaigns for university cleaners, who were contracted out and members of a different union, to win the living wage: 'A union like TEU predominantly organises people in pretty decent employment. We have an obligation to the most vulnerable. There were people on campus working all night just to pay the bills and we had to pay attention to that.'

Faith groups, too, were among the earliest members. Muslims united with Christians. Pentecostal Christians united with Anglicans and Presbyterians, who were strongly focused on social justice. Pacific ministers united around an issue they understood well: Pastor Sonny Taimalelagi was used to struggling to get by on the minimum wage and daily saw the in-work poverty among his congregation; Reverend Perema Leasi and others in the Wellington Samoan Faifeau (Church Ministers) Group shared his understanding.

Reverend Stephen King, who later became the chair of the Living Wage Movement's national governance board, says being part of the movement has given him two gifts:

> Working with other members and their organisations from the union and community streams, I have gained an understanding of the systemic justice issues that perpetuate poverty in this nation – a far more acute understanding than anything I could have learnt academically. Why? Because the movement engages you with the lived experience of others, and the stories from those in our community who work so hard without a living wage to try and support their families are far more compelling than any theory. The second gift is that participation in the movement delivers real change to peoples' lives, material change to thousands of working families, but also real change in the attitudes of those not directly affected as they are confronted with the struggle of our poorest working families.

The community stream of the alliance is perhaps the most diverse. Membership ranges from the Māori Women's Welfare League to Auckland Action Against Poverty and the Hutt, Porirua, Newtown and Waitākere union and community health services. Their roles in providing services to poorer communities give the leaders of these organisations a first-hand view of the impact of low wages on health and wellbeing.

Students associations also play a vital role in the community stream. Students understand the reality of low-paid jobs and the battle to make ends meet. VUWSA president Rory McCourt took the lead in activating student involvement in the Living Wage Movement. His successor, Rick Zwaan, arranged for the association to join the movement formally. Subsequent student leaders mobilised their peers in the campaign for a living wage for university cleaners, and some went on to be paid community organisers for the movement.

Leonie Morris of the Auckland Women's Centre had a background in social justice and union organising. She saw the Living Wage Movement as a good fit with the centre's goals. 'We were thrilled there was a group working to improve women's wages,' she says. 'Of all the people who are over 25 years and receiving the minimum wage, 67 percent are women.' Joining the community stream of the Living Wage Movement brought new relationships with other networks in the movement, such as Pacific women's groups who are committed to fighting climate change.

All too often, refugees come to Aotearoa with nothing and find the only work they can get is a minimum-wage job. Refugee-background and migrant groups have been active in the movement since the beginning, with supporters like Agnes Granada from Auckland's Migrant Action Trust playing leadership roles and bringing their organisations on board. Auckland's Aotearoa Resettled Community Coalition and Wellington's ChangeMakers Resettlement Forum have also been active. On their own, these community organisations struggle with powerlessness.

Member organisations pay a fee to join the movement. Accredited Living Wage Employers often talk about joining the movement, but the three-way alliance is separate from the employer arm. Representatives from the three streams join delegations, attend network meetings, provide leadership and are visible at every level of the movement. The three-way alliance has mobilised hundreds of thousands of individuals in the call for the living wage and ensures the breadth of community involvement required to build power far beyond that possible for any solitary union, church or community group.

The alliance was vital to the life of grassroots networks. In Wellington, regular network meetings continued at St Andrew's on The Terrace. A large and lively meeting at the end of November 2012 heard that the national Methodist Assembly had endorsed the living wage campaign with a theological statement supported by church leaders. This was described enthusiastically by Reverend Bruce Anderson from the Wesley Methodist Church as one of the most exciting things talked about at the conference. Paul Barber shared details of a new organisation called the Inequality Network. He said leading poverty commentator Campbell Roberts, of the Salvation Army, had listed the living wage as one of the three factors in the elimination of poverty, along with good housing policy and ending child poverty. A report from Muriel Tunoho about the settlement of two collective employment agreements in primary health, where the parties had agreed to work together to achieve the living wage, prompted discussion about overcoming the challenges faced by cash-strapped community organisations. A brainstorm of priorities for 2013 revealed a broad agenda, including mapping communities, expanding the network, staging a concert and reaching out further to migrant groups.

As the movement's first year drew to a close, we had new confidence. Our movement was on a roll.

CHAPTER 3

Building blocks: 2013

'Don't just do a campaign, build a movement.'
DEBORAH LITTMAN, Metro Vancouver Alliance

Changing the way the union worked

The 2012 SFWU annual delegates' conference demonstrated just how much the commitment to the living wage campaign was building within the union. The conference programme focused on maximising involvement from the union's member leaders, and every delegate attended a living wage workshop aimed at ensuring they understood the concept and could share it with others. There was training on ways to bring churches, communities and whānau to the campaign, and delegates were encouraged to tell their stories of life on poverty wages to mainstream media.

Jason Fell, a gardener at Auckland University, was one SFWU delegate who became an activist in the Auckland campaign. Jason came from a union family and was used to a working environment with solid union power. He had been working at the university in the 1980s when a job on the waterfront came up: 'My father was a wharfie, and this was a really sought-after job in Auckland. It was well paid with lots of really good perks.'

After 12 years on the waterfront, deregulation, the ECA and competitive tendering changed everything, and Jason was forced out of the job. It seemed clear to him that these changes were attempts to stifle the power of the union. 'Workers were getting paid well, employers were still making good money and it was shared more evenly,' he recalls. 'Then they brought in the ECA and we had to reapply for our jobs and become employees of different stevedoring companies.' Conditions on the job were slashed repeatedly, and one night Jason got to work and found there was no job. He returned to gardening at the university and a pay rate of $12 an hour, just above the minimum wage. He had always been a union member, and the union for the university gardeners was the SFWU.

As the living wage campaign picked up steam in early 2013, Jason stepped up to the union's regional organising committee and later the national executive. 'I didn't want to look back in 10 years and say, you could have helped, you could have said something, you could have had a voice.' He saw the Living Wage Movement as a logical step, 'a way we could address the issues that weren't being addressed across bargaining tables'. With support from students, a living wage campaign was launched on campus with the message that the university should pay all its workers the living wage – with a strong focus on the low-paid contracted cleaners who were also members of the SFWU.

Looking back, Jason is proud of the movement he helped to build:

> When I first got involved, you'd talk to people about a living wage and you'd get push-back. I never get that now. You didn't hear about the living wage then; now, it's out there. It's got people focusing on what society's about, which is that everyone's got to earn a decent amount to live on if you want a good society.

A rate to campaign on

By early 2013, work on the New Zealand living wage rate had progressed. The timing was right to announce it at a symposium at AUT on 14–15 February, on which Annie Newman and Felicity Lamm, an associate professor at AUT Business School, were collaborating. The symposium, called 'Precarious Work and the Living Wage in Our Communities', would explore how these two pressing issues might be addressed. Annie, who had returned to the union movement with a policy background, had a clear idea of the value of an evidence-based strategy. She knew the worth of identifying why some countries were more successful in certain areas than others. The symposium would tell both the academic story and the community-organising story about low pay and precarious work, and it wasn't just for academics: low-paid workers were subsidised to attend.

International guest speakers included Guy Standing – an English academic and author of *The Precariat: The new dangerous class* – and Deborah Littman, who was now leading the IAF-affiliated Vancouver Metro Alliance. Deborah knew that living wage campaigns had found success in the UK because they had been embedded in a movement. Her advice to Annie was, 'Don't just do a campaign, build a movement.'

I picked Deborah up at Wellington Airport the weekend before the symposium. She stood out in the crowd of disembarking passengers. A tiny, energetic woman with grey hair, she was engulfed in an oversized, red living wage T-shirt she had acquired from Annie on a stopover in Auckland.

Media interest was building around the rate announcement, and an *NZ Herald* reporter interviewed Deborah. Over four successive days, the newspaper ran a series entitled 'Battle for a living wage'. The first was titled 'The pay you need to survive'.[1] Journalist Simon Collins predicted that, with the announcement of the living wage rate, 'almost 750,000 Kiwis look set to be classed as the new working poor'. Following an interview with Charles Waldegrave, who explained the methodology, Collins guessed the rate would be $18–$20 an hour and included this estimate in his story. Frustratingly, he presented the work of producing a living wage rate as purely a union endeavour, writing 'when the union movement fixes the value of a "living wage" needed to have a decent life'. Educating the media and others that the movement comprised three streams working in partnership proved to be an ongoing battle.

NZCTU president Helen Kelly told the *NZ Herald* the living wage would 'take off' in New Zealand. 'The deal is that if you go to work and work hard, you should have a decent standard of living at the end of the week,' she said. 'The argument that you shouldn't have a living wage only seems to apply to the poor. Others seem to get wages that most people couldn't even imagine are being paid in this country. I think there is a moral question here.' Charles Waldegrave clarified that the living wage figure was arrived at by 'not including any luxuries at all'. He told the *NZ Herald*:

> A living wage would mean that you could have a computer in your home, you could afford for your kids to go on a school camp, and you could have a modest recreational event with friends, say once a month. It's pretty minimal. The whole idea is you could participate in society and have enough to pay your rent and food and power.[2]

Deborah Littman's background in building community alliances and leadership in the successful campaign to win the living wage at the Greater London Authority was invaluable to our movement. We were keen to learn from alliances like London Citizens. Before travelling to Auckland for the symposium and the rate announcement, at the invitation of Mayor Celia Wade-Brown Deborah gave a presentation to the Wellington mayor, councillors, community representatives and business people. Prior to this, she was scheduled to appear on Radio New Zealand's *Nine To Noon* show; however, after the *NZ Herald*'s Simon Collins guessed the rate would be $18–20 an hour, *Nine To Noon* pulled the plug on the interview. Instead, presenter Kathryn Ryan rang the mayor and challenged her about her commitment to introduce the concept without knowing the exact rate. As Deborah explained in her presentation later that morning, regardless of the rate, the living wage is about the principle of a worker's right to a decent life and to participate in society.

Deborah's presentation led to a prominent story in the *Dominion Post* titled 'Mayor pushes to give hundreds of council staff a pay increase'. This story also predicted a rate of $18–$20 an hour. Wade-Brown said she was keen to move to the living wage, but a feasibility study would be done first.[3] Deborah encouraged us to advise a staged implementation of the living wage that would start with such a study and include the benefits of implementing the living wage as well as the costs. It was sound advice, and in the years ahead the strategy was adopted usefully with numerous councils.

Prime Minister John Key, however, was unconvinced, saying the problem of low-paid workers was not as simple as a 'magic number'. The paper reported: 'Mr Key was sceptical about the practicality of the living wage and said the minimum wage would not be raised to $18 in the next 12 months.'[4] Key's statement ignored the voluntary nature of the living wage concept and confused the minimum wage with the living wage.

$18.40: The living wage

A mixed crowd of unions, workers, academics and faith and community representatives arrived at AUT for the symposium on 14 February 2013. The place was buzzing, and at the end of the day participants attended the official launch accompanied by the upbeat youth band from Jacobz Well Church. The room was full of supporters, including some MPs. Reverend Uesifili Unasa was MC, and one young business owner, Jesse Chalmers from food manufacturers Tonzu, was determined to be the first Living Wage Employer. By the time Charles Waldegrave took the microphone, with a grin from ear to ear, to formally announce the New Zealand living wage rate of $18.40, the figure was well and truly in the public domain. The diversity of those gathered, the sense of celebration and the mix of speakers with a message of

Deborah Littman (centre) and Guy Standing (second from right) with workers, including cleaners Ana Malolo (left) and Emma Endermann (third from left), at the 'Precarious Work and the Living Wage in our Communities' symposium at AUT, 14–15 February 2013.

Charles Waldegrave announces the first New Zealand living wage rate, 14 February 2013.
Photos: Jason Fell

Reverend Uesifili Unasa, MC of the event to announce the first living wage rate.
Photo: Jason Fell

SFWU member leaders Sharryn Barton (left) and Muriel Tunoho (right) join SFWU campaign director Annie Newman (centre) at the rate announcement event. Photo: Jason Fell

hope set the tone for future events. 'It established how we do things in the movement,' recalls Annie.

The public's reception was positive. Deborah Littman appeared on breakfast TV the following morning, and the *Dominion Post* ran an editorial asserting that no one could argue that $18.40 an hour was unreasonable.[5]

The *NZ Herald*'s feature articles continued throughout the week. One story, which focused on parliamentary cleaners, raised one of the most important issues in living wage campaigns: that of a living wage for contracted workers. A Parliamentary Services spokesperson argued that, since the cleaners were employed by the multi-national company Spotless, their pay rate was a matter between the contractor and the workers. It was a standard response: contracting was a convenient way to make workers invisible, along with their poverty wages. Deborah was clear: the onus should be on the client to push for a service that included higher wages for cleaners and would ultimately lead to improved productivity and morale and lower staff turnover.[6]

This strategy – of targeting the business or organisation contracting out a service rather than the contractor – would deliver the living wage to thousands of New Zealand's lowest-paid workers. As the SFWU had already discovered, it was a waste of time targeting contractors who were negotiating in a race to the bottom to achieve the lowest cost in a tender. Putting community pressure on the client who paid for the contract secured the commitment to pay workers the living wage.

The final story in the *NZ Herald* series focused on Ana and Tupou Malolo, who lived in a rented home in Ōtara with their two small children. Simon Collins pointed out that the parents of every girl attending Auckland's Diocesan School for Girls paid roughly one and a half times as much in annual fees as Ana received for cleaning the school for the entire year. Professional Property & Cleaning Services paid Ana $13.85 an hour to work from 4pm to 8pm, Monday to Friday. When she got home each night, her husband left for an eight-hour shift as a forklift driver at the Lion Nathan brewery on $14 an hour. Collins reported that lifting both parents to the living wage would raise their available income after rent from about $585 to $691 a week: 'That may not sound much to a parent who shells out $19,880 a year, plus $3600 for a compulsory notebook computer, to send a year-nine girl to Diocesan. But to Mrs Malolo, a living wage would make the difference between debt and self-sufficiency.'[7]

Diocesan School principal Heather McRae trotted out the routine employer response, saying pay rates for cleaners are up to the contractor: 'We have no control over what that employer then pays their employees. I certainly care about what people need to live, absolutely. But I guess there are things that we are in control of and things we are not.'[8]

This position was now publicly under attack. The relationship between the funder and contractor was at the heart of the living wage strategy. A week later, a front-page feature in the *Sunday Star-Times* by business commentator Rod Oram was headlined: 'A living wage is an investment in the future'. A consistent supporter of the living wage and a committed Anglican, Oram noted, '"We can't afford it" is the response of most employers to advice they would benefit if they paid their people a living wage. But "we can't afford not to pay it" is the answer from employers who understand a living wage is an investment in their people and businesses.'[9]

Oram outlined the business case: 'The upside for companies is obvious in abundant case studies overseas. Hopefully we'll start to see local leaders emerge thanks to the launch this week of Living Wage Aotearoa New Zealand.' He stressed the value to New Zealand's economy:

> We have urgent economic and social reasons for applying such practices. The median income [the halfway figure: half of incomes are above it and half are below] is around $15 an hour in retailing, accommodation and food services and around $18 in agriculture, forestry and fisheries. But while other sectors have median pay above the proposed $18.40 an hour living wage, there is widespread hardship among people paid less than the median.[10]

Pointing to the commercial cleaning industry as a 'key culprit in the low-wage economy', Oram singled out commercial office cleaning as the biggest challenge. 'It is notoriously low paying and very labour intensive. It will take brave pioneers to find a better way of doing business.'[11] It was a tough sector to crack, but the Living Wage Movement was more than ready to take it on and be that pioneer.

The detractors

It was now 12 months since the SFWU had hired Annie Newman to start a new campaign supported by a community movement, and significant momentum had been achieved. It would be easy to underestimate how radical the movement's approach was in union circles. IAF leader Sister Maribeth Larkin, who was to play an important role in the movement in Aotearoa, described the community organising approach as 'countercultural'. The prevailing culture of unions was to work from silos dependent on union power in order to win campaigns based around industrial actions and short-lived, transactional relationships with allies. The Living Wage Movement defined power differently. Power was held in the community, and although unions played a vital role, in the movement they worked in coalition with others across civil society. Building power meant building relationships across diverse organisations united around a common interest in achieving social change.

This was radical thinking in a union environment, where the usual response to workers' issues was to call on allies as reinforcements for union-determined agendas and actions. The Living Wage Movement's understanding of the need to build long-term relationships to develop the power of alliance was very different. Maribeth was right: it *was* countercultural.

The announcement of the rate was also radical because it changed the way we approached wages in Aotearoa: from employers in the post-ECA environment paying the lowest legal rate they could, to thinking about wages in terms of what workers and their families needed to lead decent lives.

There was bound to be pushback, and pushback there was. Commentator Brian Scott led the charge, claiming that the research was inaccurate and assumptions were false.[12] Charles Waldegrave wrote a response to this critique, addressing each point.[13] But blogger David Farrar on his website 'Kiwiblog' responded:

> Brian Scott has published a critique of the so called Living Wage, and it should be compulsory reading for any politician that has treated the calculations done by Rev [sic] Waldegrave as a fit basis for public policy decisions. It is quite legitimate to have a view that wages should be higher, but to insist that the correct level is that calculated by Rev [sic] Waldegrave is a surrender to symbolism over substance.[14]

In a 23-page report released in November 2013, Treasury argued that the living wage was not 'well targeted'. The writer joined the line of opponents who chose to treat the living wage as if it were a proposed minimum wage and therefore compulsory. If implemented, Treasury predicted, the living wage would have 'negative impacts on employment and inflation'. The report concluded: 'We do not think increasing the minimum wage to this extent would lead to higher average wages.'[15]

National's Finance Minister Bill English seized on this report, saying:

> Treasury advice shows that the so-called 'living wage' is not well targeted to help low-income families and, if implemented, would be likely to cost jobs and be unlikely to lift average wage rates ... Treasury analysis shows that not just the figure, but the concept, is flawed. It might sound politically attractive to be able to dial up a pre-selected made-up wage rate, but for higher wages to be sustainable they have to be based on productivity and affordability in real workplaces.[16]

An avowed Catholic, English is one of many conservative politicians whose faith sometimes underpins their political values. But while Catholic allies in the Living Wage Movement were keenly drawing on the principles of the teachings of Jesus to support the living wage, the social teaching of Bill English's Roman Catholic religion about the 'Just Wage' did not seem to influence his views on the living wage.

Detractors existed within the union movement too, including within the SFWU. Annie Newman says some could not accept that the campaign was not owned by the SFWU. Others could not countenance a non-politically-aligned campaign and argued that, since the union was affiliated to the Labour Party, the living wage should therefore be part of a Labour Party campaign. Some organisers struggled with the long-term focus of the movement and were unhappy to see resources allocated to it. Anger boiled over at one union staff meeting in Rotorua when an aspiring SFWU leader challenged a living wage organiser in the union, saying, 'When are you going to recruit some members in this fucking thing?' The ongoing support of John Ryall and rank-and-file member leaders of the union ensured things stayed on track, however, and the approach of building partnership with communities continued to be a top priority.

There were other doubters, including Australian unionist and close ally of the SFWU, Michael Crosby. While on a visit to New Zealand he advocated for a living wage campaign only on the basis that it was controlled by unions. Annie reflects, 'The prevailing view of unionism remains today that we must control the path to justice for workers, even though the mass of workers has long since left the path laid down by our union forebears and no amount of reworking the organising model would seemingly bring it back.'

Despite dissent in union ranks, with the rate announced and businesses like Tonzu and others ready to sign up, the movement was well and truly underway. Countering resistance took persistence, and with no dedicated staff, the movement had little time to undertake research and rebut misinformation. All resources were focused on building community power to achieve decent wages for low-paid workers, and there was plenty of work to be done.

Recognition

The success of the 'Precarious Work and the Living Wage in Our Communities' symposium and the rate announcement had an immediate effect on the Auckland Council campaign. With 2013 a local body election year, and although the movement was committed to the principle of political non-alignment, politicians did have a role, and it was important to gain their recognition. Meetings were held in Auckland and Wellington with politicians from all sides at central and local government levels, to introduce them to the living wage concept and articulate the non-aligned nature of the campaign. Local government politician Tracey Martin, who later became a New Zealand First MP, committed early on to advocacy for the living wage and maintained this commitment throughout her political career. Support from an ally not viewed as on the left was testimony to the strategy of non-alignment.

The Auckland network had already embarked on meetings with each of Auckland Council's local boards. Network leaders had long been trying to get a community delegation to meet Mayor Len Brown. Brown did not consider the Living Wage Movement important. 'There was zero recognition,' recalls Annie Newman. '[But] the day the *Herald* put a living wage story on the front page, I got a call from Len Brown's office saying the mayor would like to meet.' With one powerful story, the narrative had shifted, and Brown could not ignore it.

A 15-minute meeting was organised in a tiny room that had seating for just seven people. Eleven days after the symposium at AUT, 20 community leaders filed into the room to meet with the mayor. Annie saw his determination to take control of the meeting: 'He went around every person to say hello and hear from each of them. One by one the movement's delegation made a connection with the mayor.' Chris Sullivan, a Catholic deacon and social justice activist, was first. He reminded Brown of a time they had stood together, years ago, and the importance to them both of the Catholic Church. Other speakers followed, each making a powerful connection. The 15 minutes passed and then half an hour. The mayor told the community representatives not to worry about the time. 'It had never been about time,' says Annie:

> It was about us finally being recognised as a group of people who knew what we were about. It was a very powerful lesson for us, and many of those people [who were] at the meeting have remained involved. They've had the courage to stand up to power right from the very beginning because of their passion and belief in the living wage as a concept.

Having secured a relationship with Auckland's mayor, the campaign was now on its way to winning commitment to the living wage at New Zealand's biggest council – not just for those directly employed, but for the lowest-paid of all: those employed via contractors.

Concrete steps

In April 2013 Annie Newman and David Hall completed the work of making the Living Wage Movement an incorporated society. This meant national consistency around objectives and strategies, a mechanism for sourcing grants, and a formal identity beyond that of the initiating union, the SFWU.

In Auckland, large numbers of people from a range of organisations were meeting regularly. One person in particular stood out. Annie recalls an extroverted, outspoken and vivacious woman in her fifties, full of passion for the living wage. Diana Yukich and her husband, Kevin Church, owned a small fine arts printing business called Opticmix and were a clear fit with the movement. Diana had dedicated time to the community throughout her adult life; Kevin had worked in London for a union and was unafraid to share his opinions. For the first seven years in their business Diana worked two jobs, but once she had a couple of days a week free, she began volunteering at a local church's food, curtain and uniform bank. The church employed home-care workers, and Diana had already told her manager, 'If we ever get a time where people who actually work for this organisation come in for food parcels, I'm out of here.'

Diana wanted to put her energy into something at the top of the cliff, not at the bottom. One day, listening to the radio, her ears pricked up when she heard a story about the Living Wage Movement. She turned up at a meeting and offered her skills, saying, 'If you need a volunteer, I'll volunteer.'

The packed meeting had brought together Anglicans, Methodists, organisations like Auckland Action Against Poverty and the Auckland Women's Centre, and a number of unions. Most of the organisations present dealt with low-income families, and they were there to find real solutions. Diana describes those days as a roller coaster. 'When you're working with a group of people who really want to make change and that's all you're talking about, then your ideas are bouncing around really fast about how to keep the collective with you but also how to move things forward.'

With the rate identified, the next step was to set up an accreditation process that clearly established genuine Living Wage Employers. When conversations about accreditation began, Diana Yukich was at the heart of them. An accreditation project team was set up with business, faith, community and union experience included to provide a perspective from each stream. Diana was passionate about a robust accreditation programme to ensure the integrity of the movement, and she was concerned that big organisations might take advantage of the brand, promoting themselves as Living Wage Employers when they were not. 'The movement could grow, but if we didn't get an accreditation system that was credible, people would start saying "we're a Living Wage Employer" and it would be a lie. And we also didn't want it to be one of those ticks that were bullshit. We wanted a system in place that was meaningful.'

The project team set to work. Diana contacted Rhys Moore, head of the Living Wage Foundation in London, who shared with her the contract they used for employers. Diana was dedicated: she completed a copyright course online at night, found a pro bono lawyer who adapted the UK contract to the New Zealand setting, and organised the copyright work. As a result, the New Zealand movement achieved a trademark for the term 'Living Wage Employer', something that does not exist elsewhere – even in the UK, where thousands of businesses and organisations are accredited. Diana says it was 'a game changer.'

Both Diana and Kevin played major roles in establishing the accreditation programme. Opticmix was New Zealand's first accredited Living Wage Employer, and Kevin remains on the accreditation board. 'Diana was no ordinary volunteer,' says Annie. She attributes the robust New Zealand accreditation system to Diana's work: 'Only through her dedication did we bring together a model that had integrity, legality and a robustness that has stood us in good stead ever since.'

The trademark and accreditation programme sets the movement's approach apart from other strategies to lift wages. No employer can call themselves a Living Wage Employer until they are formally accredited. Simply lifting one part of a workforce to the living wage is not sufficient to gain accreditation. It is a step in the right direction, but more campaigning is needed to get that employer across the line. Adhering to this principle means no group of workers is left behind. This provides a weapon to unite groups of workers to campaign together for the living wage for all workers. And winning the living wage for workers employed by contractors lifts the veil on their invisibility. It also provides campaign goals for community networks at every stage of achieving accreditation and the living wage for every single worker in councils, businesses and with other targeted employers.

The fairest little capital

After the symposium, a living wage barbecue hosted by the TEU at AUT kicked off a series of campaigns in tertiary institutions. The Living Wage Movement had identified as key targets those institutions funded by public money. Tertiary institutions fitted that category well, and the involvement of TEU, along with other unions on site at various tertiary institutions around the country, was critical.

A campaign launched in Blackball, the home of the New Zealand labour movement, was largely driven by West Coast activist Paul Maunder and marked by a march through the town. In Kirikiriroa Hamilton, the first living wage community meeting took place at the Western Community Centre. A second community meeting in May 2013 followed a Hamilton Council vote to pay directly employed workers a minimum of the living wage over the next two years. It was an early win for the new network in the city, but one that was short-lived.

Then came a major step forward. Having taken up the challenge set by Mayor Celia Wade-Brown, the Wellington network was advancing the campaign for Wellington City Council to become Aotearoa's first accredited living wage council. Wellington prided itself on being a fair little capital. It had committed to supporting the principles of nuclear-free and fair trade.

Now it was time to adopt the living wage. With a mayor determined her city would be first, things were on the move.

Celia Wade-Brown had not forgotten the commitment she made at the Wellington campaign launch the previous year, and she was true to her word. She had seen, first-hand, the hardship faced by the council's low-paid cleaners: 'I worked quite late … I knew a number of the cleaners and the security guards as well. Quite often the cleaners were actually studying … imagine, you've got children and you're working nights, and you're earning stuff all! It seemed so unfair.'

The mayor asked council officials how many staff were paid less than the living wage. She thought it would be very few, but it transpired that it wasn't just contract workers; lifeguards, library assistants and other directly employed workers were also included. 'That was such a shock. What the Living Wage Movement did was make me aware how many staff were on a really low wage. I thought, what can I do about this? I'm mayor. What can I do that will help this happen?' Deborah Littman had influenced her thinking with her talk of London having a living wage council under Boris Johnson's mayoralty. Wade-Brown thought, 'Bloody hell … *we* should be able to do something.'

Wade-Brown wanted to achieve many things, especially around environmental issues, but without the numbers around the council table she was hamstrung. 'I would have brought light rail in overnight, but I didn't have the majority. On the issue of the living wage, it was quite clear that I had a council majority and the problem was the Chamber of Commerce and senior managers. I felt I could deal with that.'

In 2013 I was working as the SFWU media person and informally co-ordinating the local Living Wage Movement along with John Ryall, Muriel Tunoho and other network leaders. I received an email from Wade-Brown on 7 May saying the council would vote on a living wage recommendation that week: 'Details being worked through but likely to support in principle and explore a staged approach and work with LWA (living wage alliance) to create a Living Wage Wellington coalition. It will amend our forward programme and be in time for annual plan deliberations.' I replied that this was great, but pointed out that we already had a coalition called Living Wage Wellington and suggested adding wording to commit the council to 'support, lead and champion Wellington as a living wage city'.

Living Wage Wellington prepared a submission for the annual plan process. It was the first of many and the demands were clear: support the living wage in principle; ensure that all staff, including those employed by contractors, were paid the living wage; support local businesses to become Living Wage Employers; commit to taking a lead in creating a living wage city; and work with Living Wage Wellington to prepare an implementation plan to achieve this. Living Wage Wellington wasn't there to pussyfoot around. We were asking for the lot. The written submission was supported by stories of low-paid workers employed by the council and their lives in the community.

SFWU member and council cleaner Maliki Rahman was one of these. Maliki lived in the Hutt Valley. He had come from Malaysia two years before with his wife and two small boys, and they had since had a baby girl. Maliki and his family loved living in New Zealand, but with just one earner on the minimum wage, money was tight. The living wage would mean healthy food for the children and a warm home. Maliki was happy to speak out for fair wages for the cleaners and was the first of many workers to tell their stories to Wellington City councillors. It was by no means easy. Council management actively discouraged workers from speaking out, and workers employed via contractors were vulnerable. They could not afford to lose their jobs and incomes. But their willingness to share their stories was driven by a sense of justice, a commitment to the union and the need to change things for their families and communities.

Mayor Wade-Brown invited a Living Wage Wellington delegation to present to council on 16 May 2013. That morning, more than 20 community leaders and a large group of supporters carrying the living wage banner and wearing the movement's distinctive red T-shirts assembled in the rather small council foyer. The delegation represented thousands of people and reflected the diversity of the city. There were leaders from community health, homelessness and budget advice services, as well as union leaders and church ministers.

Reverend Margaret Mayman led the presentation. The speakers included local primary school principal and NZEI Te Riu Roa member Justine McDonald; Fatuatia Tufunga, a minister from the Taranaki Street Wesley Methodist Church; and Phil Jones, general manager of the Wellington printing firm Thames Publications, who told councillors that his business wanted to become one of Wellington's first official Living Wage Employers

BUILDING BLOCKS: 2013

On 16 May 2013 the first Living Wage Wellington delegation converged on Wellington City Council. Photo credit: Fairfax

A delegation to Wellington City Council on 11 December 2013. Left to right: Rebecca Matthews, Alan Wendt, Esau Taniela, Reverend Bill Herbert, Rick Zwaan, Eleanor Haggerty-Drummond, Eileen Brown, Peter Conway, Marianne Bishop, Vera Williams, Nick Kelly, Reverend Tric Malcolm, Fiona Osten, Prue Hyman, Father Gerry Burns, Stephanie McIntyre, Reverend Brian Dawson, Marama Mayrick. Photo: Lyndy McIntyre

as 'it was the right thing to do'. Surrounded by living wage supporters, the councillors heard Maliki's plea for the council to adopt the living wage. He told them his pay was not enough to support his wife and children and they could not afford shoes for winter. His story was moving.

One of the ministers in the chamber that morning was Reverend Brian Dawson, who was emerging as a leader in the Wellington network. Brian had taken up the role of vicar at St Peter's on Willis Anglican church. He recalls being introduced to the Living Wage Movement when Max Rashbrooke walked into St Peter's and said, 'You really do need to become involved in this living wage thing.' Although he knew the concept from the British Methodist Church, Brian hadn't come across it in New Zealand. Then he got a call from Bruce Anderson at the Taranaki Street Wesley Methodist Church, inviting him to lunch with Margaret Mayman: 'In true Margie fashion, she said "You have to be involved, Brian". It wasn't really an invitation. It was a directive. They were keen to have all the inner-city churches behind the campaign. They sold me very quickly that St Peter's would be a good fit.' Brian was enthusiastic. St Peter's was a parish with strong activist roots and he was looking for a new cause. 'The vast majority of the parish jumped on board, boots and all.'

In June Living Wage Wellington took another delegation to Wellington City Council, and once again the council chamber was packed with supporters. The worker speaker was a library assistant and PSA member, Eleanor Haggerty-Drummond. Despite a clear message to council employees from their managers, discouraging them from speaking out, Eleanor told her story, which focused on the need for library staff to be valued in their work. Later that day her story was broadcast on the Radio New Zealand news. It was not what council management had in mind.

Mayor Wade-Brown thanked the delegation for 'a fantastic presentation' and said the council would consider requests to support the living wage in principle and become a Living Wage Employer. She later said it was the approach of the movement and the strategy of strong community representation that made the difference: 'What was so good was having a range of people speaking at council and to have the particular mix of councillors committed to working for people on low incomes.' While we were confident of support, the demands of Living Wage Wellington were pretty radical. In keeping with the principle of leaving no workers behind, the movement called on council to commit to all the demands – while recognising it would not happen all at once. This would be the strategy of all the movement's campaigns, and the determination to eventually win everything was successful time and again.

On 12 June 2013, Wellington City Council held the first of many votes on the living wage. The following resolution was moved by the mayor and seconded by Councillor Justin Lester in the Strategy and Policy Committee:

> That the Str*ategy and Policy Committee:*
> - *Recommend that council agree to support the principle of becoming a living wage council and a living wage capital.*
> - Request officers to work with stakeholders to develop a 'living wage framework' and report back in November 2013 that:
>   a) Provides for the phased implementation of a living wage for directly employed council staff, staff employed by council-controlled organisations and contractors who deliver council services
>   b) Advises of the impact on council's procurement policy and future tendering arrangements
>   c) Determines the role(s) for council in advocating for a living wage capital.
> - Make provision in the 2013/14 annual plan for $250k, funded from general rates, for commencing implementation from 1 January 2014.[17]

Straight after the vote, I received an email from Councillor Paul Eagle:

> Kia ora everyone! Some great news: WE DID IT! In favour of the council supporting in principle becoming a living wage Council and Capital were the Mayor, and Cllrs Ray Apihene-Mercer, Ngaire Best, Stephanie Cook, Leonie Gill, Justin Lester, Bryan Pepperell, Helene Ritchie and Iona Pannett. The opponents were: Jo Coughlan, Andy Foster, Simon Marsh, John Morrison and Ian McKinnon.[18]

The *Dominion Post* ran the story the next day under the headline 'Wellington leads the way with living wage policy'. It reported that two hours were dedicated to the living wage debate, and councillors had allocated $250,000 in the council's annual plan towards implementing the living wage for staff. The mayor said it was important for the council to show leadership: 'There's a really important ethical issue here. Let's get on with it.' Councillor Simon Marsh opposed the recommendation, saying, 'It's not a no-brainer. This actually relies on a lot of brain power … to look at what the effect on the ratepayer is.' Reverend Margaret Mayman, Living Wage Wellington's spokesperson, summed up the community voice: 'There is a lot of work to be done in determining how this will be achieved, but it is good news for council workers and their families, especially the lowest paid.'[19]

The Wellington City Council resolution was confirmed on 27 June 2013 by the full council, with a 10:5 majority vote. Councillors Andy Foster and John Morrison would later switch from opposition to backing the living wage when faced with the pressure of overwhelming community support during subsequent mayoral campaigns. But a lot more campaigning happened before that. Mayor Wade-Brown's office issued a media release endorsing the living wage. 'Wellington has taken a major step toward becoming New Zealand's first truly living wage city. We want a successful high growth, high value economy in Wellington.'

For the Living Wage Wellington network and others campaigning across the country, this was cause for celebration. However, not everyone was happy with the outcome, including Wellington City Council officers and the Wellington Chamber of Commerce. They would continue to attempt to block the council from implementing this decision for almost five years.

CHAPTER 4

The game changer: 2013

'When I first heard the words "power building", that was a game changer.'

IBRAHIM OMER, ChangeMakers Resettlement Forum

Sabotage

Buoyed by the victory, Living Wage Wellington's leaders were keen to translate Wellington City Council's June 2013 vote into pay rises for workers as soon as possible. The local network delegated John Ryall, Paul Barber and me to attend meetings with council staff. We pushed to meet with the chief executive and officers to get agreement on the framework councillors had voted for. It was not easy and, when meetings were eventually held, it became clear that turning the elected representatives' commitment to the living wage into a reality would be a major challenge.

The staff member charged with meeting Living Wage Wellington representatives did not see that it was the role of officers to implement council policy. He insisted that, regardless of political decisions, it was not possible to extend the living wage to contracted workers. He put up countless barriers. Council, he said, didn't know how much workers were paid: John Ryall said he could find this out, and promptly did so. The staff member said it wasn't possible to compel contractors to pay a specific rate to their workers: John explained that this already happened in businesses where clients wanted their contracted workers to be paid more and were prepared to cover the cost. It would be too expensive, came the reply, and ratepayers would baulk at the cost. We explained that Living Wage Wellington brought together thousands of ratepayers, and those ratepayers had elected the representatives who had already voted for this.

From the outset, council staff seemed intent on sabotaging the living wage implementation. Meetings with them were few and far between, and those that did occur were fractious. The new chief executive, Kevin Lavery, did not attend. Lavery, council officers and the Chamber of Commerce believed it was illegal to require contractors to pay the living wage because the Local Government Act 2002 required councils to undertake all procurement in the 'most cost-effective' way. In response the Living Wage Movement commissioned a legal opinion, thankfully, for the underfunded movement, paid for by the PSA and prepared by Dr Matthew Palmer, which provided the legal backing necessary to achieve the movement's goal: the living wage for Wellington City Council's contracted workers.

The delays and opposition were frustrating and prompted many strategy meetings between John, Paul and myself, and later Brian Dawson. We became increasingly aware that constant campaigning would be necessary to cross the finish line.

Action in Ōtautahi

In Ōtautahi Christchurch, too, a campaign had been brewing around the city council. Chas Muir from SFWU was one of the early leaders, along with Reverend Jolyon White from Anglican Advocacy (a division of Anglican Care Canterbury Westland) and Jo McLean from the Engineering, Printing and Manufacturing Union (EPMU). Chas was a parishioner at the Anglican cathedral. He'd heard about the success of community organising in other countries and was keen to be part of it: 'My faith, together with being a unionist, were the drivers for me to become active in fighting for the living wage.'

In March 2013 Chas and Jolyon began to deliver living wage presentations to interested groups and community boards in the city. 'Jolyon was an advocate for social justice, so we shared the same values,' recalls Chas. 'He had just delivered a sermon ... about inequality and poverty. We met for coffee and decided that the Living Wage Movement had to happen in Christchurch.'

Karena Brown from EPMU was another early leader. Karena grew up in a low-income family in Addington, Christchurch. 'Social justice is in my blood ... Dad was a delegate for the Engineers' Union. Mum was a strong Labour member in Norman Kirk's electorate.' Karena followed her parents' activism. After leaving school at 15 and a stint in the air force, she got an office job and became a delegate in the New Zealand Clerical Workers Union and later a member of the union's national executive. She moved to an administration job at the union office. 'Then the ECA came along and

Backed by local supporters, Kate Day and Reverend Jolyon White from Anglican Advocacy appear before Christchurch City Council, February 2014. Photo credit: Fairfax

killed the Clerical Workers Union and I went to the Engineers' Union.' She's still there – as a researcher in E tū, an amalgamation of the EPMU and the SFWU.

The Christchurch team set up a steering group to target the council. Through the advocacy of Councillors Phil Clearwater and Yani Johanson, there was a push for the living wage for both directly employed workers and those employed by contractors, such as cleaners. Council staff agreed to do a feasibility study. Then Chas invited SFWU member Moli Fataua, a night cleaner at Christchurch International Airport, to tell her story to the Spreydon/Heathcote Community Board. Karena recalls, 'Moli spoke from the heart. She had them all in tears.'

The *Press* reported on Moli's story with the headline 'Struggling mum backs living wage call'. The article described how Moli worked full time as a cleaner but couldn't afford to feed, clothe and keep her children warm.

'Situations like hers are behind a growing international movement calling for companies to adopt a "living wage" policy to help the working poor survive.'[1] Councillor Johanson told the *Press* that while directors' and chief executives' salaries rose constantly, wages at the bottom failed to keep up with the cost of living.

The *Press* article took the living wage message to the people of Christchurch. The early champions, Councillors Clearwater and Johanson, were both in People's Choice, an umbrella group of left-leaning politicians in council that adopted the living wage as a core principle; at future council election forums, all those who stood under the People's Choice banner signed a living wage pledge.

The fledgling network was building in Christchurch. Joining SFWU, EPMU and Anglican Care were the Problem Gambling Foundation, NZEI Te Riu Roa and the Local Government Union, which had become part of the PSA. Karena recalls, 'We started putting in submissions to the council about why we needed the living wage and turning up and speaking to it in the annual plan … We got into the ears of the mayor, Lianne Dalziel. She was supportive, but she was very much tied into the cost. We slowly got her there.'

In July 2013 Hamilton City Council reversed its vote in support of the living wage that it had passed two months earlier. Unfortunately the work of community organising required to sustain the political commitment hadn't underpinned the original vote. For the new Hamilton network, it was back to building more community power to campaign and win.

Brand power

The living wage brand was becoming increasingly well known, and some mainstream businesses were beginning to take advantage of it, misrepresenting themselves as Living Wage Employers. One of the first to do so was The Warehouse. Out of the blue, The Warehouse made a public announcement that the company was a Living Wage Employer, despite not being accredited and the term being trademarked. The fact that the company expected its workers to complete 5000 hours or three years' service to qualify and, in the high-turnover retail sector, that over 80 percent of staff would likely leave before qualifying, was lost in translation. But the media was quick with congratulations. Economic commentator Bernard Hickey reported this development in the *NZ Herald*:

The Living Wage Movement is one response to the growing realisation that slowing economic growth is partly because of a falling share of income going to wages, which depresses demand and investment. Circuit breakers are needed to boost productivity and wages, and this is one of them. The Warehouse is hoping it will be a circuit breaker for their sales, profits and share price. For now, the Red Sheds have become the place where everyone gets enough of a Living Wage to buy those bargains.[2]

Annie Newman and Diana Yukich met with The Warehouse chief executive. Annie recalls, 'We said to them: you're not living wage, and you can't talk about being living wage because you're going to undermine the efforts of those who are starting to step up and become living wage.' Although angered by The Warehouse action, Annie and Diana believed it was essential to maintain a relationship, but despite an amicable follow-up meeting, the company refused to change its position. In 2019 it happened again: The Warehouse received considerable publicity for agreeing to a living wage – for 'most' of its workforce.

An exercise in democracy

As the clock ticked, the Wellington movement became impatient with the lack of progress from the council. Paul Barber recollects that council staff seemed to view the living wage as an annoying peripheral issue: 'We needed to set the agenda by taking the initiative. What the council leadership wanted and what the council officials wanted were a long way apart.' The Wellington movement decided to write the council's policy for them. Paul recalls: 'We'd keep going to these meetings and they hadn't done anything ... and we realised that, if we don't do it for them, it won't happen.' One reason for this lack of response from officers was, no doubt, the prospect of local body elections and the possibility of a different regime emerging after the elections – one more aligned with the ideology of the chief executive and the council's officers.

Local body elections, set for 12 October 2013, provided an opportunity for an exercise in local democracy around the living wage. We embarked on our first national campaign action, and large groups attended network meetings in Auckland and Wellington to organise election forums. We'd heard about the powerful London Citizens assemblies from Deborah Littman and others; now, in Aotearoa, we set about organising a new kind of election forum modelled on the IAF-style assemblies. Rather than providing a platform for politicians, these would be firmly centred on giving communities a voice. Candidates from across the political spectrum would be invited to a community venue full of local people. Filling the space was not left to chance: member organisations were asked to make a clear commitment to mobilise their people.

The forum organisers – the emerging leaders in the movement – set out to demonstrate people power in their communities. Candidates would be invited to hear workers' stories of lives lived on low wages and to listen to community leaders' calls for the living wage. They would then be challenged to make a public commitment to clear demands, or 'asks', as IAF called them. Those issuing the challenge were called 'pinners'. It was the job of the pinner both to put the ask to the candidate and to pin them down to a yes or no answer. The format was very different from previous election forums run by unions and progressive groups seeking social change, and was a major step in the Living Wage Movement's success in gaining political commitments.

The Auckland network organised an ambitious eight forums. The first was jointly hosted with Unions Auckland at the Papatoetoe Cosmopolitan Club. There was also a faith groups forum, and another hosted by women's organisations. Former refugees and migrants organised a forum, and another, attended by around 70 health workers, challenged district health board candidates to support equal pay and the living wage. The range of groups prepared to host living wage election forums demonstrated the diversity of the movement, and forum venues were decorated with colourful handmade banners that further spelt this out: 'Quakers for a Living Wage', 'Westies Deserve Living Wages' and 'P.I.C. Otara Supports the Living Wage Campaign'.

'The forums were a new way of doing things,' recalls Annie Newman. 'People were asked a direct question about whether they supported a living wage and were asked to respond yes or no. That was not something any local or central government politician was used to.' At the heart of these events was the tactic of securing public commitment from candidates that would enable networks to hold them to account after the elections. Some politicians weren't used to this level of directness and honesty. At a West Auckland forum organised by the Tuvaluan community, Councillor Linda Cooper said yes to the living wage; when this was picked up by the local press, however, she denied having made the commitment.

SFWU national president Barbara Wyeth (centre) and members Orquidea Tamayo Mortera (left) and Alicia Heremaia (right) at 'Do Women Matter?', a living wage election forum at the Ellen Melville Centre, Auckland, 2 September 2013. Photo: Jason Fell

Most election events take place without rules. Candidates are invited to talk about what they believe in and what they think, leaving plenty of room for a lack of clarity on specific changes they are prepared to commit to. The living wage forums were firmly led by co-chairs from within the movement. They were serious, but were also a celebration of community and featured music, entertainment and shared food. Politicians did not own these events.

The other defining element was accountability. 'Previously we were used to running election events then waiting passively to see what would happen,' recalls Annie. 'It's only if you get that rock-solid commitment that you've got something to make them accountable.' This was difficult for politicians like Linda Cooper, who made her commitment to a room full of witnesses and media representatives. Others welcomed the opportunity to make an emphatic commitment that was then publicised by the movement's member organisations throughout their networks.

The living wage forums were pieces of theatre, and labour-intensive. They were formulaic, but the organisers were cautious not to lose the energy that comes from people telling their own stories. Auckland had two dedicated organisers employed by SFWU who worked on the coordination and turnout to make the forums there a success; in Wellington a young activist was employed in a coordination role, which was funded by unions. Sam Gribben contacted candidates, sought their commitment to the living wage asks and invited them to attend the main forum at St Peter's Church in Willis Street. With a mayoral commitment and council vote already secured, Wellington candidates were asked to commit to 'taking all possible steps to support Wellington City Council becoming a living wage employer by paying a living wage to directly employed and contracted staff' in the next council term.

VUWSA ran another forum at the Victoria University student hub at which president Rory McCourt ensured that commitment to the living wage was among the questions put to candidates. Two university cleaners at the event, both SFWU members, spoke of the struggle of living on the minimum wage and the long hours cleaners were forced to work to get by. Mata, a Sāmoan mother of four, spoke first, followed by Ibrahim Omer, a refugee from Eritrea.

Ibrahim was an SFWU delegate but was not confident about standing up to speak. His union organiser, Yvette Taylor, saw Ibrahim as a future leader. 'She wouldn't leave me alone, and over a coffee she convinced me [to do it],' he recalls. When he arrived, the hub was full:

> I thought there were only going to be 40 to 50 people. When I saw the hub was packed, I wanted to run away. I was freaking out until I actually spoke. After I spoke, something changed in me – that I could do something with my life, rather than just doing two and a half cleaning jobs.

At the end of his speech Ibrahim told the students, 'I didn't come here to be just a cleaner. I want to be like you. I want to be a student.' He won the student audience over, and afterwards the candidates flocked to this cleaner who had so powerfully articulated his story of life on low wages. A *Dominion Post* headline the next day read 'Cleaners upstage the candidates'.[3] Ibrahim recalls, 'The day was fantastic and we got lots of support. Then all the candidates invited me to have morning tea with them if they won.' All mayoral candidates at the forum supported the living wage except Councillor Nicola Young, who continued her opposition – although not as stridently as in those early years.

The main Wellington forum was at St Peter's. The church was full, and Reverend Brian Dawson chaired the event. Mayoral candidates were given two minutes to speak and council candidates 30 seconds – plenty of time for living wage supporters like Councillors Iona Pannett and Paul Eagle to make a clear commitment. Celia Wade-Brown demonstrated her commitment by wearing a living wage T-shirt.

Also in contention for the mayoralty was Councillor John Morrison, and it was vital to secure his public commitment. Morrison did not attend the forum at St Peter's, but came to a smaller one in the Pacific Islanders' Presbyterian Church hall in Newtown. Speakers there included two staunch Sāmoan women. Malia Falanai-Andrews worked for a Pacific budgeting organisation and had a clear message about the lives of local families on low incomes. Lalopua Sanele, an SFWU delegate and a cleaner at Wellington Hospital, put the ask to the candidates. Lalopua had a strong presence and had led her workmates in many successful actions in the past 25 years, including a long cleaners' strike at Wellington Hospital. Her job was to challenge the candidates to say yes to the ask, and she was just the kind of forthright and persuasive leader to do this. The community pressure was real, and Morrison made the public commitment that Living Wage Wellington was seeking.

This was the outcome the movement always sought – not just a commitment from a preferred candidate. There could be no preferred candidate. The IAF mantra was 'no permanent friends, no permanent enemies'. There would be no backing for candidates who did not commit, regardless of which party they came from or whether they were known to those in the movement. For those who did commit, no matter where they sat on the political spectrum, their support on this issue would be publicised across the movement.

As far as Living Wage Wellington was concerned, the mayoral election was won that day. Sam Gribben had found it difficult to get hold of John Morrison, but when he did, Morrison said he would attend the third forum, where he made the commitment to the living wage. 'There was a question around whether the living wage was an election issue between the two front runners, John Morrison and Celia Wade-Brown,' recalls Sam. 'We won the living wage issue before the election even happened by securing John's commitment. That was when it felt like a mainstream political consensus in Wellington. Since then, every mayor elected in Wellington has supported the living wage. It has become a benchmark for election.' The successful candidate Celia Wade-Brown later mused about her opponent's new-found commitment to the living wage: 'He probably would have done it, but he might not have fought back against Kevin Lavery [Wellington City Council's chief executive during the adoption of the living wage] and the others quite so hard.'

Wade-Brown brought with her a narrow majority of councillors who supported the living wage. Sam attended her celebration party in his red T-shirt to send a clear message about Living Wage Wellington's expectations of the mayor and her council. They would be held to account.

In Auckland a commitment to adopt the living wage was obtained from the current mayor, Len Brown, who was standing again. Brown won the mayoralty, but only nine of the 20 elected councillors had pledged to the living wage ask. Diana Yukich later reflected: 'He talked the good talk, he was very positive and he opened the door, but it became clear very early on that he wasn't going to be able to get his councillors onside.' A few weeks after the election, Annie Newman announced to the movement's inaugural annual general meeting, 'The work continues toward the next election.'

The broad coalition

With the election forums completed, our focus was on building a national movement. Work continued on the development of a process for accreditation of employers, largely led by Diana Yukich. To inform future rate updates, Charles Waldegrave's living wage research team sought ongoing input from economists and others well versed in industrial relations. A reference group of Felicity Lamm, Prue Hyman, NZCTU economist Bill Rosenberg, policy advisor Lee Tan, Annie Newman and John Ryall was set up to grapple with thorny issues, such as whether a cell phone should be considered a standard item in every family. (The answer at that time was no, but it changed to yes in the 2018 update.) They also questioned whether the rate should be updated on the basis of the Consumers Price Index (CPI) or average annual earnings, and decided on the latter since the living wage was now a wage in the market.

From the start, and in contrast to similar movements overseas, Living Wage Movement Aotearoa NZ had strong backing from the central trade union organisation. Peter Conway, NZCTU national secretary and living wage portfolio holder, provided the main link to the wider union movement and coordinated discussions around contracted workers: who should be included and who should not? What is 'regular' work and what is 'ongoing'? Peter drew up a definition for the movement.

In October 2013 the Wellington network farewelled Reverend Margaret Mayman, who was moving to Sydney. Her contribution to the establishment of the Living Wage Movement in Aotearoa was acknowledged at a special gathering of the Wellington network, and at her formal farewell in the St Andrew's hall.

But the most significant event on the movement's 2013 calendar was the inaugural annual general meeting on 30 October. Held at the Auckland Council of Trade Unions' office, it was linked by video conference to Wellington and Christchurch. I joined 24 people at the Auckland meeting. Even at this early stage, the movement was a broad coalition. Among the attendees were many who would go on to take leadership roles and mobilise their own people in future living wage actions. The largest group was from the union stream, but the strong attendance from faith and community groups showed that the idea of three streams working in partnership was becoming a reality.

Annie Newman presented an annual report that described the work to date: 'In six months, the organisation has progressed from an idea to a fully functioning body providing oversight of an emerging community coalition, an employer accreditation system and a vibrant public debate about the Living Wage.'[4] The movement was based on the principles of local organisation, political neutrality and community ownership. Coalitions had blossomed in Auckland and Wellington, and interest was building in Christchurch, Hamilton, Dunedin and Blackball. Council elections had stimulated activity, particularly in Auckland and Wellington, and a grant of $30,000 from the JR McKenzie Trust would enable five-day residential courses in leadership to go ahead at the end of the year in Auckland and Wellington.

The annual report provides insight into the financial support for the movement. Much of the work was being carried out by SFWU staff; Sam Gribben's employment was paid for by local unions in Wellington; and in Christchurch, emerging leaders Jolyon White and Kate Day were supported by Anglican Life. Adding to the movement's funds was the number of fee-paying member organisations. Much-needed financial stability and credibility were provided largely by treasurer Shirley Zhuang and accountant Marina Kokanovic. Both from the SFWU finance team, these two gave countless hours of voluntary time, as was required for the ambitious and underfunded movement. Diana Yukich's voluntary contribution was also noted.

The annual report noted the announcement of the rate as a major achievement. The research had been largely uncontested, and had received support from across the political spectrum and captured media attention. Annie noted the 'critical impetus' this gave the campaign:

> The debate about wages has begun to change to reflect the growing concern about poverty in working families in New Zealand, and the idea of a wage based on need rather than a product of the market has gained momentum since the May 2012 launch of the Living Wage Movement … The living wage has arguably entered the lexicon of public debate in a remarkably short time.[5]

The inaugural AGM laid the groundwork for the future. Goals for the following year included the launch of the accredited employer programme, deepening engagement with community partners and building capability among community leaders. The upcoming general election would bring not only challenges but also opportunities to address inequality. We needed, Annie said, to 'build an organisation that is robust, that is grounded in sound principles, and that establishes clear boundaries for our activity'.[6]

The name, Living Wage Movement Aotearoa NZ, was formally adopted. Rules were endorsed, and annual subscriptions from member organisations were set (large groups, such as unions, would pay $1000–$5000; smaller groups $50–$100). Guidelines were approved for local networks, and also for local boards consisting of leaders drawn from the three streams. The meeting established an employer accreditation advisory board (also drawn from the three streams) to grant licences to accredited employers and endorsed a policy stipulating that Living Wage Movement Aotearoa NZ was a non-party-political organisation.

The meeting then elected the first governance board: from the faith stream were Reverend Jolyon White, Reverend Brian Dawson, Ivoni Fuimaono and David Hall; unionists included John Ryall, Robert Reid and Brenda Pilott; and from the community stream were Muriel Tunoho, Dr Siobhan Trevallyan from Waitakere Union Health Centre and student leader Sonya Clark from VUWSA. The last item on the agenda was a motion that Annie Newman be the national convenor for a three-year term. Agreement was unanimous.

The AGM was a significant milestone for the Living Wage Movement and brought together the planning, thinking and activity of the past two years since John Ryall had voiced his idea. It cemented the concept of the partnership of faith, community and union, and put in place the building blocks needed for the movement to achieve its goals.

A DIY framework

In Wellington the November deadline for the city council to produce an implementation framework for presentation to councillors approached, but so far council officers had produced nothing in writing. By way of assistance, Paul Barber and I wrote a framework and circulated it among elected representatives and council officials.

Our framework demonstrated how Wellington City Council could implement the living wage. We promoted the living wage as a sound investment in economic and social wellbeing as well as a fiscal cost. We showed how the living wage could be implemented over the next three years so that the council could become a fully accredited Living Wage Employer by 2017. The framework proposed to begin pay rises for directly employed workers in 2014; those employed via contractors would move to the rate as contracts came up for renegotiation. The council would also have an advocacy role in promoting the living wage in the city.

Wellington City Council eventually achieved accreditation in September 2018, but not without a long battle against organised opposition from council officials, the Wellington Chamber of Commerce and the Taxpayers' Union. The latter, a right-wing lobby group set up in 2013 with the goal of reducing taxes, was co-founded by David Farrar and Jordan Williams. It dedicated considerable energy to attempts to overturn democratic decisions supporting the living wage, which were themselves driven by communities that included the very ratepayers the Taxpayers' Union claimed to represent. The Taxpayers' Union relied on executive director Jordan Williams and researcher Jim Rose parachuting into communities to tell them how they should spend their money. Williams in particular became a familiar sight at council meetings debating the living wage, and they monitored progress in cities and towns where grassroots alliances were determined to ensure that their councils delivered on commitments made at well-attended public community forums.

Living wage leaders were learning that a good argument, a sensible and clear pathway and a legal opinion made little difference to ideologically driven officials or the Taxpayers' Union, who focused solely on the immediate cost. The only way to win was by publicly demonstrating community – and therefore voter – support for the living wage. The movement needed to send a clear message to local body politicians: to get elected, it was in their interests to back the living wage. But securing employer or political commitments was not enough when gatekeeper chief executives and senior officials were determined to keep elected representatives out of decision-making around wages.

The movement's leaders knew there was a lot to learn. What did it mean to build power in community? How could we mobilise communities to pressure employers and win the living wage? How could we transform from a campaign to a genuine movement based on partnership and long-term relationships? To answer these questions we needed a deeper understanding of the countercultural approach of broad-based community organising. The Living Wage Movement turned to the IAF and our friend Deborah Littman to learn the strategies of their approach.

Adopting the IAF approach

The IAF was established in Chicago in the 1940s and based on organising principles developed by Saul Alinsky. Although cultures have changed over the 80 years since its formation, the principles have endured. At the heart of the model is the strategy of creating power in disempowered communities by uniting diverse institutions, or civil society organisations, around a commitment to build community power for change – exactly the problem the SFWU sought to resolve.

'The basic understanding that Alinsky came to was that the people he was dealing with, although they were poor, were not powerless, and their power rested in their civil society institutions,' says Deborah. But those institutions did not speak to one another. 'The game-changing thing that IAF did was to understand the power of institutions as opposed to the individual, and to understand the power that came from bringing those civil society organisations together.'

As the IAF organising model won campaigns and united organisations into alliances, the movement grew. IAF alliances appeared across the US, then in Canada, the UK, Germany and Australia. Countries adopted the model to suit their own culture and issues. In Aotearoa in 2012, the model offered a way to bring together organisations to build power in a fragmented civil society.

One of the strongest principles of IAF is first to build the alliance, and then to identify the issues. New Zealand's Living Wage Movement differs on this key point, having gone out specifically to build an alliance around a single issue. 'This could have been a point of tension between the New Zealand movement and IAF,' says Annie Newman. 'But IAF supported our movement from the start, providing training and mentoring and the opportunity to learn IAF's power-building philosophies and skills. From this point forward, the movement adopted all the IAF principles. The New Zealand movement's focus is on power building the IAF way.'

Those principles included building a movement based on enduring relationships and partnership, and strengthening the capacity of member organisations to mobilise members. Another core principle is developing leaders through training. It is IAF's practice to place a high priority on training community leaders intensively in the skills of building alliances that are committed to creating the community power needed to win real change.

The IAF principles and techniques became the basis of the New Zealand Living Wage Movement's initial five-day residential courses in Auckland and Wellington. These would be led by Deborah Littman with the support of Sister Maribeth Larkin, an IAF organiser based in Los Angeles.

Sister Maribeth grew up in California in the fifties and sixties, a time of social revolution in youth politics and culture. She took her vows to become a nun in the 1970s as a 20-year-old, and joined a social service order. Her order, the Sisters of Social Service, was founded in Hungary under the umbrella of the Benedictines. In 1976, while doing parish-based social work at Dolores Mission Parish in East Los Angeles, Sister Maribeth became involved in the United Neighborhoods Organization (UNO), a local organisation affiliated with IAF.

Maribeth soon became a leader. She was hired as a UNO organiser in 1978 and continued working in various roles for the IAF until 2019. She helped to develop a state-wide network in Dallas, El Paso and San Antonio, and in Los Angeles she helped to lead the building of a powerful community organisation able to mobilise thousands of people to public assemblies and actions, called One LA. Sister Maribeth brought vast experience in community organising, largely with Hispanic and black communities.

Learning about power

The first living wage training course was held in Auckland at Vaughan Park, an Anglican retreat and training centre. Many early Auckland leaders attended, including Fala Haulangi, Diana Yukich, David Hall and Annie Newman. 'A whole lot of things stood out,' recalls Annie. 'One was the diversity of participants and how each stream had its own language, which could be alienating, but the training overcame those barriers to create trust … strong bonds formed between leaders in institutions with quite different missions.'

The Wellington course took place in Akatarawa near Wellington. Although resources were tight and the venue was basic, the trainees were committed and eager to learn. The group of 20 was evenly split between the three streams. The faith group was dominated by Anglicans, including Brian Dawson, Jolyon White and Reverend Tric Malcolm; community participants included Muriel Tunoho and the current and future student presidents, Rory McCourt and Rick Zwaan. I was a union participant, along with Sam Huggard from FIRST Union, Rebecca Matthews, Karena Brown and Yvette Taylor, who also arranged release from his cleaning job for her delegate, Ibrahim Omer.

The training programme, used by IAF organisations around the world, revolved around understanding power, alliance-building and action in order to empower communities. At the heart were relational organising and building power. These concepts were framed by two things: the first was an ancient text by Greek writer and historian Thucydides called *The Melian Dialogue*. Throughout the five days, this text provided a tool for understanding power. The second was an activity on the final evening in which we put into practice the concepts and skills learnt during the week. The programme was unlike anything we had participated in before. Annie recalls, 'We were used to modular training. To take five days to focus on a few concepts was a pretty radical approach for unions.'

The course began with intensive sharing in which participants told of their personal experiences of standing up to power. As people shared their stories, the level of trust grew. We threw ourselves into a role play based on

The Melian Dialogue. Reading this text was the only preparation we had been asked to do, and it was perplexing: what did a collection of speeches from leaders of opposing sides in a fifth-century BC battle have to do with modern-day campaigning for wage justice? Faced with an invasion by the powerful Athenians, the inhabitants of the island of Melios believed they would win because their cause was just. They had faith in their allies but ignored the fact that these allies were weak. The Athenians were prepared to negotiate, but the Melians stubbornly remained in the 'world as it should be' rather than the 'world as it is'. Role playing these two groups was a challenging start and caused us to dig deeply into the principles of power and powerlessness. We learned about the qualities of leadership required to attract followers and maximise participation. For the trade unionists attending, this was a big shift from a transactional approach to organising.

At the training, all the learning about power, leadership and working in alliance is in preparation for action. On the last evening, participants work together to produce an action aimed at exerting community pressure on a political target and gaining a commitment. Guests are invited to watch participants put into practice what they have learnt. Newly elected Wellington City Councillor Sarah Free attended the Wellington action. In just a few hours, we participants had organised a programme with music, theatre and the sharing of real workers' stories, which culminated in a challenge to Councillor Free to make a commitment to the living wage.

The event was Councillor Free's introduction to the Living Wage Movement and she wasn't sure what to expect. Mayor Celia Wade-Brown had asked her if she would support the living wage, and she had agreed. She already had social justice values and had witnessed the inequality of those on low incomes in her work as an advisor at the Sustainability Trust, where she had assisted people to make their homes warm, dry and healthy. Introduced to the Living Wage Movement that night, she recalls, 'I was pleased to see so many people from Christian churches. That really interested me because I didn't see the church as political.' Free felt inspired and 'went away resolved to do my best to make it happen'. Common ground was firmly established and Councillor Free, who became Wellington's deputy mayor in 2019, remained a loyal ally of the Living Wage Movement and a vocal supporter of Wellington City Council becoming New Zealand's first living wage council.

The training helped the movement to take a step forward. Paul Barber, who attended the Wellington course, describes it as 'a pivotal moment. We came from different streams that don't necessarily interact. It built our relationships and what it means to be movement-building. And having the international input from Deborah and Maribeth … got us thinking: how would that work in Aotearoa New Zealand?'

For many of us, the course changed how we looked at life, our work and our activism. Rebecca Matthews recalls, 'It had an impact on the way I worked. It appealed to things I have anyway, like a curiosity about people and their lives and a desire to have a genuine connection with people … It was not just about political organising. It was about how you think and relate to people.'

Ibrahim Omer also found the training life-changing. 'When I first heard the words "power building", that was a game changer. It changed the way I think. It changed the way I think of myself. I'd always thought I was good with people but I didn't see that I could use those people skills and make an impact on people's lives.' After the course, Ibrahim went straight to Victoria University to enrol as a student. Seven years later, as a new member of Parliament, he recalled this experience in his maiden speech: 'One Sunday night I was cleaning a lecture theatre. The next day I had my first lecture, Politics 111, in the same lecture theatre. It was a very emotional moment that I will never forget.'[7]

The training resulted in determination from some faith groups to take a leadership role. Brian Dawson recalls, 'I loved that training. I've gone on to use those principles in other work ever since.' Afterwards, he and other faith leaders took the initiative to coordinate a Christmas event to support Wellington City Council cleaners, called Carols for Our Cleaners, in Civic Square. Brian was MC, the mayor's cleaner Angela Toa was speaker, and a large crowd sang carols led by SFWU organiser and minister Alan Wendt with a Pacific choir from the Wesley Methodist Church.

At the next Wellington network meeting, Reverend Norman Wilkins proposed that we seat ourselves in a circle as equals. We elected the first local board for the Wellington region: Muriel Tunoho and Rick Zwaan representing community, Paul Barber and Brian Dawson representing faith groups, and Rebecca and myself from the union stream. The local board has since overseen all work of the Wellington movement.

And then came a breakthrough. Wellington City Council officers finally produced a paper with recommendations for councillors to vote on. It was presented to the council on 11 December 2013. At the meeting, council parking wardens staged an action. The wardens, members of SFWU, arrived together and met their union organiser, Yvette Taylor, at the front door, where they all donned living wage T-shirts. When the living wage delegation entered the council chamber, the wardens also marched in and assembled along the wall directly behind the councillors. A dramatic photo of the parking wardens, lined up in their red shirts, appeared in the next morning's *Dominion Post*. Yvette recalls: 'The wardens were minimum-wage workers employed by Armourguard. They were a tight crew at work, mainly young Pacific Island guys … and the delegates made sure everyone was there. [They] were happy to take part in the action. They wanted to win.'

Despite the parking wardens' action and a compelling speech from one of their delegates, it was not yet their time. However, it was time for a commitment to the directly employed workforce. The council officers' paper acknowledged council's 'in principle' decision made in June and proposed a living wage rate be phased in from 1 January 2014 at a cost of $750,000. It also proposed that council-controlled organisations consider how to achieve the living wage within their current budgets and that further work be done on workers employed via contractors in preparation for the 2015 long-term plan.

This vote lifted over 450 workers to the living wage. The movement's first major victory had been won by the power of community.

CHAPTER 5

Trailblazing: 2014

'The legacy of this movement will be a stronger democracy where voices unite across diverse groups to advance social justice. It will be built by forging deeper relationships between organisations, through shared community leadership skills, and the participation of grassroots communities in pursuing solutions to poverty and inequality.'

ANNIE NEWMAN, Living Wage Movement Aotearoa NZ

An explosion of events

Hundreds of directly employed Wellington City Council workers moved to the living wage rate in January 2014, the first large group to do so as a direct outcome of the campaign. It was certainly something to celebrate, but it was just a start. Contracted workers were next. No worker would be left behind. Although it was tempting to run quick campaigns for small achievable goals, the movement stuck to campaigning for whole workforces.

The year began with an explosion of events as local networks enthusiastically took the living wage message into communities, especially in Auckland and Wellington. One of the first, a Whānau Day held in Auckland, offered free entertainment, music, food and information stalls. The event received financial support from the Māngere–Ōtāhuhu Local Board, and its success was largely due to SFWU member Alicia Heremaia. 'Alicia was passionate about her community and paying living wages. She was the main driver and we were the support team,' recalls Diana Yukich. 'We were celebrating the community, informing the community and growing the movement.' The inclusive and community-focused approach set the standard for future events.

Inspired by the living wage concept, requests came from the regions for meetings, speakers and information. In January Annie Newman addressed a public meeting in Palmerston North that brought together faith and community groups and unions around a shared commitment to establishing a network. Unfortunately, the meeting was disrupted by aspiring politicians who insisted on speaking. 'This created a backlash from participants, who had been promised the movement was not political,' Annie recalls. 'It impacted on our chance of building trust and commitment.' We were learning the value of the IAF principle of keeping grassroots organising in the community and engagement with politicians in a separate arena.

The Auckland network was everywhere, spreading the message through stalls and information stands, and local activists engaged in thousands of conversations with organisations and individuals. Annie recalls one with Jackie Blue, a National Party MP who was immediately supportive despite her party leader's opposition. Blue left Parliament and became New Zealand's Equal Employment Opportunities Commissioner, a strong and vocal supporter of unions and equal pay and an ally of the Living Wage Movement. 'New Zealand's a small country,' says Annie, 'and you get a lot of mileage from spending time in the community and talking.'

Network members continued to lobby local boards, uncovering both support and opposition. Although these boards had no voting power on the council, they could put pressure on political leaders. When Fala Haulangi and Diana Yukich heard that a Henderson–Massey Local Board meeting would include a vote on the living wage, they hurriedly organised a strong living wage presence. The board voted in favour of the living wage, against the explicit wishes of local councillor Linda Cooper, who told them it was not their place to make this decision. Afterwards, board member and later Auckland councillor Shane Henderson emailed Fala: '[You] are a real inspiration with your tireless advocacy of a fair go for low-wage workers. It was a real privilege to be in a position to bring this to the public forum … cheers to those that could make it on the night. I think their presence and support really made a difference in that vote!'[1]

The movement was also increasingly active in other places. In March 2014 a public meeting was organised by the Fabians in Wellington with leader of the Anglican Diocese of Wellington Bishop Justin Duckworth and Charles Waldegrave as speakers. And in Hamilton a range of groups – the interfaith network, the disability advocacy organisation People First NZ, Methodist City Action, Anglican Action and a raft of unions – came together to establish a network. A living wage 'teach-in' was held at Auckland University, and in Christchurch a public meeting drew a crowd from faith and community groups and unions.

Then came celebrity endorsement. In March, UK singer-songwriter

Billy Bragg gave a shout-out for the living wage at an event in Auckland. When he visited New Zealand again that October he offered his endorsement of the living wage during performances in Auckland and Wellington, in support of local network members who were collecting donations. Other overseas celebrities, including US singer Bonnie Rait, lent support to the movement, and many New Zealand artists and performers, among them Don McGlashan, Robyn Malcolm, Reb Fountain, Gary McCormick, The Eastern and Jennifer Ward-Lealand, gave their voices and time to events. The movement's determination to transform the lives of low-paid workers struck a chord.

A rate that is living

In February 2014 the national governance board met in Auckland, then moved to a Mt Eden café for the formal launch of the Living Wage Employer accreditation scheme and logo and the announcement of the 2014/15 rate. The café, O'Sarracino, later named Ika, was part-owned by former Alliance MP Laila Harré and her husband Barry Gribben. Ika would become Auckland's first accredited living wage restaurant in March 2016.

An orange and blue employer logo differentiated the employer stream from the community movement and would be available under licence to Living Wage Employers. Some people found the distinction between the two hard to grasp. The role of the community movement of grassroots organisations was to build local power and drive campaigns. The living wage accreditation board dealt with inquiries from employers. When employers became accredited, the community celebrated.

At the launch Charles Waldegrave announced the updated living wage rate of $18.80, an increase of 40 cents an hour. It was important that the rate kept up with increased costs and wage movements. Waldegrave later explained, 'The living wage is not a welfare benefit. It is a wage in the market and so the annual updates should relate primarily to movements in wages.' The rate increased by the movement in average earnings recorded by the Stats NZ Quarterly Employment Survey. Most accredited employers and commentators considered this reasonable, but some Wellington City councillors felt they should have been consulted as the council was the largest and most high-profile employer to adopt the living wage, at least for some of their workforce. In an email to Celia Wade-Brown and councillors, on behalf of the movement I pointed out that 'the process of setting the living wage and now accrediting Living Wage Employers involves many employers around the country. We are pleased to let you know that LWMANZ [Living Wage Movement Aotearoa NZ] has been swamped with inquiries today from interested employers, and the announcement has been very positively received.'[2]

Contest of ideas

In April 2014 the Living Wage Movement's national governance board came together for a two-day strategic planning retreat at Willow Park, an Anglican conference centre in Auckland. On the agenda was discussion about where the movement wanted to be in five years' time, how the board would work together in the future, and what relationships were required to build the movement further.

The meeting revealed different views about the partnership model and how the three streams would work together. What emerged was a contest of ideas. One proposal was to take some church leaders into union negotiations with a large corporate employer to give the union side an advantage. 'There was a view in the union movement that this new campaign was about using the leaders of faith groups and communities to back a union strategy to leverage wages up,' Annie Newman recalls:

> It was almost like 'you can do something for us, by putting your bishop's hat on when we go to see the CEO'. We were standing alongside people with integrity, history, analysis and constituency. These were our partners and we were past reducing them to the symbols of their tradition. If we did that, our movement would have turned into a union-brokered campaign.

That moment epitomised the difference between the transactional approach we were used to in the union movement and the relational approach we had embraced in the Living Wage Movement. 'The old union strategies weren't serving workers,' reflects Annie. 'We needed a real game changer to do something about that. What we were looking for was a whole new way of relating as part of a bigger civil society and we found this in the Living Wage Movement.'

Susan Adams recalls some tension in that discussion: 'It was a power struggle, a struggle for ideological supremacy.' The movement was growing increasingly into the relational model of sharing power with community and leaving the transactional, rent-a-crowd approach behind. This new power was based on long-term partnership.

The power of the plan

A vital aspect of winning the living wage for local body workers was gaining political commitment and ensuring this was written into annual budgets or plans. By law, a council must consult with its community on its annual plan, and this necessity provided an opening for the movement to employ local democracy as the lever to win the living wage. A united community voice had a greater chance of influencing the commitment to deliver a living wage. Accordingly, the Auckland network threw everything into a campaign to influence Auckland Council's 2014/15 annual plan and produced a well-researched document, authored mainly by FIRST Union's Ed Miller.

The Wellington network also organised a strong presence in Wellington City Council's annual plan deliberations. The mood was positive – after all, councillors had already voted for the living wage, and the mayor was a strong supporter. But the draft plan prepared for public consultation was disappointing: the question on the living wage was framed negatively and included inflated cost estimates. The tactic was used by a number of councils to frighten communities into rejecting implementation. But where the local movement is active, this strategy is seldom successful – and it was not successful in Wellington. The network swung into action, organising submissions. The community's response was overwhelmingly positive.

Alongside the submission process, council officers conducted a series of independent polls. The results showed that a clear majority supported the living wage and a small number were strongly opposed. Clearly, there was a mandate for council to move on with implementation. Not one for mincing words, Brian Dawson said, 'Wellingtonians have obviously not been frightened off by scaremongering around the cost, which will be met by a range of measures, including from the council's current wage budget and through negotiations with relevant contractors.' Despite the negative presentation, the people of Wellington were ready to be citizens of Aotearoa's first living wage city.

In March 2014 Living Wage Wellington brought another delegation to council. Contracted parking wardens and cleaners presented submissions calling for the living wage for council's contracted workers. In April the mayor introduced the annual plan, saying, 'It was gratifying to receive so many submissions congratulating us for already adopting a living wage for staff directly employed by council … This rate will also be extended to council's parking team when the service is brought in-house.'[3] A statement of intent had been sent to council-controlled organisations, and officers were carrying out work to extend the living wage to contracted workers for the 2015–25 long-term plan.

Everything seemed to be on track. There was well-demonstrated support from a diverse movement representing thousands of Wellingtonians. There was broader community support, demonstrated through the council's own polling, and strong political support from the elected leaders. Officers were instructed to undertake the necessary work. Instead, they dragged the chain and ignored the will of the community and their political leaders. Three years would pass before serious steps towards implementation were taken.

Expansion

Although SFWU had adopted the campaign for the living wage as a strategy in 2012, other unions joining the movement were now wrestling with the concept. What did it mean for their membership? NZEI Te Riu Roa was one of the first to embrace the living wage and explore its relevance for members. In March 2014 NZEI Living Wage for Learning rallies were held in Auckland and Wellington.[4] Rebecca Matthews, who organised these well-attended events, recalls, 'We were trying to make the connection between a living wage for people working in schools and children and their families.'

> Poverty doesn't support learning if children are coming to school hungry, if they're not able to participate in sports because their parents can't afford the fees or the uniform or the boots, if their parents are having to work multiple jobs and never see their children, or the children are having to be dragged around at night to jobs. Also for the educators themselves, and particularly for support staff, if they're on poverty wages, they're not in the best position to support children either.

In Auckland, networks continued to grow in the sprawling city. Yvette Taylor had moved to Auckland and took on a leadership role in the movement. The only way to organise effectively was at the grassroots, area by area. There was an Auckland central network and a West Auckland one, where Diana Yukich was a leader. A 'Westie' herself, Diana recalls that people there were coming together every Friday, with meetings in between. West Auckland was a mainly low-income area with a diverse range of organisations and individuals, from the Tuvaluan Church to the PSA, SFWU and the Kiribati community, all keen to be involved.

Inspired by the South Auckland Whānau Day, activists organised West Fest for a Living Wage in May 2014 'to bring together different communities that were interested in the living wage around the West Auckland network,' says Yvette. 'It was a festival-type event to raise awareness and the profile of the movement.' Hundreds attended. Television and film actor Robyn Malcolm was MC, and there was food, music, stalls and a photo booth for people to record their image alongside statements about what the living wage meant to them. This time, leaders of political parties were invited so they might get a sense of the importance of the living wage to this community. Those who attended included Labour Party leader David Cunliffe and the high-profile leader of the generally conservative New Zealand First Party, Winston Peters. The movement was keen to gain support and commitment from politicians for the adoption of the living wage in the public service. Winston Peters' attendance demonstrated that the concept was making an impact across the political spectrum.

These creative events were good for raising awareness, and they also built the confidence and relationships that were the glue of local networks. Some wanted the events to be staged every year, but they required a lot of energy and organisation that was also needed to focus on specific goals, like winning the campaigns in local councils.

The Parking Services saga

In December 2013 I had received a call from Wellington's deputy mayor, Justin Lester, who said he had good news. The council would take Parking Services in-house and the workers would move to the living wage. This was good news indeed. These staff were largely minimum-wage workers, and this would be another step towards accreditation for the council. I sought his assurance that the existing workers would all be kept on. Lester gave that assurance, and I have no doubt he believed this would be the case.

Around 30 workers were employed in Wellington City Council's Parking Services. Those managing fees and fines were employed by a different contractor to the wardens. On 18 December the *Dominion Post* had reported: 'Service and Food Workers Union national secretary John Ryall said raising the pay of wardens – at present about $14.10 an hour – to the $18.40 living wage was great news, provided existing wardens were able to shift to working for the council.'[5]

John said SFWU's members in Parking Services were working up to 70 hours a week for as little as $14.10 an hour, regardless of their experience. A council representative, however, was reported as saying the contractors had been informed of the council's decision and 'would provide opportunities for their staff to apply for jobs'.[6] Although this rang a few warning bells, we thought it was just a formality and all would be successful.

When the councillors endorsed the proposal to bring parking wardens in-house in December 2013, the rationale was that these workers would become 'ambassadors'; their roles would expand with more focus on dealing with the public and they would be upskilled. In June 2014, before Wellington City Council took the workers in-house and moved them to the living wage, the council hired Madison Recruitment to manage the process of the workers reapplying for their jobs. It became apparent that council officers did not intend to keep all workers and provide training to upskill them for the new roles if necessary. SFWU and the Living Wage Movement opposed this process vehemently but council officers went ahead anyway. As a result of this process, a small number of Parking Services workers lost their jobs. To our minds, the loss of any at all was unacceptable.

Once the council took over Parking Services, the number of workers increased and so did their skills and incomes. Moving to the living wage rate does not limit future union bargaining success or take away the option of industrial action. With the support of their union, Wellington wardens went on to negotiate significant pay rises: between 2017 and 2020, they achieved a 22 percent wage increase when inflation was just over 7 percent. 'They improved their wages, with the base being the living wage and then other qualifications steps above it, through collective bargaining,' John recalls. 'There have also been considerable benefits for the council. Through moving to the living wage, taking it [Parking Services] back in-house and transforming the way that people work jobs through technology, the productivity gain has been enormous and it has meant far better conditions for the workers.'

Two years later the Taxpayers' Union released an 82-page report entitled *Best of Intentions, Worst of Results*. Author Jim Rose exaggerated the job losses among council's parking workforce and concluded that this was a failure of the living wage approach, when in reality, council management was responsible.[7] John Ryall recalls the Taxpayers' Union dredging up the saga at a council meeting in Lower Hutt and arguing that if you implement the living wage, people lose their jobs: 'Their position was that we were depriving poor people of jobs, implying that all poor people are useless and couldn't do their job if you demanded more from them,' recalls John. 'The Living Wage Movement strongly supports upskilling workers. A very high level of workers in Parking Services today have a level four NZQA qualification: a certificate of regulatory compliance. They complete this in work time. The council pays for it all.'

Stevan Carlyon, an SFWU delegate, had been a minimum-wage parking warden. He shared his story in the union's magazine *Our Voice*. Stevan had been living at his brother's home, feeling isolated and depressed. 'All I could do was exist. I struggled to make ends meet,' he said. The move to the living wage enabled Stevan to save for his wedding and honeymoon. 'I'm just lucky I have food in my pantry,' he said: 'People who are solo parents, they cannot feed their children very well if they are not on the living wage. We do have that money, and when friends come over we supply them with a good home-cooked meal.'[8]

Trailblazing employers

In July 2014 the first group of fully accredited Living Wage Employers was announced. Living wage leaders gathered to celebrate at O'Sarracino, the Auckland café where the updated living wage rate had been announced in February. Most of the 11 newly accredited employers attended the event, including James Crowe and Tommy Holden, the creators of Nice Blocks. Each of these employers had made sure that all directly employed and contracted workers in their business were paid a minimum of the living wage.

These early accredited employers were trailblazers. Although wealthy corporates and institutions funded by public money were the main targets of the movement, it was small businesses that showed the way. Large organisations seemed challenged by the idea of including contracted cleaners in their adoption of the living wage; these small, ethical businesses proved it could be done when an employer was committed. Opticmix was the first and smallest Living Wage Employer. At the launch of the accreditation programme, director Kevin Church told media: 'If a business can't afford to pay the living wage, really it is questionable how valid the business is to run.'[9]

On the day of the announcement, the Wellington network held a flash mob and a Nice Blocks 'lick-in' at Victoria University. Living wage supporters, university cleaners and students were joined by the TEU bargaining team, fresh from putting a living wage claim on the table with their employer. The action kicked off a long-running campaign to win the living wage at the university.

With the announcement of the first accredited employers, the path was now laid for any business or organisation to come on board. Networks were more determined than ever to achieve the goal of accreditation at their local council.

Two years on

In August 2014, Living Wage Wellington held a second birthday party at Loaves and Fishes, the large hall attached to the Anglican Cathedral. It was jam-packed with supporters, including the Anglican Bishop of Wellington Justin Duckworth, local MP Grant Robertson, Mayor Celia Wade-Brown and other local body politicians. Reverend Brian Dawson welcomed performers from the community, including a kapa haka group, a primary school Pacific group and jazz singer Lisa Tomlins. Over 300 turned out to the upbeat and somewhat chaotic celebration for a movement that was making a difference.

A few weeks later Living Wage Wellington organised the first community meeting in Porirua, chaired by Brian Dawson and Stella Teariki, a local PSA organiser who became a valued leader in the movement. Around 50 people from across the three streams came to Porirua Union and Community Health Service in Cannons Creek, where they broke into small groups to discuss the impact of low wages. There was plenty to talk about: Porirua had some of the poorest communities in Aotearoa. By the end of the night the discussion had moved to setting up a local network.

The first Porirua network meeting was held in September at Mana College and included future leaders in the network Stella Teariki, Andrew Chick from the CTU, Reverend Cath Growcott from Porirua Anglicans and Reverend Hiueni Nuku from Porirua Union and Community Health Service (PUCHS). Hiueni soon signed up PUCHS as a member of the movement, and quickly ensured that the health service achieved accreditation as a Living Wage Employer.

In October students, general and academic staff, cleaners and alumni met at the VUWSA office to brainstorm ideas for a campaign in the university community, and the Living Wage for Vic campaign was born. I was more than keen to see my old university take up the living wage.

Also in October, AGMs for Living Wage Movement Aotearoa NZ were held in Wellington and Auckland (Hamilton members travelled to the latter and Christchurch people joined online). The movement's second annual report was full of stories of growth. There were now over 50 paid-up member organisations of the community movement and nearly 30 fully accredited employers. Networks were active in Auckland, Hamilton, Wellington, Porirua and Christchurch.

The Aucklanders elected a new board with representatives from Aotearoa Resettled Community Coalition, the Public Service Association (PSA), St Matthew-in-the-City, the EPMU and SFWU; and a new national governance board was elected, with David Hall, Brian Dawson and Jolyon White (faith stream); Warwick Jones from the PSA, Robert Reid from FIRST Union and John Ryall (union stream); and Dr Rose Black from Poverty Action Waikato, Muriel Tunoho, Rick Zwaan and Leonie Morris (community stream).

Residential training programmes were held again in 2014, this time led by IAF trainer Joe Chrastil from Seattle. The first was in Auckland. Susan Adams attended, and was struck by how different the movement was, with 'training, energy and enthusiasm and a clear focus of what we were on about. We could all bring our own perspectives from the different experiences ... That was a strength.'

The second course was in Wellington. Hiueni Nuku, Andrew Chick, Stella Teariki and Teau Marama came from Porirua, along with Kieran Monaghan (who would later establish a group called Aotearoa Artists for a Living Wage, and introduced the living wage stage at the annual Newtown Festival) and Lyn Williams, an SFWU organiser who lent solid support to a group of Quakers who established Living Wage Whanganui.

Hiueni Nuku was from the Tongan village of Hautu. He came to New Zealand as an adult, took on work as a labourer and later enrolled in a polytechnic course. He and his wife, Tongi, had four children. The student allowance was not enough to feed the family and Hiueni took on a full-time cleaning job. Living on a cleaner's wage was hard, and he joined the queue at the food bank. He eventually gained a Bachelor of Commerce, became the manager at Porirua Union and Community Health Service and was ordained as a Methodist minister in 2010. He later said, 'I really want to support the living wage because I experienced that struggle. Some days we didn't have bread on our table.' Hiueni would become a wise and valued leader in the movement – in Porirua, on the Living Wage Wellington local board, the national governance board and on the accreditation advisory board.

Networks are the heart of the Living Wage Movement. In the Wellington region, supporters in Porirua had established their own network, and others in the Hutt Valley later also set up an independent network. Unlike Auckland, the Wellington region includes a number of different cities and districts, each with its own identity and council. Hutt and Porirua cities wanted their own living wage networks. The movement has two goals: to create local movements with the capacity to mobilise people, and to build a national membership organisation. There was always a balance required between creating genuine local grassroots organisations and maintaining the critical mass whereby large-scale mobilisation is achieved. But local movements were also a strength, as they ensured networks that were focused on mobilising locally to campaign to win the living wage, especially at their own councils. As well, local leaders emerged who were grounded in their own communities.

Momentum continued to grow. Eighty South Auckland leaders gathered in November to talk about what mattered in their communities. All their concerns related to the need for decent pay. The Living Wage for Vic campaigners held an event hosted by TEU and attended by a large group of university cleaners, many of whom were refugee-background workers. And in Auckland a delegation of living wage leaders met with AUT leaders to challenge them to ensure that university contractors paid the living wage to their cleaners. They met resistance from the unsympathetic vice-chancellor, Derek McCormack. Local board member Susan Adams recalls, 'He wasn't too happy when I reminded him he couldn't even open his doors if the cleaners hadn't cleaned the toilets.'

Nobody ever expected to achieve every goal immediately, but in the minds of leaders like Susan, all the delegations and campaigning had a cumulative effect: 'Many small incremental steps need to be taken and, years later, you look back and see the significance of those early achievements.' Such steps were being taken all over the country.

On 4 December Stella Teariki and Andrew Chick led a network meeting in Porirua, where Stella, Andrew, Hiueni and Teau Marama, a social worker at Porirua Union and Community Health Service, shared what they'd learnt at the residential training course. The meeting had a full agenda: planning a presence at local summer events, community mapping and supporting activity in the region and nationally.

Challenges

The year 2014 was one of building and consolidation. The accreditation programme was in place and the first employers were formally accredited. With the adoption of the living wage for its directly employed workers, including parking wardens, Wellington City Council had taken the first step towards fulfilling its promises. The rate had been updated, the original networks were strong and new ones were springing up. Successful residential training courses had identified new leaders.

Although the movement was still not formally affiliated with the IAF, we continued to benefit from this relationship through support with training and advice from IAF leaders. Thousands of supporters had been involved in actions across the country. A clear challenge had been issued to the corporates, which employed thousands of the lowest-paid workers in New Zealand via contractors, to follow the lead of the small, ethical employers, NGOs and unions.

But the challenges were huge. Winning the living wage for the lowest-paid workers in Aotearoa would take sustained campaigning and more resources than the movement had at the time. Although plenty was happening, our ambitions for the movement were not matched by our capacity to deliver on goals. The lack of dedicated community organisers was a major obstacle to achieving our vision.

Annie Newman put together a proposal for the J R McKenzie Trust, to fund three half-time community organisers to coordinate campaigns and actions, relationship-building and training. The trust's goal – to create a socially just and inclusive society – aligned well with ours. Annie's application described a movement focused on the broad community alliance essential to shift the debate about in-work poverty, and committed to action to transform the lives of workers and their families. The legacy of the movement, Annie wrote, would be 'a stronger democracy where voices unite across diverse groups to advance social justice'.[10] It would be built by forging deeper relationships between organisations, through shared community leadership skills and the participation of grassroots communities in pursuing solutions to poverty and inequality.

Living Wage Movement Aotearoa NZ wanted to emulate the IAF, develop more leaders and expand the number of member organisations and commitment within those organisations beyond that of a few enthusiastic leaders. In the UK, US and Australia, IAF alliances were led by paid community organisers dedicated to building those alliances. Building power in communities was a slow process, but the Living Wage Movement was impatient and ready to effect real change.

CHAPTER 6

Organising everywhere: 2015

'Action is the oxygen of organising.'
SISTER MARIBETH LARKIN, Industrial Areas Foundation

Community organisers on the job

A major obstacle to achieving the vision of the Living Wage Movement was the lack of dedicated community organisers. By the beginning of 2015 Annie Newman had found the solution. The J R McKenzie Trust provided funds to organisations committed to addressing poverty and inequality. But was our movement too political? Non-alignment to any political party had always been a key principle; we had charitable status on the basis that the movement was not a political lobby group.

At J R McKenzie Annie dealt with executive director Iain Hines, who was an enthusiastic advocate for the living wage. Iain considered the trust's role was to enable organisations like ours to contribute towards addressing inequality. He recalls that the trust was trying to assist by funding programmes that would make the biggest difference; it focused on Māori and Pacific communities and programmes that changed structures and systems, rather than helping a few families out. 'We were thinking, how can we ambitiously embed differences in the way things work?' he says. 'Living wage is a clever example of that.' Iain would work hard to maintain ongoing support until 2018, when he stepped down from his role.

In February 2015 I received a phone call from Annie. The application to the J R McKenzie Trust had been successful: we had received funding to employ two half-time community organisers in Auckland and Wellington for three years. That grant was followed by another three – over $750,000 in total. The community organisers would coordinate and support the work of local networks and their campaigns, build relationships and ensure that leaders were trained and supported. Diana Yukich, who was now a leader in the West Auckland network, secretary of the national governance board and coordinator of the accreditation programme, was appointed to the Auckland role. I was appointed to the Wellington position, which I would hold for five years. My position was full time, thanks to additional funding from the movement and TEU.

TEU had embraced the living wage concept from the start. Tertiary institutions purport to be the critics and conscience of society, with a commitment to equality and taking a lead in the socio-economic life of their cities. But workers in the sector – both directly employed staff who were TEU members and contracted workers such as cleaners and caretakers – were often on low wages. Staff, students, alumni and other groups with a stake in local tertiary institutions wanted them to walk the talk of their lofty principles. This was backed by leadership from TEU, in particular from national president Sandra Grey and secretary Sharn Riggs. There had been active campaigns at AUT and Auckland University, and in Wellington the Living Wage for Vic campaign had been brewing since mid-2014. The Victoria University branch of TEU decided to fund an organiser for one day a week to coordinate the campaign, topped up from TEU's national budget. That work was included in my role.

Victoria on the radar

Sandra Grey had previously been the Victoria University TEU branch president and had long been concerned about the injustice of low pay for some workers in universities. As a lecturer at Victoria, she was impressed by an SFWU campaign to lift the contracted cleaners' wages, and she attended night-shift cleaners' campaign meetings to tell them that TEU members supported them.

Sandra credits her activism to 'a couple of left-wing schoolteachers who showed me a world beyond the world I lived in'. Sandra hadn't grown up in a union household, but under compulsory unionism she had joined the journalists' union, JAGPRO, at 17 because 'that's what you did to get your press pass'. She became a delegate and experienced negotiations and pickets while working at Independent Radio News. In 1991 she witnessed the impact of the ECA first-hand: 'We were one of the first sites to be de-unionised and go onto individual employment agreements. I was handed an individual agreement that took away my penal rates, meal allowances and the taxis to get home after midnight shifts.'

Sandra left the sector and eventually became a political scientist at Victoria University of Wellington, where she taught courses in social movements. She became active in her own union and the wider trade union movement, which was lamenting the losses brought about by the ECA. 'The movement was still licking its wounds. There was a hyperthermic reaction to defend the core of what you were, which was wages and conditions for your members only.' Sandra and many of her colleagues were interested in a more outward-focused approach, rather than just workers' rights in the workplace. 'The union movement, in its history, had done big campaigns and I don't understand why we wouldn't be in that space.'

TEU adopted the living wage as part of its industrial strategy, focusing on AUT and Victoria University – where there was already activism. For Sandra, all the components for shifting the public narrative about low pay and wage justice existed in the Living Wage Movement. 'I saw the success the living wage could bring because of the way the movement was organised. I saw in the Living Wage Movement things I didn't see in other parts of the union movement. We shift the world through values-based campaigning, where you get ordinary people to talk about how it changes their lives. The genius of the movement is that once upon a time nobody talked about a living wage, and now everybody does.'

Sandra recalls that TEU made a determined effort to say: 'We will protect the most vulnerable. That's our first and foremost job.' Backing the Living Wage for Vic campaign was a good way to put this into action. There was optimism about the campaign, the TEU branch was united and the students were ready to get active. The aim was to win accreditation at Victoria University and create a domino effect across the tertiary education sector.

Seeking a community voice

In February 2015 the updated living wage rate of $19.25 was announced at an accredited Wellington restaurant, La Boca Loca. The atmosphere was festive with a touch of theatre. The Brass Razoo Solidarity Band, dressed in living wage T-shirts and sombreros, welcomed guests at the door with a spirited mariachi set. La Boca Loca's owner laid out dips, salsa and corn chips, and the place was packed with the usual diverse group from across the three living wage streams. Ibrahim Omer and care worker and SFWU delegate Tamara Baddeley unveiled the rate. The spirit of the event was captured by TV3 and, in line with our strategy to ensure the movement's faith leaders were visible, speaker Bishop Duckworth was interviewed on Radio Live.

Action requires energy, but it is also energising. By now we were well schooled in the IAF principle Sister Maribeth Larkin had shared at residential training: 'Action is the oxygen of organising.' As community organisers, Diana and I were continually assisting networks to demonstrate active community support. Emerging network Living Wage Porirua was itching to build support for their council to adopt the living wage, and local activists decided to have a presence at Porirua's Waitangi Day celebration, Festival of the Elements. Leaders from around the Wellington region joined Stella Teariki, Charmaine Reihana, Cybèle Locke and other Porirua City residents to engage with the community. In subsequent years there would be plenty of locals to lead activities in Porirua, and the community was supportive from the start.

In contrast, the movements in Auckland and Wellington were now well practised at organising large community delegations to front up to council meetings at short notice. Susan Adams recalls getting people to fill Auckland Council's public gallery: 'It was exciting to watch and listen. That provided huge energy and impetus for the group of living wage support people to do it again.'

Community actions and events kept coming, from a talanoa (dialogue) about a living wage in Ōtara to a breakfast at the University of Canterbury. The movement joined allies in a march to end child poverty in Auckland, and teamed up with Te Wharepora Hou and the Auckland Women's Centre for an event called Wise Wāhine Speak. Women's Centre manager Leonie Morris was on the living wage national governance board. From the mid-1980s to the early 1990s she had worked closely with Annie Newman, myself and other women employed as organisers at the Northern Hotel and Hospital Workers Union, then at SWU. Now she was keen to get the Auckland Women's Centre involved in the Living Wage Movement, which she considered

> ... a brilliant counter to all the neo-liberal ideas that had become so entrenched in New Zealand since 1984. It was looking at people first and the simple concept that people needed enough so they could thrive and be part of society. The message was repeated over and over again, and it was such an important message.

By 2015 this message was gaining traction. More unions and groups wanted to campaign under the living wage banner, and this prompted the national governance board to create criteria for the endorsement of campaigns. These ruled out alignment with political parties 'except for the purposes of lobbying and dialogue with those parties in their capacity as decision-makers', and noted the requirement to involve faith, community and union streams in local networks and involve those networks in the campaign.

The criteria demonstrate how seriously the movement took the three-stream partnership. This was a broad-based alliance. The requirements reinforced the grassroots networks where those streams came together as the powerhouse of the movement: the place where activism and relationships drove organising and campaign action.

The local body campaigns in Auckland and Wellington ticked the boxes and were endorsed by the governance board, and the networks launched into the 2015 councils' long-term plan processes. In Auckland, action occurred all over the city: there was a get-together at the Birkenhead Community Centre on the North Shore, a 'Picnic Out West for a Living Wage' at a Uniting church in West Auckland, and a 'Picnic for a Liveable City' at Papatūānuku Kōkiri Marae in Māngere, where volunteers gathered community views. These events provided opportunities to build support and gather signatures calling for the inclusion of the living wage in the council's long-term plan.

This new way of campaigning wasn't always easy. Relational organising took time. Sometimes there was a tension between building long-term relationships and the pressure of mobilising turnout for events and actions. In Auckland, Diana Yukich was also running a business and carrying out her role of accreditation coordinator. 'You wanted bodies on the ground, but you also wanted relationships to be authentic,' she recalls. 'So we were growing the movement, contacting people, going to see people as well as organising events.'

In March 2015, funding from the Think Tank Charitable Trust (now the Te Muka Rau Charitable Trust) enabled an extension of Diana's hours. Reverend Clay Nelson, from the Auckland Unitarian Church, took up the paid position of accreditation coordinator. As the movement grew and campaigns took off around the country there was a sense of really achieving something – despite continued opposition from the government, Treasury and employers' groups, who underestimated the power of community. As Diana said, 'They didn't see us coming.'

There was now a tangible connection between the success of campaigns and the commitment to grassroots community alliances. This commitment sometimes meant stepping out of our comfort zones. It was years since I'd spent time in churches, but I enjoyed my relationship with faith-group partners and their reflective approach. The style and spirituality of the various faith traditions enriched our meetings and our relationships. Diana had never in her life been to so many churches, but in those that backed the movement she found people listening to each other: 'I saw churches in a whole different light. I saw that churches help the community.'

Living Wage Wellington campaign actions to extend the living wage to contracted workers in Wellington City Council's long-term plan delivered thousands of signatures in support of the network's submission. The submission noted that the council's commitment to the principle of becoming a Living Wage Employer meant the next stages of implementation should be included in the plan. In all our campaigning we now adopted the IAF approach: our submission was positive and encouraging, welcomed the steps taken and emphasised our willingness to work together. But that didn't soften the demands. The time had come to deliver the living wage to Wellington's lowest-paid workers. We needed to mobilise local communities to make a very visible call for political action.

The power of self-interest

As the movement grew, so too did the understanding of the relevance of the concept. Identifying self-interest was a core IAF principle, and member organisations in the Living Wage Movement found their own ways to talk about what the living wage meant to their people and their culture. An organisation where leaders and members could articulate the need for the living wage in ways that made sense to them was an organisation with an investment in committing to the movement. In the broader community, too, the movement invited people to talk about what the living wage meant to them.

Principles of social justice and equality are an integral part of the spiritual teachings in the faith community and the drivers of a commitment to seek a better world. At a gathering of Anglicans from the diocese at the Wellington Cathedral of St Paul, those present were invited to answer the question 'What does the living wage mean to you?' They wrote: 'Good news';

'Living life, loving people, journeying together'; 'Fairness, life, freedom'. At Porirua's Creekfest event, responses reflected the poverty in that community: 'That a parent could afford to stay home with their kids and the other parent would earn enough for their family'; 'Able to buy proper nappies for my daughter'; 'Security in my retirement.' In Newtown, a community generally considered progressive and where support for the living wage has been strong, people answered: 'Breakfast for families' tables'; 'Mana motuhake'; 'Equality'; 'Living not existing'.

Inspired by the Auckland Whānau Day, New Zealand Nurses Organisation member Kieran Monaghan organised a similar event in Newtown. The community celebration began with a procession to the community centre led by the Brass Razoo Solidarity Band in living wage T-shirts. Brass Razoo's regular attendance at living wage events was coordinated by trumpeter John Maynard, a regular at Living Wage Wellington meetings and actions and a participant in the 2014 residential training. Food was largely donated by Commonsense Organics, a business that later became an accredited Living Wage Employer – the first retail chain to do so. Poet Karlo Mila gifted and performed a living wage poem, Dayna Kosega from TEU organised a Pacific band, and workers shared their stories.

All this activity around the country was focused on building the movement and demonstrating community support for campaigns. Again and again, events centred on community turnout, local entertainment, worker and community speakers and the sharing of food. The atmosphere was always one of celebration and hope, with workers, their whānau and the wider community at the heart. Events were colourful, creative and, above all, grassroots demonstrations of people power.

A sea of red

In Wellington this activism was sorely needed. Progress at the council had stalled. Despite the elected representatives' commitment to include contracted workers, when the draft long-term plan was published these workers were invisible. The living wage network decided to turn that around. The council organised community forums in the five wards, and the network mobilised to organise a large turnout at each. We would be easily identifiable in living wage T-shirts, and one strong spokesperson from each ward would speak for the movement. The forums would be a sea of red.

As the crowd of living wage supporters gathered outside St John's Hall in Willis Street in preparation to march into the Lambton Ward forum, it was clear we would be the largest group inside the packed venue. After her presentation, Mayor Celia Wade-Brown called for questions. Reverend Brian Dawson spoke. He was a large man with a big presence. He observed that councillors had voted in 2013 to ensure that the living wage was implemented, and asked why there had there been so little progress, and why the living wage for contracted workers was not included in the draft long-term plan when community support for it was so strong.

At the Onslow–Western Ward meeting, Michael Gilchrist, a PhD student active in the Living Wage for Vic campaign, put the same questions. Andrew Casidy, a leader in the finance union Finsec, spoke for the movement at the Northern Ward meeting. In the Eastern Ward it was Georgi McLeod, a Miramar resident who worked for the Council of Trade Unions. By the time of the Southern Ward consultation meeting, living wage activists were confident and determined. Ibrahim Omer and fellow SFWU organiser Anthony Leaupepe climbed onto seats and erected a large living wage banner across the back of the venue. When question time started, Reverend Norman Wilkins, a retired minister and St Andrew's on The Terrace parishioner, jumped to his feet. Norman was a true enthusiast and passionate about the living wage. He introduced those who had come from his inner-city church and asked the parishioners to stand. It was clear that the living wage contingent far outnumbered any other group present. There was power in the room, and that power was held by the Living Wage Movement.

The local movement swamped the council with submissions, and delegations from member organisations made oral submissions. In May, Living Wage Wellington again crowded out a council meeting to ask councillors to include a comprehensive commitment to the living wage in the long-term plan. As a result of the campaign, councillors voted on an amended plan that included the living wage. This resulted in a final draft that included $750,000 to move contracted workers to the living wage and an additional $100,000 to lift the pay of workers at the council-controlled Museums Trust. Trust chief executive Pat Stuart had made an emphatic submission in which she maintained this was the necessary figure to afford to pay the living wage. Despite this, Stuart continued to resist paying the living wage even after the funds were provided – demonstrating the problems with organisations funded by the community but set up at arm's length from council.

The Wellington Chamber of Commerce was outraged by the amendments to the draft long-term plan. The chamber's chief executive John Milford fired off a furious three-page letter to councillors that included a paragraph in bold type: 'We are also concerned to hear that, without adequate consultation, the council will be considering as part of its LTP deliberations a policy which will require one of the council's contractors to implement the living wage as part of the contracted services.'[1] Milford decried the decision to include provision to extend the living wage to council-controlled organisations. He also attacked, at length, the methodology of the living wage calculation, quoting from Brian Scott's flawed analysis.

Local movement leaders were confident that a clear majority of elected representatives would back the amended long-term plan. But the battle was far from over. Councillors were under pressure to abandon the commitment to the living wage for contracted workers because of the Local Government Act's requirement to 'provide local public services and infrastructure in a way that is most cost-effective'. They were called to a closed-door meeting and presented with confidential legal advice.

The vote to adopt the revised draft plan took place on 27 May 2015. An amended version of the resolution shows the impact of that public-excluded meeting. The plan included continuation of the living wage for directly employed workers, but the wording around contracted workers was watered down: contracting must be provided in 'the most cost-effective way'. However, the plan did include specific steps towards a living wage for contracted workers: $250,000 for 2016/17, a further $500,000 towards future contract negotiations for the living wage, and an instruction to officers to progress the living wage on a contract-by-contract basis, taking into account legal advice and efficiency.

This rather modest resolution incited the Wellington Chamber of Commerce to declare their intention to seek legal advice on the decision. Hot on the heels of the chamber's press release was one from the Taxpayers' Union. Spokesman Jordan Williams said the Local Government Act 2002 required the council to ensure efficient and effective use of its resource:

> The living wage policy is a deliberate sabotage of efficiency by choosing to pay more for something than it's worth. No wonder this decision was made in secret. Councillors that really care about poverty and want the council to be providing the best service at the least cost will be hanging their heads in shame.[2]

Wellington City Council's revised long-term plan was a step forward: the next step was to make sure it passed the final vote. The mayor was keen for the movement to demonstrate community support again on the day of the vote, but after repeatedly taking large delegations to the council chambers, it was time to find a new strategy. Our solution was the Mop March.

Taking to the streets

The Mop March was the brainchild of a Living Wage Wellington network meeting. It was promoted among supporters as a march to 'clean up low pay in Wellington'. Early on 24 June 2015, cleaners all over Wellington came off their nightshifts and headed for the Wesley Methodist Church in Taranaki Street. They were dog-tired, and some took the opportunity to nap in a café beside the church while others snoozed in their cars. Around 8am, hundreds of people began to assemble. The smell of barbecued sausages promised a hearty breakfast, marshals in hi-vis jackets gathered in the church for a briefing and, as the Brass Razoo Solidarity Band entertained the crowd, mops and buckets began to appear.

It had been Ibrahim Omer's job to get the cleaners to the church for the 8.30am march. It was a big ask:

> Most people finished work at 4am, but they realised how important this was. If we don't march, if we don't make a noise, nothing will change. It was a hard thing to do because most of them … have kids and they probably won't get a sleep and they have to go back for the nightshift. They knew the living wage was making an impact and the only way was supporting the movement and standing up for themselves.

Reverend Motekiai Fakatou, a Tongan minister at the church, welcomed the crowd, and Helen Kelly, president of the Council of Trade Unions, led the march alongside Bishop Justin Duckworth. The brass band was followed by rows of cleaners with their mops, beating on buckets. The march proceeded down Taranaki Street and Wakefield Street, crossed the road at the town hall and entered Civic Square, where a strong media presence awaited.

When the mayor and councillors arrived at Civic Square to address the marchers, the crowd sensed victory. The mayor reiterated her support and then headed back to the council chambers, where council voted to endorse the living wage section of the final long-term plan by nine votes to six.

The Brass Razoo Solidarity Band leads the Mop March in Wellington from the Wesley Methodist Church in Taranaki Street to Civic Square, 24 June 2015. Photos: Georgia Choveaux

The demonstration of community support throughout the long-term plan consultation had worked. Although actions in the plan fell short of promises made in election forums, the strategy of continually moving forward and eventually securing Wellington's accreditation as the first living wage council was on track. The stage was set to transform the lives of workers and their families. But despite clear community support, that stage remained a battleground.

'Heaps of aroha'

Although the Wellington City Council campaign dominated the movement's work in the city, other campaigns were underway. On 1 April 2015 there was a forum at Victoria University, the first of many living wage actions in the hub. One speaker, economist and former Victoria academic Prue Hyman, told a large group of students, academics, general staff and supporters that the living wage made economic and social sense. 'We should be going for a high-wage, high-skill, high-productivity economy,' she said. 'VUW should be part of that.' Students should be able to attend a university that valued its employees and took leadership in the campaign to make Wellington a place where employers paid a living wage. It was also of benefit to students, who needed decently paid part-time jobs.

In June, Diana Yukich, Brian Dawson, Muriel Tunoho and I travelled to Australia for a six-day IAF residential training. It was an opportunity to network with the Sydney and Brisbane alliances and see their work firsthand. We also caught up with our IAF friends Sister Maribeth Larkin and Joe Chrastil, who led the training. We were impressed by the diversity of participants and the active involvement of Muslim women.

Back in Aotearoa, 2015's accredited Living Wage Employers were announced at the Tūaropaki Trust. A group of the movement's leaders travelled to Hamilton where the trust was based. The Māori television programme, *Te Karere*, announced that the trust was 'the first Māori organisation in the world to be awarded the living wage accreditation'.[3] Sharryn Barton, from the E tū rūnanga and with Waikato Tainui, Ngāti Maniapoto and Ngāti Raukawa iwi affiliations, described it as 'awesome for workers in Aotearoa and their families that there are more Living Wage Employers stepping up to the mark and caring about their workers. Heaps of aroha to them. It gives us hope. If they can do it, so can everybody else.'

It was significant that New Zealand's first corporate business to embrace the living wage was a Māori organisation. But where were those massively profitable businesses, like the overseas-owned banks?

CHAPTER 7

People vs Institution: 2015

'The most cost-effective way to employ workers is slavery.'
PETER CRANNEY, employment lawyer

Solidarity for Selwyn

In the Hutt Valley, Muriel Tunoho, John Ryall and others had been meeting regularly to plan a local network. They called for interested organisations to attend a meeting on 27 July 2015 in the Pōmare Community Hall. Over 60 people attended. Anglican minister Charlie Noanoa opened the meeting, and after waiata, worker stories and presentations, small groups discussed the next steps. Follow-up meetings were held next door at the Hutt Valley Union and Community Health Service, and Living Wage Hutt Valley was up and running.

In Auckland a campaign was developing that centred on Selwyn Village, a residential care home in Point Chevalier owned by the Anglican Church. Yvette Taylor was the SFWU organiser of the Selwyn caregivers and kitchen and laundry workers. Previous campaigning by SFWU to win the living wage for Selwyn workers had been unsuccessful despite the workers' commitment and activism. This time, residents and their families were invited to support them. 'The idea was to see if the union, combined with the Anglican group, residents and family members and other supporters, would be able to put enough pressure on the Selwyn Foundation to hold them to their Christian values and get them to be a Living Wage Employer,' she recalls.

The first step was to talk with the workers about the living wage. Yvette says they were excited: 'The cleaners and the contracted workers were all on the minimum wage or a little above. A lot of time was spent identifying leaders, like caregivers and union delegates Bernie Chand and Petria Malloch.' The Selwyn Supporters Coalition was set up, bringing together Point Chevalier residents, Anglicans, residents of the facility, Grey Power and unions. The coalition distributed information leaflets to rest-home

POWER TO WIN

Selwyn Supporters Coalition held a public meeting in Auckland on 5 August 2015. Pictured is Agnes Granada from Migrant Action Trust and Earth Action.
Below: Selwyn Village E tū delegate and caregiver Bernie Chand (second from right) and other workers joined forces with the community in the Selwyn living wage campaign.
Photos: Jason Fell

visitors and gathered signatures on a petition calling for the living wage for caregivers, cleaners, laundry and other service staff at Selwyn Village.

On 5 August they held a public meeting at Point Chevalier Primary School. More than 200 people from the Selwyn Supporters Coalition, the Human Rights Commission, academics, aged-care advocates and other supporters attended, and the meeting received widespread publicity. The *NZ Herald* ran a story headlined 'Selwyn Village targeted by living wage campaign', which included comments from a resident's family member. Don Cotter's family was paying $60,000 a year to support his father-in-law, and he believed the Selwyn Foundation could afford to pay its caregivers more. Cotter was a retired businessman. He decided to back the living wage after talking to his father-in-law's caregiver, who had to bike to work because her car had been stolen. When Cotter said to her, 'I hope you had insurance,' she replied that she couldn't afford to pay for it. 'I know that no adult can live on the minimum wage and be involved in society in a meaningful way,' Cotter told the *NZ Herald*.[1]

There was no quick win in this campaign; Selwyn Village resisted the community pressure. For Anglicans like Susan Adams, it was a tough campaign. She was embarrassed and found it hard to believe they couldn't get movement from the chief executive, the board and others she had thought would be allies. 'Those of us in the faith movement, and the Anglican church in particular, met two or three times with the board CE to try to pin those people down. We felt very disappointed.' But she felt the time had not been wasted, saying, 'We learnt a lot about power.' It was hard to be patient in campaigns like these, but the public pressure paid off and the Selwyn Village workers eventually won large pay increases and the living wage.

Actions too many to mention

The day after the Selwyn Village public meeting, Living Wage Porirua held a formal community launch at the Pacific Islanders' Presbyterian Church in Cannons Creek. This was Reverend Perema Leasi's church, and the launch was an opportunity to bring him closer to the local movement. Reverend Perema, as he was known, gave everything to his community and had a wonderful way with words. Born in Saipai on the island of Savai'i in Sāmoa, Perema always brought God into events with welcomes and prayers, and left everyone in no doubt that God was on the side of the working poor and the Living

Wage Movement. Sadly, he passed away in 2019. His obituary spoke of 'his big heart, his belief in social justice, his love for his community and his never-failing support for the underdog … he was a leader, a man of unflinching faith, a quick-witted joker and a lover of life and all those who lived it.'[2]

At the Porirua launch, the entertainment, food and prayers all reflected the Pacific community. Two young Sāmoan men who worked as parking wardens in Wellington shared their stories, and everyone laughed when one said the living wage meant he could now afford to have a girlfriend. The MC was Caroline Mareko, a parishioner at Reverend Perema's church and a leader in the Sāmoan, union and early childhood communities. At the conclusion of the evening people were invited to sign a banner to demonstrate their commitment to work for the living wage in Porirua. One of many who stepped up was Porirua Mayor Nick Leggett. I leaped from my seat when I saw him heading for the door, seizing the opportunity for a conversation. He had been reported in the local newspaper as an opponent of the living wage at Porirua City Council, but now maintained that he was a supporter; the paper had got it wrong. We arranged a meeting and the campaign to win the living wage at Porirua City Council began in earnest.

Other actions and events continued around the country. Living Wage for Vic launched a postcard blitz on campus, and a team of activists, including TEU president Katy Miller, union organiser Nicki Wilford and student leaders, invited students to sign up to support the campaign. 'Our cleaners work so hard for such low pay. At VUW our cleaning cohort is largely made up of Māori, Pacific and people of refugee backgrounds. Many of them are working long and sometimes split shifts to support their families,' Nicki said later. 'Surely they are entitled to be remunerated at a level that allows them to live with dignity.' Students were overwhelmingly supportive. They saw how hard cleaners worked, and many were themselves working long hours in low-paid jobs to pay their rent and bills.

In October 2015 the SFWU amalgamated with EPMU to form E tū, now New Zealand's largest private-sector union. Former EPMU national secretary Bill Newson became the E tū national secretary and John Ryall the assistant national secretary. The commitment to the Living Wage Movement continued in the new union.

The 2015 AGMs were again held in Auckland and Wellington. The annual report described a vibrant and growing movement with 'actions too many to mention.'[3]

A dog's breakfast

Meanwhile, the power struggle at the heart of the Wellington City Council campaign continued. Network meetings focused on ways to ensure political commitments were honoured, but it was clear that powerful forces were preventing this. The council's chief executive, council officers and the Wellington Chamber of Commerce seemed determined to block the living wage commitments. The Chamber of Commerce continued to cry wolf over their legal action and a myth grew around their supposed legal case, which never went to court. The chamber's president, employment lawyer Peter Cullen, was a former student leader and, interestingly, a former Hotel and Hospital Workers' Union secretary. John Ryall rang his former colleague and asked him to back off from the legal challenge, given his history of working for low-paid workers, but Cullen refused to commit.

As the close of the year approached, interest in the 2016 local body elections was growing. In Wellington there were rumours that Councillor Nicola Young – an opponent of the living wage – would stand against Mayor Wade-Brown. We viewed the success of the Wellington City Council campaign as the catalyst that would encourage and pressure other councils around the country to follow suit, and maintained community pressure. We would keep workers' stories at the heart, ensure that the living wage was an election issue, and get a commitment from the next Wellington mayor to the council becoming an accredited Living Wage Employer.

To do this it was vital to have active involvement from the council workers, including those employed by contractors. For the unions on site, it was an opportunity to bring workers together in one campaign. This went against the often siloed approach in the union movement, where individual groups of workers generally campaign separately, even when they are on the same site, thus diminishing their power. A workplace organising committee was set up with delegates and organisers from the PSA, E tū and the Manufacturing and Construction Workers Union, which represented the recycling workers.

Those of us charged with representing Living Wage Wellington continued to raise outstanding issues with council officials, although meetings were infrequent and always at our instigation. Despite councillors having voted to become a living wage council, there were plenty of issues.

When the directly employed workers were lifted to the living wage rate of $18.40 in January 2014, we assumed this would be updated each year to the new rate. But by August 2015 the living wage was $19.25; directly employed staff at Wellington City Council were receiving only $18.55. Council officers were resistant to an 'outside agency' setting pay rates. In an attempt to opt out of the official rate, they dreamed up what they called the 'Wellington Wage' – the original living wage rate with CPI increases added on. Meanwhile, the Museums Trust ignored the fact that it had been allocated public funds specifically to pay the living wage, and established a rate of $15.64 – an action that threw into question the accountability of council-controlled organisations, given that the facilities they managed belonged to the people of Wellington. As well, an increasing number of workers were on what council staff chose to call a 'training rate'. It was a dog's breakfast.

Living Wage Wellington battled this out with council staff. We met them and wrote to them, pointing out repeatedly that they were not meeting their commitments. In December we wrote to the mayor, the deputy mayor and the chief executive about the Museums Trust's failure to allocate the additional funding for the living wage to the purpose for which it was provided, saying: 'This is clearly totally contrary to the commitment to move forward with the living wage. It makes a mockery of the public consultation to extend the living wage to the Museums Trust.'[4]

The Wellington City Council story demonstrates why the commitment to accreditation is pivotal to locking in the living wage. Simply gaining agreement to pay the current rate does not make an employer a Living Wage Employer, and battling for each successive increase is unsustainable. Living Wage Wellington's leaders gradually edged the council closer to accreditation, but the resistance from council officers and council-controlled organisations meant this would take nearly three years to achieve. Inch by inch, however, the campaigners moved forward. The next step was to win the living wage for the first group of contract workers, and that was a battle royal.

Living Wage Wellington had meetings with Mayor Wade-Brown and her deputy, Justin Lester, who began to play a leadership role in the living wage issue. Lester grew up in Invercargill with his brother and his mother, who was a beneficiary and a part-time cleaner. 'To me it was all about fairness and respecting the employees of the organisation and their right to be paid well,' he says.

He recalls meeting with Living Wage Wellington:

What I immediately jumped to was: here are the values, this is what we want to achieve, so how do we implement it at a council level, given that it was quite a polarised council. You had Celia's leadership at one end of the spectrum and some quite conservative council members, but also a new chief executive in Kevin Lavery.

Lester recalls the approach was effectively to give the chief executive an ultimatum. 'Having the living wage community behind it just made it so much easier.' Moving the directly employed to the living wage had been relatively straightforward: there was a cost, but there was solid support around the table.

The mayor's courage and her deputy's style of leadership were pivotal to Wellington City Council adopting the living wage for contract workers. That courage and leadership were put to the test at one of the most dramatic meetings of the campaign, which turned out to be a battle for power and the maintenance of democracy.

The battle of Wellington

Most Wellington City councillors wanted to get on with delivering their commitment to extend the living wage to contracted workers. The issue had come to a head with a proposal to begin with the low-paid contracted security workers. Council officers recommended against this and the issue was to be voted on at a council meeting on 28 October.

The episode attracted a great deal of media coverage. A story published in the *Dominion Post* on the day of the vote gave a leg-up to Living Wage Wellington's campaign. One of the opponents' arguments was that the living wage was unaffordable, but commentator Max Rashbrooke had researched the pay rises of higher-paid council staff, including the chief executive, and proceeded to decimate the argument:

> My analysis of that data shows that the number of staff earning more than $100,000 a year has increased from 148 in 2011–12 to 192 last financial year. The payments to those staff have increased from $20.4 million in 2011–12 to $26.8 million last financial year – a rise of 30 percent. Chief executive Kevin Lavery, meanwhile, has had his salary increased from $400,000 in 2013–14 to $416,000 this coming year. What these figures show is that if councillors are concerned about the cost of the living wage, they could easily meet it by restraining top pay. The cost of paying the living wage to all staff, on the campaigners' estimates, is only 6.4 percent

of the salary bill for the highest-paid staff. A few years of restraint there would have created ample room for the living wage.⁵

Living Wage Wellington organised a large presence for the October meeting. Just beforehand I received a phone call from Justin Lester, who said the chief executive had asked to make a personal statement and the mayor had agreed. What happened at the meeting demonstrated the lengths to which those with institutional power will go to undermine democracy. Lester remembers this as a 'great night'; I recall an inspiring evening when a united community movement, committed to wage justice, stood up and spoke truth to power and won.

As 60 Living Wage Wellington supporters entered the council foyer to hold elected representatives to account, security guards informed us that only a small group of the delegation could be present in the council chambers. We'd taken many delegations to the chamber before and people had lined the walls, but this time only 10 from our group would be admitted. I was one of that group; everyone else crammed into an adjacent room to watch proceedings on a screen.

The meeting opened as formal council meetings do: with a public participation session, when individuals and groups can have their say on the issues on the agenda for that meeting. Because we knew the officers would focus on the legal issues around extending the living wage to workers employed via contractors, we had invited employment lawyer Peter Cranney to speak for our delegation. Peter had prepared a speech, but discarded it and spoke off the cuff. Memorably, he addressed the issue of the requirement in the Local Government Act 2002 to ensure that contracts were awarded on the basis of the most cost-effective option, declaring, 'The most cost-effective way to employ workers is slavery.'

After public participation, the mayor announced that the chief executive wished to make a personal statement. Kevin Lavery delivered a lengthy speech in which he told councillors they had a duty of care to him as his employers. That included not putting him at risk by compelling him to carry out what he believed to be illegal. It was a threatening display of institutional power in which Lavery, an employee, attempted to change the vote of elected representatives. It did not have the desired effect. When his speech ended, Wade-Brown rose to her feet, thanked her chief executive, and moved the motion to extend the living wage to the contracted security guards. The motion was promptly seconded by Justin Lester.

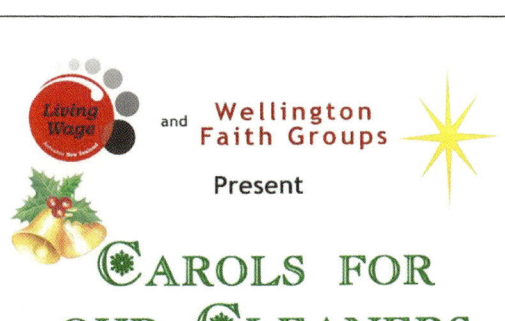

Carols for Our Cleaners poster, December 2013.

Living Wage Movement and Living Wage Employer logos.
Design: Eleanor McIntyre

Living Wage for Learning rallies were held in March 2014. New Zealand Educational Institute, Te Riu Roa Collection. Design: Meredith Biberstein

A billboard errected outside St Matthew-in-the-City in central Auckland in Living Wage Week, November 2016. Design: Sam Gribben in collaboration with local activists

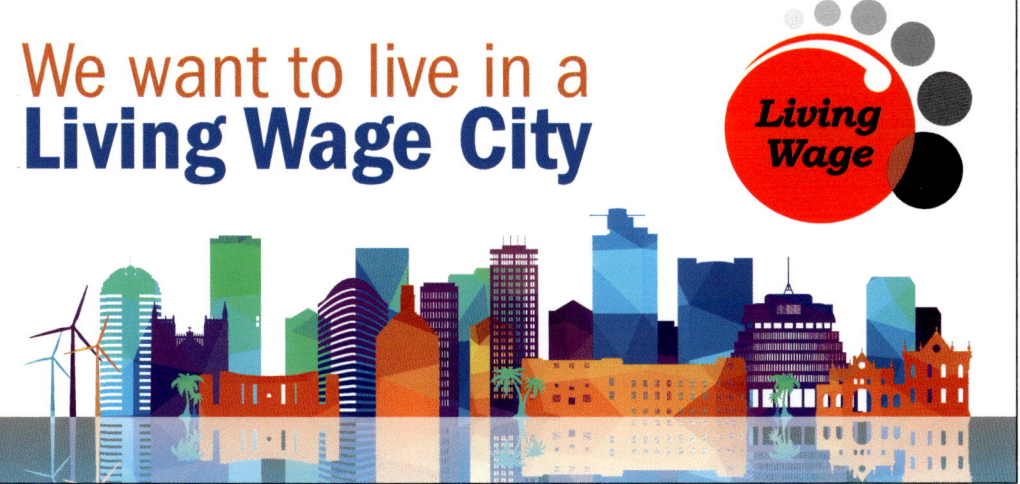

A 'Living Wage City' billboard created for the living wage stage in Newtown, Wellington, on 6 March 2020. Design: Sam Gribben

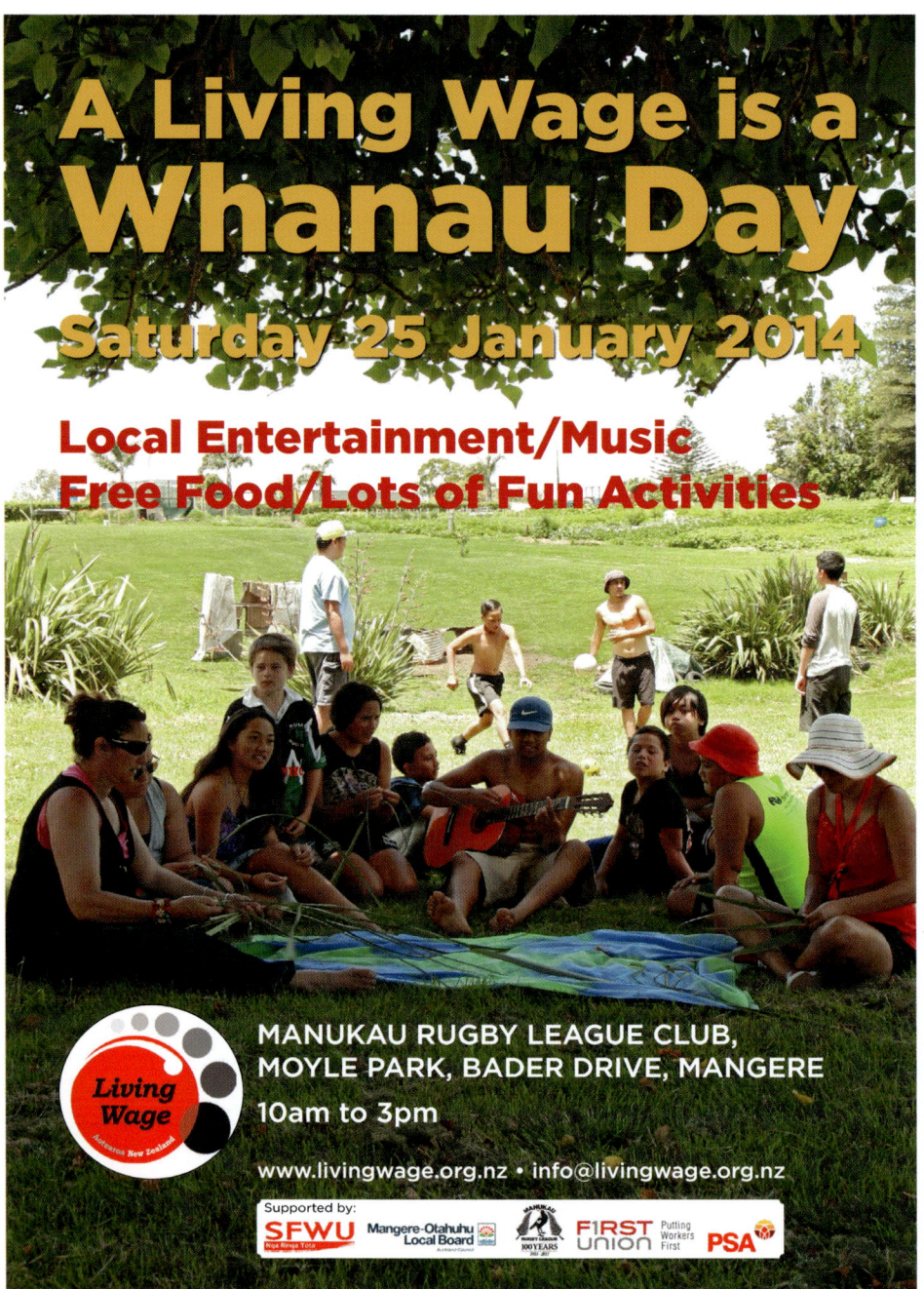

Poster advertising the Living Wage Whānau Day, February 2013, at Manukau Rugby League Park in Auckland. Design: Chris McBride, Photo: Jason Fell

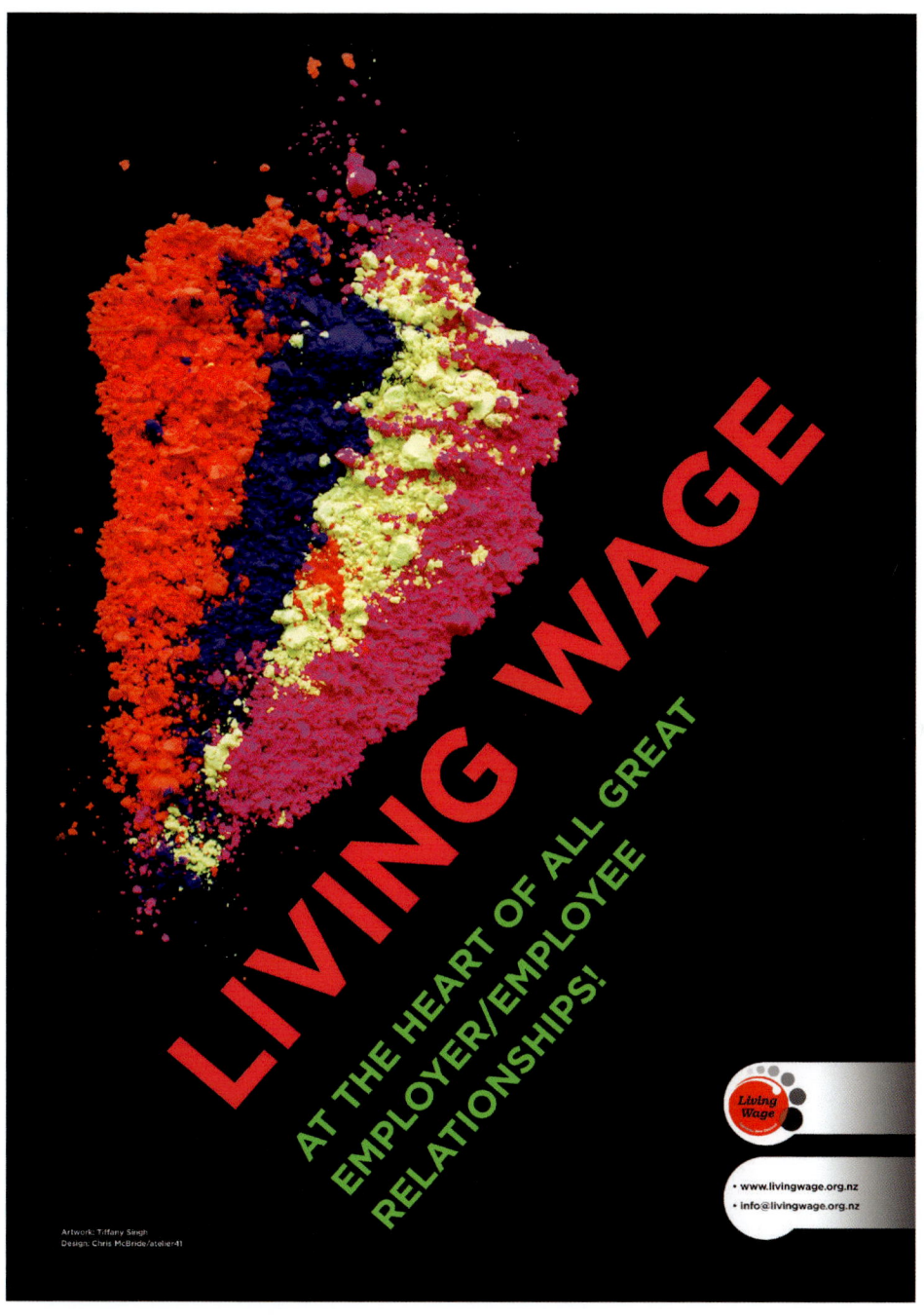

Promotion poster for Living Wage Employers, 25 February 2014.
Artwork: Tiffany Singh, Design: Chris McBride

MOP MARCH

Clean up low pay in Wellington

Support Wellington City Councillors voting to extend the Living Wage to low paid workers employed by contractors.

- Meet at the **Wesley Church forecourt,** 25 Taranaki Street at 8.15am, Wednesday 24 June for a BBQ breakfast.

- March to **Wellington City Council** at 9am.

The Mop March, 24 June 2015.
Design: Sam Gribben

Promotion of Living Wage Day at Victoria University of Wellington on 10 March 2017 featured university cleaner Awak Apiak (above) and student president Rory Lenihan-Iken.

The 2017 Wellington general election forum was advertised under the banner 'A Fairer Aotearoa'. Design: Andrew Chick

The atmosphere was tense. The motion was passed, and councillors voted nine to six to award the security and noise-control services contract on the basis of the living wage. Lester then moved that the cost of paying the security guards the living wage be covered by reducing the council's personnel and travel budget by $250,000 to maintain a fiscally neutral position. This was seconded by Councillor Iona Pannett, and the motion passed. An adjournment was called and everyone spilled out into the foyer.

The crowd of living wage supporters emerged from the overflow room singing the living wage song. There was victory in the air. Looking back, Justin Lester recalls thinking, 'We'll do what we need to do. Kevin got up, and he spoke, and in many respects posed some ultimatums, whether or not he was going to continue in an organisation where elected representatives were going strongly against his own recommendations and advice.'

It was a tough call for the mayor, but Wade-Brown stood fast:

> I was in no doubt. I find it hard when I can see both sides of the argument, and when your senior managers are very against something they've usually got a reasonable reason. On this one I was quite clear about what the right thing to do was, so I wasn't fazed at all. I thought it was slightly embarrassing for the chief executive to be a little emotional in his advice. We're used to that from the politicians, not the managers. And we won. Kevin was unhappy about it. I think he really thought we were getting into management territory when we were talking about pay and conditions, and we thought we were getting into human territory.

That vote ensured that Wade-Brown was on the way to achieving her goal of being the mayor of New Zealand's first living wage council.

> I was very conscious I was mayor in the capital city. It was leadership for the country, not only for the people living and working in Wellington. It feels good to lead something so worthwhile. I think it's fortunate that I had a very explicit set of values that all people are worthwhile. It doesn't matter what kind of job they are doing.

The next morning the *Dominion Post* editorial carried the headline 'City council move on living wage is modest and sensible', and said Wellington City Council was not doing anything extreme in deciding to require its security service contractors to pay a living wage.[6] This was followed the next day by another editorial headlined 'Living wage the right thing to do'.[7]

A story in the business section had a different tone. Reporter Michael Forbes wrote:

Wellington City Council is sticking to its guns on the living wage – a move that could cost it an extra $1.7 million and expose it to costly legal action. The council, which has been paying its own staff a living wage since 2013, took the bold step on Wednesday of requiring contractors who provide its security services to do the same. In doing so, it flew in the face of warnings from its own officers and chief executive Kevin Lavery that it would effectively be paying 19 percent more than the going rate for guarding, noise control and cash collection services over the seven-year life of the security contract without seeing any extra benefit.[8]

The most notable headline was in the *National Business Review*. Taxpayers' Union founder David Farrar's piece was headed 'Wellington City Council does the "big FU" to ratepayers'. The article listed councillors' names and how they voted, and urged readers: 'Remember the names when you get your rates bill.'[9]

The media interest was not surprising. It was clear this decision would pave the way for other councils. It was also the beginning of achieving the goal set by SFWU leaders when the Living Wage Movement was initiated: to unlock a strategy to win pay rises for large groups of low-paid workers employed via contractors. Wellington City Council had shown that it could be done.

The Wellington Chamber of Commerce was not ready to throw in the towel, however. On 6 November the chamber announced it would take a judicial review of the council's decision to extend the living wage to contracted security guards and noise control officers.[10] Chief executive John Milford commented that the chamber did not take delight in heading to court, but the council needed to be held to account. Justin Lester hit back, saying the chamber was silent when council spent hundreds of thousands of dollars on events like fireworks and the Santa Parade, but stamped its feet over a few extra dollars for workers. Celia Wade-Brown was steadfast and claimed there was a clear benefit from paying staff a living wage: 'Decent pay and good performance are connected.'[11] Living Wage Wellington spokesperson Reverend Brian Dawson described the chamber's legal action as 'a mean-minded waste of money', saying, 'the chamber seems determined to do everything it can to keep these workers on poverty rates, deny Wellingtonians the right to decide to be a fair city and spend a lot of money on pointless litigation'.[12] Ten days later, legal firm Chen Palmer Partners announced that the Wellington Chamber of Commerce, in conjunction with the Taxpayers' Union, had issued a judicial review of the decision by

Wellington City Council to require its independent contractors to pay their employees the living wage.[13]

End-of-year action

Building community power depended first on building leaders in the movement. In October and November, residential training took place once again in Auckland and the Wellington region, with Sister Maribeth in the lead role. Over 40 new leaders were trained.

One participant in Auckland was community development facilitator Cissy Rock. Cissy would soon take over the community organising role from Diana Yukich and become busy organising Auckland activities for the first national profile-raising Living Wage Week. This included the erection of a huge billboard outside St Matthew-in-the-City, which showed a man in business attire eating an oversized piece of cake while a crowd of people below held up their hands for crumbs.

There was no complaint from parishioners about the church promoting the rather provocative billboard. St Matthew-in-the-City had been supporting the working people of Auckland City since the late 1880s, and

The billboard, designed by Sam Orchard, erected outside St Matthew-in-the-City in central Auckland to mark Living Wage Week, November 2015. Photo: Jason Fell

was considered to be the workers' church, from which Selwyn Village and the City Mission were founded.

As the year of action came to a close, Living Wage for Vic held another event at the Milk and Honey café on campus. The venue was full of supporters from the university and the local movement. A campaign was launched to invite alumni to sign a letter to the vice-chancellor, Grant Guilford, expressing pride in their university – a pride that would be enhanced when the university adopted the living wage. As a graduate from 1972, I welcomed the opportunity to send a clear message that I expected my university to do the right thing.

In December a delegation went to Porirua City Council to challenge Mayor Leggett and city councillors on the living wage. The delegation included PSA president Mike Tana, who would soon mount a successful mayoral campaign of his own. Tana called on the mayor and councillors to adopt the living wage. Single mother Charmaine Reihana, a union member, a regular at Living Wage Porirua meetings and campaign actions around Wellington and a cleaner at the police college, shared her story of supporting five children on an income just above the minimum wage.

So ended 2015. It was a year of collision between institutional power and people power, and demonstrated that the strategy of organising across communities to fight for decent wages was working.

CHAPTER 8

The power of assembly: 2016

'We are not asking for a luxury life, but we want a fair wage.'
FAEPEPELE TAITUAVE, contract cleaner

Going the extra mile

The year 2016 began with two events to announce the annual update of the living wage rate. The updated rate of $19.80 was a modest rise of 55 cents an hour but would mean an extra $22.00 a week for a 40-hour-week worker on the living wage.

The first announcement event was at the Manukau Rugby League Club in Māngere. The clubrooms were packed with people, many from local Pacific communities, and there were speakers, lots of food and a festive vibe. The second was in Wellington at New Zealand's first living wage printing company, Pivotal Thames (formerly Thames Publications), which later became Pivotal.

This long-established business had a track record of printing for both social justice organisations and commercial clients. Here was a classic, medium-sized mainstream business demonstrating how to become a fully accredited Living Wage Employer. Pivotal Thames general manager Kyle Radersma proudly told members of the local movement, supportive politicians and media that he had started paying the full living wage to all staff a few months earlier. This now included the contracted cleaners. 'They come to work and feel valued,' he said. 'They are happy to go the extra mile.'[1] Some businesses said that requiring cleaning contractors to pay the living wage was too hard. Pivotal Thames, however, contracted its cleaning to New Zealand's first fully accredited cleaning company, Fresh Desk, whose owners, Nicole Oxenbridge and Caroline de Castro, were at the new rate announcement with some of their workers.

Pivotal produced a special wine label for the event and threw in some wine to celebrate the occasion. Workers from the printing company spoke, as did CTU president Richard Wagstaff, who told those gathered that the announcement of the living wage rate was a reminder of what needs to happen with the minimum wage: rather than small top-ups, there needed to be a policy to sustain a higher minimum wage rate.

Although it was great to welcome businesses with a conscience, most of the movement's energy continued to be focused on building the grassroots networks required to win campaigns. Our experience with Wellington City Council had showed that a sustained demonstration of community power was necessary. Continual activity was required to create visibility, develop leaders and expand the movement.

Demonstrating community power

In early 2016 a number of events across the Wellington region once again provided opportunities for networks to be visible and engage with local communities, including the Newtown Festival, the Festival of the Elements in Porirua and postcard blitzes at Victoria University during orientation week. There, students and academics joined low-paid cleaners to demonstrate support for Living Wage for Vic. This lively campaign had solid backing from the TEU and E tū.

In March the formal launch of Living Wage Hutt Valley took place at Pōmare School. The Hutt Valley network organised the event, again with leadership from Muriel Tunoho and John Ryall. They were joined by local activists Dina Awarau from Hutt Union and Community Health Service, Reverend Norman Wilkins representing Presbyterians, Michelle Maguren from NZEI Te Riu Roa and Betsan Martin, the Public Issues Coordinator of the Methodist Church NZ.

The commitment of these activists was vital. Michelle, a former low-paid school secretary, was now a union organiser and mobilised the Hutt Valley branch of NZEI to support the event. Local primary and early childhood teachers and school support staff provided a spread of sandwiches, sausage rolls, cakes and pies for the 120 people who filled the school hall. This was what the living wage grassroots movement was about: NZEI Te Riu Roa was a member organisation, and the union's members wanted to support this event in their own community to raise awareness of issues of inequality and poverty wages. Education workers know the impact of low wages in communities. Pōmare School was a low-decile[2] school with few resources,

The South Sudanese Dancers, led by E tū member and caregiver Margaret John (right), take to the stage at the movement's Hutt Valley launch at Pōmare School, March 2015. Photo: Sam Gribben

Living Wage Hutt Valley met regularly at Hutt Union and Community Health Service. Left to right: Dina Awarau, Robyn Winther, Christine Pattison, Tina Birch, Archie Kerr, Muriel Tunoho, Dorothy Wilson, Kim Ellis, John Ryall and Reverend Norman Wilkins. Photo: Lyndy McIntyre

but the spirit of community was strong and it was the right place for the launch, which ended with a long queue of people signing a pledge to support the movement. A security guard and a cleaner shared their stories; the South Sudanese Dancers, a group of refugee-background workers based in the Hutt Valley, entertained; and the *Hutt News* carried supportive coverage. Another network was officially launched.

Soon after the event, and largely under Muriel's leadership, the Hutt Valley network made submissions to Hutt City Council, calling on it to adopt the living wage. This led to a meeting with chief executive Tony Stallinger and some senior staff. Stallinger appeared sympathetic. The meeting was positive, and a commitment was made to produce a report for councillors. All well and good – but progress was agonisingly slow. As with Wellington, the experience of fighting for the living wage at Hutt City Council showed that securing solid commitment from elected representatives was a more effective strategy than battling it out with council officers.

Across the harbour in Wellington, the living wage network prepared another submission on Wellington City Council's annual plan, this time under the name of St Andrew's parishioner Paul Barber and endorsed by 26 organisations from the three living wage streams, which represented thousands of Wellingtonians. Three sentences of the submission were highlighted:

> Council has voted for this. The people of Wellington have backed it. Now it's time to make the commitment a reality.[3]

A slap to the voters

One unexpected ally in the Wellington City Council campaign was the *Dominion Post*. On 4 March 2016 Wellington's daily paper carried an opinion piece complaining that the vote to extend the living wage to security guards over four months earlier had not yet been implemented. Under the headline 'Council churlish on the living wage', the author wrote:

> While everyone waits for the chamber [of Commerce] to formally make its complaint, the security guards should be paid the wage the councillors decided on.
>
> Councillor Paul Eagle believes that Lavery, who seems ill-disposed towards the policy, is using a 'delay tactic' to hinder its introduction. If that's true, he is well out of order. Eagle also rightly points out that 'the

chamber have had time to act' and haven't done so yet. Instead, its threat is hanging over a policy decided upon by elected councillors. That's ultimately a slap to the voters, and a bad precedent for how other council decisions might be stalled.[4]

By this time the Wellington Chamber of Commerce had woken up to the reality that, despite the threat of legal action, councillors would likely defy their opposition to the living wage. The chamber's previous chief executive Raewyn Bleakley and John Milford, while he was president, were regular oral submitters at meetings concerning the living wage. Our team was often in the council chamber at the same time and found it telling that the Chamber of Commerce rarely brought anyone from among the business community; their main ally was the Taxpayers' Union.

When the council first voted to adopt the living wage in December 2013, Bleakley had described the decision as a waste of public funds, saying, 'We implore the council to use ratepayers' funds to drive economic growth for our city so everyone can benefit from higher wages.'[5] When the first accredited employers were announced, the chamber was again vocal in their opposition, even though the adoption of the living wage was obviously a voluntary decision. Bleakley said the concept was flawed, especially when adopted by the council. 'Wage increases should be about performance and productivity,' she said. 'This is not what the living wage is based on. The message the living wage sends is that there is no incentive to invest in your education, improving skills or your future because the living wage cuts across all of those. It's a blunt and ineffective instrument.'[6]

An extraordinary amount of energy was poured into this campaign of opposition. Since the dramatic council meeting in October 2015, and after failing to persuade councillors to their view, the chamber ramped up its rhetoric around legal action. Although the case never went to court, the chamber managed to use the threat of the untested possibility to cook up an agreement with the chief executive, Kevin Lavery.

Deputy Mayor Justin Lester recalls thinking, 'If they want to do that, good luck to them. They're entitled to have their opinion. We're going to call their bluff, because we think we're on a steady course and legally robust.' He didn't believe legal action would succeed because there was already a precedent of council decisions, such as for events or grants, that were based not on best price but on serving the community. 'So we called their bluff, and there was no legal action.'

The dead rat

In May 2016, John Milford of the Chamber of Commerce and Wellington City Council chief executive Kevin Lavery reached an agreement behind closed doors that demonstrates how far power had shifted from elected representatives to the chief executive and officers. Councillor Pannett described councillors as being forced to 'swallow a dead rat' when a motion to extend the living wage to security guards carried a proviso that this would not be extended to other contracted workers without consultation with the chamber. Pannett disagreed with the process of making a deal behind closed doors and councillors being faced with a fait accompli. Other councillors were also uncomfortable.

The confidential agreement, which described the position reached between the chamber and Wellington City Council as 'mutually acceptable',[7] prevented the chamber from challenging the three-year security contract at the living wage rate. The council would move regular, core cleaning contracts in-house and to the living wage, but the living wage would not apply to the council's other cleaning contracts. If, in the future, the council wanted to require other contractors to pay the living wage, the council would consult the chamber before implementation. If disagreement ensued, the parties would seek a declaratory judgment in the high court.

The document ended with the words, 'The chamber and the council acknowledge that these terms represent a mutually agreed position and are not intended to be legally enforceable.'[8] Reverend Brian Dawson would later say that it wasn't worth the paper it was written on. Justin Lester also viewed the agreement as meaningless and face-saving for the chamber:

> It allowed them to get out of their threat of litigation with some dignity and respect, thinking that they'd achieved or won something, when ultimately the letter said council couldn't be held to it and it wasn't legally binding. What it did do was allow us to put another stake in the ground.

The *Dominion Post* described the move:

> Wellington Chamber of Commerce has backtracked on threats to take Wellington City Council to court over its living wage policy. In a joint statement … both parties said legal proceedings had been halted and they were working towards a way to pay contractors the living wage that was acceptable to the council and the chamber.[9]

It was not the public message the chamber would have wanted, but Living Wage Wellington's Paul Barber saw things differently: 'The people of Wellington will be pleased that the democratic decision of council to value these workers by paying them the living wage, made nearly five months ago, will now go ahead.' The movement, he said:

> would celebrate the fact that Wellington City Council will extend the living wage to council's security and noise control workers, who are among the lowest-paid workers in Wellington, noting there was still work to do to ensure that those in council-controlled organisations and other council workers, employed via Wellington City Council contracts, got the living wage.[10]

The broad-based organising kaupapa

Elsewhere, other less dramatic council campaigns were underway. Thanks to the leadership of Titahi Bay resident Andrew Chick with Hiueni Nuku, Stella Teariki and others, Living Wage Porirua was campaigning at full tilt to ensure progress was made in the council's annual plan. The network set out to show that the community was behind this, collecting nearly 1000 signatures on submissions in support of the council adopting the living wage.

Around this time, at the invitation of Porirua Anglicans' minister Reverend Cath Growcott, Reverend Jenny Dawson joined Living Wage Porirua. Jenny had moved to Porirua from Hawke's Bay, where she'd seen the impact of poverty in her neighbourhood of Marewa. Her concerns about poverty were driven by her theology, 'the sort that says we're here to make a difference for everyone'. Jenny had lived in Christchurch in the mid-1980s, where she became an activist for social justice causes, initially in the anti-racism movement. With others from Corso and HART, she had organised a protest at Christ's College against the Cavaliers' rugby trip to South Africa in 1986. When accepted for ordination training, she wanted to make a difference: 'I couldn't stand up and be a priest in this church without asking hard questions about how things got to be good for some people and not others.'

Now, 30 years later, Jenny found herself drawn to the concept of faith, community and union strands working together: 'It just seemed perfect that we have three quite different groups who don't necessarily talk well to each other.' She liked the way meetings were run:

139

> We did things like going around everybody, saying what their organisation was, why they were here and what they were doing. I got to know people. All those good things about how people belonged, they are really important for inclusiveness. It's so simple, the way we organise ourselves, but a lot of groups don't. I learnt lots of things about where people fitted in and I belonged.

Jenny and other Anglican parishioners became regulars in campaign actions and joined a large group supporting Living Wage Porirua's oral submission at the council in May 2016. Then, at a council meeting in June, Mayor Nick Leggett announced that council would allocate $200,000 towards lifting the pay of the lowest-paid directly employed council workers. The mayor's resolution passed easily. The proposal included deleting the lowest pay bands and was welcomed by the network as a good first step. But still, three years passed before that win was built on.

Numerous thorny issues continued to emerge with Wellington City Council's implementation of the living wage. Between the chief executive, the officers and the contracting companies, every effort was made to avoid delivering on the mayor's and councillors' political commitment. Security guards, employed by Recon Security, were told they would only receive the living wage if they achieved an additional qualification; cleaners were told the living wage would only apply to those employed by Spotless at the main Wakefield Street building. It was a far cry from the commitments made at election forums. 'Wellington City Council cleaners still waiting on the living wage', Stuff reported.[11]

In July 2016, new Living Wage Employers were announced at Christchurch Transitional Cathedral and Auckland's Holy Trinity Cathedral, both of which were fully accredited. The list included a software company with 70 employees, an early childhood centre and a coffee-roasting business. A number of employers gathered at Holy Trinity to share stories of the impact of the living wage on their businesses and organisations. Among them was Labour MP Tamati Coffey, who with his partner owned the living wage-accredited Ponsonby Road Lounge Bar in Rotorua. Annie Newman said on the day:

> These employers are doing the right thing by their workers, but also reaping the rewards of a stable, happy workforce and the ability to market themselves as an official Living Wage Employer. Increasingly New Zealand employers understand that becoming a Living Wage Employer is not only the right thing to do, but a sound business decision as well.[12]

On 1 August the hourly rate of around 60 Wellington City Council cleaners and security guards employed by contractors went up by $3 an hour as part of the council's implementation of the living wage. As this did not include all cleaning contracts, the fight continued to ensure that every cleaner received the pay rise.

In August Deborah Littman returned to Aotearoa for a few weeks, her visit supported by Mayor Wade-Brown with funding from the mayoral fund. Her main purpose was to meet the mayor, councillors, chief executive and officers to share her expertise and experience of implementing the living wage. The meeting was small, however, and the chief executive notably absent. There was a great deal more interest from the community, and a public meeting at St Peter's in Willis Street was packed with Wellingtonians keen to hear Deborah talk about the successful living wage campaign in London. The campaign resonated strongly in Wellington. People wanted to know how it was done.

Living Wage Movement AGMs were again held in Auckland and Wellington, and community action, concrete wins and the steady growth of local organisation were all noted. 'With our sights set on the big goal of contributing to a reduction of poverty and inequality through the living wage, our movement has focused on the democratic project of building connections within organisations and across civil society,' Annie Newman reported.[13] The big news at the AGM was Living Wage Movement Aotearoa NZ's endorsement of a proposal to formally affiliate with the IAF. The annual report outlined the importance of this step 'to secure the relationships and support that have provided a strong basis for our development so far':

> The Living Wage Movement now has a governance body with experience and understanding of the model of building power in society ... We know the Living Wage Movement provides the only broad-based organising kaupapa in NZ and so this relationship is important if we are to see the fruits of our investment in Aotearoa.[14]

The art of doing public business

The 2016 residential training courses, which also took place in August, provided vital preparation for leaders and activists for the upcoming September local body election forums. With the 2013 experience behind us,

Auckland mayoral candidates listen as council cleaner Malia Lagi shares her story at a living wage election forum at St Matthew-in-the-City, 1 September 2016. Photo: Jason Fell

we knew what was required to achieve success. Local networks needed to secure solid public commitments from as many elected mayors and councillors as possible, and this wouldn't happen without effective, well-attended election forums. The training ensured that networks were well prepared to run these.

After what Diana Yukich called a 'brilliant and energised' forum in West Auckland, it was back to St Matthew-in-the City for the main Auckland forum. Annie recalls, 'The art of doing public business through an election forum was evident.' Mayoral candidate Phil Goff said yes to a living wage and honoured his campaign pledge to establish an advisory group before Christmas 2016. Diana says Goff told the forum he wouldn't extend the living wage to workers employed by contractors in his first term, but he would do it in the second, 'and he said he never breaks promises. He said he'd set up a committee and he'd pay the directly employed and he'd plant a million trees.'

Phil Goff used his first interview as Auckland's mayor to put a stake in the ground. When asked by a Radio New Zealand reporter what was the first thing he would do as mayor, he declared it was time for elected representatives to take back power from appointed chief executives and officers:

Newly elected Auckland City Mayor Phil Goff greets living wage supporters at a meeting to set the council's budget, 15 December 2016. Photo: Jason Fell

> I will be meeting with my chief executive officer and my leadership team to make it clear that my anticipation is that the people who make decisions at the council level have to be elected representatives. Elected representatives and the mayor are not there simply to rubber-stamp decisions. Right across government in New Zealand there's a strong element of 'Yes Minister', and probably in local government it's stronger than in most areas.[15]

This was music to the ears of the Living Wage Movement.

The Wellington forum was at the Wesley Methodist Church. Andrew Chick and I walked there at lunchtime to check it out. We'd held our launch there in 2012, but suddenly the church looked very large. We needn't have worried. Living Wage Wellington had done the work on turnout, and over 250 people filled the church that night. This forum was a partnership with Downtown Community Ministry (DCM), a homelessness agency and a member organisation. Mayoral and council candidates were asked to make commitments to ending homelessness as well as to implementing the living wage. We needed rock-solid support to finish off the living wage job, and for the first time candidates were also asked to commit to achieving formal living wage accreditation.

Celia Wade-Brown had pulled out of the Wellington mayoral race and the front runners were Justin Lester and the current Porirua mayor, Nick Leggett. Although Legget had strong conservative backing, he had already experienced the movement in Porirua and could see there was public support for the living wage in Wellington City. At other Wellington mayoral candidate meetings he signalled much greater support for the living wage than he had demonstrated in the Porirua mayoralty. On the night of the forum, candidates were asked to make a clear commitment to finishing off the job of becoming a Living Wage Employer, to ensure that every council worker, including all those employed via contractors, was lifted to the living wage. Commitments were secured from a clear majority of candidates, including the eventually successful mayoral candidate Justin Lester. But it was another Justin – Bishop Justin Duckworth – who made powerful concluding remarks in which he spelt out how thousands of Anglicans living in the city would hold candidates to account to deliver on their promises, a warning to them not to stand if they lacked the courage to deliver.

This time the Christchurch network also ran an election forum, at the Trade Union Centre. All mayoral candidates were invited and allocated time to speak, and questions were put to them on the living wage. At the end of the session candidates were asked to sign pledges. The front-runner and ultimately successful candidate was the current mayor, Lianne Dalziel, who was cautious about signing the pledge – particularly as Christchurch City Council had holding companies employing contractors. Karena Brown recalls, 'She was comfortable and happy to have the discussion around direct employees, but the whole point of accreditation and that issue really concerned her.' The Auckland network had the same issue with Phil Goff. Winning the living wage sometimes requires a staged implementation to get to the end goal. Christchurch organisers changed the words in the pledge to 'work towards' in relation to getting the holding companies on board, and Dalziel signed.

The Hutt City forum in September was the first living wage election forum in the Hutt Valley. A fierce southerly storm did not deter people from supporting the forum at St Paul's Anglican Church in Waterloo, and it turned out to be the largest meeting of the election campaign in Hutt City. Council cleaner Faepepele Taituave was one of the worker speakers. 'My name is Faepepele. My name means look after with care,' he began. Faepepele was from a village in Savai'i, Sāmoa. Eight years earlier, he and his wife had brought their young children to New Zealand for a better life. 'In 2009 I started working as a Hutt City Council cleaner,' Faepepele told the crowd. 'The cleaners are employed by a contractor. We work very hard. Even in heavy rain. We have to carry heavy vacuum cleaners. We work with strong chemicals. Some of the cleaners have been sick because of the chemicals.' After seven years in the job, 51-year-old Faepepele was paid $15.60 an hour, 35 cents above the minimum wage. His wife was a caregiver, also on a low wage. He told the candidates:

> We try very hard to budget. We always put our kids first. But it can be tough. I don't want to complain about my pay, but it can be very hard bringing up two teenagers. On low wages, it's hard to find the money for our kids' sports and school activities. I want to buy the things they need to do well and make sure they have a future. We are not asking for a luxury life, but we want a fair wage.

The network now had an active and visible campaign and an established group of local leaders to drive it. Candidates at the meeting were asked to commit to paying directly employed staff the living wage, extending the living wage to workers employed via contractors next, and working with Living Wage Hutt Valley.

The majority of candidates who were elected supported the commitments, but Mayor Ray Wallace, who again won the mayoralty, was hard to pin down. He did not attend the forum, saying he had another appointment. However, he made a verbal commitment in his office at a meeting with Muriel Tunoho and myself, prior to the forum. Although he didn't sign a pledge, he read the written asks and said, 'I can agree to that.' But Wallace was slippery, and Muriel and I regretted not securing his signature. It was a lesson learned.

A Porirua election forum was held at Reverend Perema's church. A large crowd of aspiring mayoral and council candidates lined up that evening, including the former PSA president Mike Tana. Some months earlier I had run into Tana at a café in Wellington, where he informed me of his intention to stand for the Porirua mayoralty. It was clear that he saw himself as a champion of the living wage and he expected the support of union members and progressives. At the forum, Living Wage Porirua challenged candidates to support the principle of Porirua City Council becoming a living wage council, to put in place a plan to achieve the living wage for all council workers, and to work with Living Wage Porirua to do this. The majority of

Pinner Reverend Jenny Dawson at the 2016 Porirua election forum, Pacific Islanders' Presbyterian Church, Cannons Creek. Photo: Sam Gribben

successful candidates did so, and the successful mayoral candidate, Mike Tana, was unequivocal in his support, throwing his arms dramatically into the air and crying 'Yes, yes, yes!' There was huge applause.

Holding politicians to account

It is one thing to get a public statement and another thing altogether to get action. The people of Porirua had elected a mayor and a clear majority of councillors who had made firm public commitments to the living wage. What could possibly go wrong? Well, things did not go as smoothly as the network hoped they would, and much more activism was required to get Porirua City Council over the line.

Soon after the election I joined representatives of Living Wage Porirua, including Jenny Dawson, Andrew Chick and Stella Teariki, at a meeting with chief executive Wendy Walker, HR manager Jeremiah (Jerry) Wren and Mayor Tana, to discuss how the living wage would be progressed and how we would work together. The new mayor had little to say and handed the meeting over to his chief executive. What he did say, however, was that now he was elected, he could see that Porirua had a lot of expensive jobs requiring attention. A recent earthquake and floods had changed everything, and many of the councillors were new and feeling overwhelmed by the unexpected workload and costs from these natural disasters. He spoke of concerns about rate increases and opposition in the city's northern ward. Was this the same man who cried 'Yes, yes, yes!' to all the asks of the community? Apparently it was.

Wendy Walker was in firm control of the meeting. She said the council had no plans to progress the living wage in next year's annual plan; it would be better to leave it until the long-term plan process in 2018. When we reminded them of the new mayor's commitment to the living wage in the election campaign, they became defensive. I was quietly fuming, but Andrew Chick was a peacemaker and a diplomat. He asked to meet Tana again in the new year and agreed to supply the mayor with the names of councillors who had made the commitment to the living wage. This was shaping up to be a frustrating battle – and it was only the beginning of the term.

It was a different story in Wellington City. New mayor Justin Lester was clear that he had campaigned on Wellington becoming a living wage council and that the promise must be upheld. Although support was not unanimous, a comfortable majority on the council would support it. He was equally clear that the 'treaty' with the Chamber of Commerce was not going to get in the way, saying, 'We had a clear triennium plan and got in, so we had the mandate.' With the writing on the wall, the Wellington City chief executive fell into line.

Lester wasted no time. Soon after the elections he called a summit of community stakeholders at the Wharewaka on the waterfront. Living Wage Wellington was among the organisations represented. Following the summit, a three-year work programme was published. This included a clear commitment to action on the living wage and described what success would look like in three years: the official living wage rate for all council employees and staff of council-controlled organisations; implementation of the living wage in contracts delivering core services; and council accreditation as a Living Wage Employer. Living Wage Wellington was very happy with that. The campaign's goal – accreditation of New Zealand's first living wage city council – was within reach.

The Auckland election forum was also a trigger for action. In November 2016 Annie Newman set up a meeting with the new mayor, Phil Goff.

Bronwynn Maxwell also attended, as a representative of PSA, the main union at the council. Annie sent a briefing paper to Goff, reminding him that a majority of elected councillors had pledged to support the living wage and seeking the establishment of the advisory group the mayor had committed to at the election forum. The paper pointed out that the living wage was aligned with current council strategy, in particular the Auckland plan. Its adoption would support Auckland Council to turn around its record of unequal distribution of income.[16] In 2015 the Auckland Council Group had 1912 employees who were paid more than $100,000 a year, while 1840 workers were paid less than the living wage – and that number was rising. The briefing paper pointed out that Auckland Council could afford to pay the living wage. In 2013 Living Wage Auckland had estimated the cost as being less than one percent of the wage budget. 'The figures involved are tiny compared with the overall scale of council's business', wrote Annie.[17]

The black hole of Greater Wellington Regional Council

In Wellington, former Green Party MP and current Greater Wellington Regional Councillor Sue Kedgley planned to put up a motion for the regional council to become a Living Wage Employer. She had long supported low-paid workers and worked hard to get this on the council's agenda.

In September 2016 the Greater Wellington Regional Council (GWRC) voted for the first time on the living wage. Backed by other enthusiastic councillors and a crowd of living wage supporters present at the meeting, Councillor Kedgley spoke passionately for the council's adoption of the living wage.

Before proposing the resolution, she reasoned:

> Paying the living wage is one of the most effective ways of reducing the gap between the rich and the poor in New Zealand. Every year the wages of the chief executives and managers increase and you seldom hear a complaint or anyone opposing the endless increases for staff at the top of an organisation on the grounds that they are unaffordable. Yet when we propose a meagre increase in the wages for staff at the bottom, everyone says they are unaffordable.

GWRC voted unanimously to become a living wage council, but in reality this vote turned out to be fairly hollow. Only a small group of directly employed workers was affected and, to progress the living wage for contracted workers, another framework would have to be produced by council officers. On the day, however, Living Wage Wellington leaders took GWRC's affirmative vote to become a living wage council as a clear indication that the council intended to do just that. John Ryall was reported as being 'ecstatic' and called the vote a major step forward. He drew the obvious conclusion that a large number of contracted workers providing services to the regional council, including cleaners and security guards, could look forward to a considerable lift in pay. 'Once this is implemented,' he said, 'they will get a major increase in their income, by as much as 25 percent, so this is a pretty powerful resolution.'[18]

Living Wage Wellington spokesperson Paul Barber said GWRC's commitment was fantastic news for those on low incomes and the wider community: 'It's also good for the regional council as an employer, because we know having a decently paid and valued workforce brings benefits in terms of increased morale and reduced turnover.'[19] Kedgley was thrilled to get this over the line and immediately posted on social media that GWRC was a 'Living Wage Employer'. Unfortunately, this was premature: there was a long way to go before all GWRC's workforce, including the contracted workers, were paid the living wage.

The framework, which council officers were supposed to produce in 2017, did not appear. Once again the Living Wage Movement was bogged down in a process captured by council officers with no inclination to implement the vote of democratically elected representatives. The movement campaigned persistently, however, and seven years later, in August 2023, GWRC finally voted to become an accredited Living Wage Employer by 2026. The 10-year delay in implementing the 2016 vote was reflected in the *Post*'s (the rebranded *Dominion Post*) headline: 'Councillors embarrassed, irritated by delay in living wage'.[20]

Across the Wellington region we learned the hard way that leaving implementation to council officers was like sending it into a black hole. It was not the way to lift workers' wages, and not the way to achieve the democratic outcome of a council vote. No amount of negotiation and persuasion would move reluctant council officers, who were doubtless comfortable in their own employment terms. The only way to win the battle over decent pay for low-paid workers was to continue to build community power and exert that power on the elected representatives by securing a public commitment and then holding them to account on delivery of that commitment.

At Christmas time, the Wellington network gathered again in Civic Square for Carols for Our Cleaners. Reverend Tric Malcolm led the event, a council cleaner told his story and Councillor Paul Eagle appeared as Father Christmas. Wellington City councillors, regional councillors and other supporters attended. It was more than time for Wellington City Council to deliver on the commitments made. Surely 2017 would be the year.

CHAPTER 9

Lives transformed: 2017

'At five o'clock I go home, clean the house and cook for my kids. They shower, we eat, then I help them with their homework. I'm awake again at four-thirty. I make my lunch and the little ones' lunches and drive to work.
If I got the living wage, oh my God! Life would be different!'

REBECCA NYAKUONG KUACH, Victoria University of Wellington cleaner

Two thousand pay rises

In contrast to the uphill battle at Wellington City Council, Auckland Council forged ahead with implementation of the living wage across its directly employed workforce. In January 2017 the Auckland Council advisory group met for the first time. The group of 10 included the mayor and three representatives of the Living Wage Movement: Annie Newman, Leonie Morris, and Bronwynn Maxwell from the PSA. Its immediate priority was to advise council officers on a formal public consultation document and the plan to roll out the living wage if the elected council agreed to proceed. The group was tasked with assessing such things as how to address relativity issues for staff paid above the living wage, the adjustment of the rate over time, and options for a staged implementation. An implementation process was agreed on: there would be pay increases each year, and the first adjustment would be of most benefit to those on the lowest rates.

It was a mammoth task to ensure that around two thousand council staff who were paid less than the living wage got a pay rise. It was a big win and affected a wide range of workers: library assistants and shelvers, lifeguards, customer support and recreation assistants, ushers, café staff, venue set-up and bar workers, cleaners and building maintenance staff. The cost was estimated to be $7.5 million.

The process was thorough and involved frequent engagement with Living Wage Auckland. As a result, the implementation went smoothly and reinforced the value of candidates' election forum commitments to an ongoing relationship after the elections. Auckland Council officers were supportive, and any idea of an 'Auckland rate' was quickly dismissed. The Living Wage

Advisory Group's record of actions from an early meeting reflects the enthusiasm of council staff and an understanding that adopting the living wage was good for the city and for the council as an employer.[1]

'From the start the process was constructive and cooperative. The council officers and the representatives of the Living Wage Movement shared the belief that adopting the living wage was the right thing to do and good for the city of Auckland. The role of the advisory group was to work out the best way to do this,' Annie Newman recalls.

Auckland Council officers' support of the living wage concept meant the narrative was completely different to the Wellington experience. A draft report for public consultation prepared by council officers reveals their supportive approach:

> Our preference is to introduce a living wage for council staff as we believe this is the right thing to do. It will ensure people working for the council can meet their basic cost of living, but we will make sure we do this without the need for higher rate increases. At the same time, it will help address pay equity issues between male and female employees. We believe Auckland Council should play a key leadership role on these important issues.[2]

Phil Goff does not recall any resistance from staff. He assumed officials would follow the instructions of those who were elected to office and says, 'It would be a funny sort of democracy if that weren't the case.' He believed his chief executive and staff were pleased with the decision and viewed it as fair for their employees: 'They were willing collaborators in the process.'

How different from the battle with the chief executive and officers in Wellington, Porirua and Hutt City. The contrast raises the question of where power lies in a council. If candidates stand on clear platforms, make commitments to the living wage and are elected and supported by communities, how do chief executives and council management assume the right to block the delivery of these commitments?

Listening campaigns

Fala Haulangi returned to the Auckland community organiser's role in February 2017 keen to focus on South Auckland, where the need for the living wage was great. She activated her Pacific networks and began working with Sanele Poluleuligaga, a Sāmoan Catholic deacon, to organise 'tabletop' meetings with South Auckland communities. The concept came from the

IAF. Tabletop meetings brought neighbourhood groups together to sit around tables and talk about what mattered to them, what impacted their families and what pressures they faced. IAF-affiliated alliances used such meetings to decide which issues to campaign around.

The Living Wage Movement was a single-issue movement, initiated by a union, and a different kind of listening campaign had taken place over the years when SFWU members clearly told their union that poverty pay was the biggest issue facing them and their families. Low incomes contributed to the issues these workers faced, of poor housing, inadequate health services, debt, parents working long hours and a lack of social cohesion. The same issues came up over and over again. With the general election not far away, Fala and Sanele decided this was a good time to sit down and listen again by holding tabletops in South Auckland to check these communities' concerns. Fala recalls that income and the related issue of housing were predominant: 'Even now they are the two pressing issues: income and housing.'

In February I travelled to Whanganui for a public meeting to generate awareness and build local support for the living wage concept. This was largely organised by Marion Sanson and other Quakers with support from Lyn Williams, an E tū organiser based in Palmerston North. Largely because of the work of Marion and a small group of mainly faith supporters, Living Wage Whanganui continued as a grassroots movement despite not having the regular support of a community organiser.

The successful strategy

Many of the Wellington City Council cleaners had still not received the living wage despite the numerous commitments made to it. A *Dominion Post* reporter rang me, clearly looking for a complaint about council leadership. Although there were countless media opportunities to participate in negative stories, this was not our strategy. The IAF principle of working together in a relational way, publicly celebrating incremental wins and keeping up the community pressure to move to the next step, was what secured the achievements of the movement.

In April 2017 the updated living wage rate of $20.20 was announced, and Mayor Justin Lester announced that all Wellington City Council cleaners would get their pay rise and the council would start paying the full and updated living wage rate. The long-term and annual plan committee agenda included a proposal to lift the rate paid by the council to $20.20, as well as a commitment to the staged implementation of the living wage on 'relevant contracts for regular and ongoing core services, to be processed on a case-by-case basis'. The *NZ Herald* reported:

> Staff working directly for the council already get the living wage, such as those working in parks, gardens, recreation or libraries. But because cleaning and sanitation work was contracted, those workers weren't initially included. Now the latest long-term and annual plan committee agenda shows cleaning work will be included from July 1 this year. The 'living wage' rate of $18.40 an hour for all workers will also be adjusted to $20.20. The changes will cost $700,000 for 2017/18.[3]

The mayor said it was a 'no-brainer' to include the contracted cleaners: 'We wanted a prudent budget, a budget that was affordable but that also ensures we treated our staff well.' He said experience had shown that paying a living wage could actually save money. He cited the example of the council taking the parking wardens in-house and employing them at the living wage rate, which resulted in overall savings by removing the contractor's cut. 'Previously the contractor was taking the majority of the benefit from the contract, and not the staff. We've had greater loyalty from staff, reduced turnover and increased services, at a lower burden for ratepayers.'[4] The council, he said, was looking at other contracts to bring in-house and up to the living wage rate.

The shift to the living wage transformed the lives of contracted parking wardens, security guards and cleaners. Ann Simone and Alana Moss were employed by Spotless as cleaners at Wellington City Council. They were E tū members, and I met Ana through her union organiser, Ibrahim Omer. She worked a day shift at the council's main Wakefield Street building while Alana cared for their toddler. Like many cleaning couples, at the end of the day they exchanged care of their child, and Alana started the night shift. Before the pay rise they had to work long hours just for the necessities. 'We were squeezed into a tiny room, as we couldn't afford anything else. We never made ends meet.' After shifting to the living wage, Ann said, 'We managed to move into a two-bedroom place with more space for our baby to play in.'

Making headway

In March 2017 Hutt City Council voted to support the living wage in principle, and the chief executive was instructed to draft a remuneration and employment policy to address paying the living wage to direct employees. This paper was supposed to materialise by July. John Ryall and I immediately prepared a paper on options for ensuring that contracted workers got the living wage and fired it off to relevant parties. Unfortunately our enthusiasm wasn't matched by that of the council officials, who directed their energy into commissioning costly legal opinions from law firm Simpson Grierson.

A seven-page opinion from the law firm contained such gems as: 'Paying a wage higher than the market rate (or paying a council contractor more so that it can pay its employees a higher-than-market rate) could arguably be seen as not in accordance with sound business practice nor the prudent stewardship of resources.' On the obligation of council to be a good employer Simpson Grierson had this to say:

> … an argument could be made that paying a living wage could lend support to or assist the achievement by a local authority of providing fair and proper treatment of its employees. Of course, these comments are not applicable in respect of requiring council contractors to pay a living wage to their employees (because the council is not the employer of these persons).[5]

'These persons', of course, included invisible workers like Faepepele, the Hutt City Council cleaner who had shared with council candidates at the election forum the previous year the reality of the demanding, dirty and sometimes dangerous work of the low-paid council cleaners, and who told them, 'We are not asking for a luxury life, but we want a fair wage.'

Making headway with their council was also front of mind for Living Wage Porirua. After the 2016 elections, the network was confident the council would act quickly. Early meetings with the new mayor and chief executive had dented that confidence, but the network continued to campaign persistently. In March 2017 a Living Wage Porirua delegation was back at the council chambers making a submission on the council's annual plan. Stella Teariki invited Awhina Kauwau, a PSA member and customer service officer from Te Rauparaha Arena, to tell her story to councillors. 'I love my job, but it's challenging and I am good at it. I want to be valued and have recognition for my work. Part of that recognition is a fair rate of pay,' she said:

> Last year I got a pay rise of a dollar an hour because of council's commitment to the living wage. Thank you for that. It's really made a difference, not just to me but to my co-workers as well. But I'm still not on the living wage and life's still tough. We all work hard. Our jobs are important. We want to be valued for the work we do and our contribution to the community.

As a result of the call from the community, Porirua City Council decided to lift wages again for directly employed workers – but not to the full living wage rate.

In May 2017 Hutt City Council approved a policy that would deliver the living wage to direct employees, provided it was done in a 'cost-effective' way. Councillors asked chief executive Tony Stallinger to continue working with Living Wage Hutt Valley on the issues around contractors and report back to the council's September meeting. Stallinger was a personable man, but he was also cautious and not about to show leadership on the living wage.

Through the initiative of the 'Man with a Plan', as Councillor Chris Milne called himself, Hutt Valley Chamber of Commerce was invited to join the group considering the living wage, which also included John Ryall and myself as representatives of the local network. The chamber's president, Neville Hyde, was friendly and easy to work with, but he had no idea how the minimum wage was calculated, let alone the living wage. The council officers did nothing to progress the political decisions, stalling continually, refusing to discuss the implementation paper we had prepared, cancelling meetings and filling up the few that took place with legal misinformation.

John and I kept reporting back to the network, but after the Wellington experience we'd grown tired of these pointless meetings. There was one highlight, however. Neville Hyde asked if he could share a local Chamber of Commerce confidential survey. We replied that he could be assured of our confidentiality, as long as the chamber did not misrepresent the position of their members at future council meetings. Hyde shared the survey, which revealed that the chamber had received 70 responses to the question: 'Do you support the Hutt City Council enforcing businesses that contract to council paying the living wage to those staff providing services to council?' The result was interesting: 'The outcome of the responses was closely balanced between those in support and those against or unsure.'[6] This did not provide the ammunition for the chamber's strong opposition and, since

LIVES TRANSFORMED: 2017

they continued to oppose the living wage, we felt at liberty to speak out about their survey. The council officers pushed on with barriers, roadblocks, spurious legal arguments and general opposition. Living Wage Hutt Valley campaigned relentlessly throughout Ray Wallace's term. There were wins, but each was hard won.

Courage under fire

On 10 May 2017 a campaign event took place in the student hub at Victoria University. Living Wage Day had been weeks in the planning. The lunchtime event was organised with support from the talented student president,

Rebecca Nyakuong Kuach (left), student Sophie Coomber and librarian Thomas Martin wait to address the crowd at Living Wage Day, Victoria University of Wellington, 10 May 2017. Photo: Lyndy McIntyre

Rory Lenihan-Iken. A student, Sophie Coomber, shared her story of life in a low-paid city job. E tū member Rebecca Nyakuong Kuach, a former refugee from South Sudan who cleaned the main university buildings, also spoke. Rebecca had experienced tremendous hardship and danger when her family fled from war-torn South Sudan and during years of living in a refugee camp. Like many refugees, the only work she could find in New Zealand was minimum-wage cleaning. A single mother with five children, Rebecca had no option but to work long hours in her low-paid job at the university. She was an E tū delegate and a staunch advocate for the living wage for herself and her fellow cleaners. Rebecca shared her story with over 300 living wage supporters gathered in the hub.

Rebecca's life as a Victoria University cleaner and single mother was tough. She would later say:

> At five o'clock I go home, clean the house and cook for my kids. They shower, we eat, then I help them with their homework. We go to bed. I'm awake again at four-thirty. I make my lunch and the little ones' lunches and drive to work. If I got the living wage, oh my God! Life would be different![7]

Rebecca was employed by cleaning contractors OCS. After the event in the hub she was called in for a disciplinary meeting and threatened with the sack. Fortunately Ibrahim Omer was her union organiser and acted swiftly to make sure she kept her job. Rebecca had told her story despite knowing that to do so was risky for a vulnerable, low-paid worker like herself.

It was always clear that real workers' stories were essential to win public support and political commitment. The power of the story is at the heart of the Living Wage Movement, but this does put pressure on workers. It takes real courage for them to share their lives publicly in this way. When leaders in the movement searched for storytellers, workers who lived hand-to-mouth and could ill afford to lose their livelihoods always put their hands up first. They did it because they were constantly looking to the future of their families. Rebecca Nyakuong Kuach was one of the most courageous people I have ever met, and her courage was tested as she continued to risk her job by speaking out about the life of poverty that was the lot of the low-paid contracted cleaner.

Central government in our sights

In August the hard work and campaigning of Chas Muir, Karena Brown, Jolyon White and others in Christchurch began to pay off: Christchurch city councillors voted to move all directly employed staff to the living wage. The *Press* reported that this would benefit about 470 staff, or 16.5 percent of the council's workforce.[8] Councillor Aaron Keown, who moved the recommendation, told colleagues this was their chance to 'look working-class people in the eye and say: "We value you."' Councillor Pauline Cotter thought the council should lead the way: 'We need to move towards a more equitable society where people have dignity. If you work really hard and still can't make ends meet, where's the dignity in that?'[9] Although there was still much to do to win the living wage for the contracted workers and to achieve accreditation, it was a big move forward for the Christchurch network.

A bigger challenge loomed for the national movement: to win a commitment to the living wage from the next government. Prime Minister Bill English had announced there would be a general election on 23 September 2017, and the networks set about planning general election forums. Local body election forums had been successful in 2013 and 2016; surely demonstrating widespread community support and calling for firm commitments from politicians at a national level could be equally successful. Adopting the same strategy had the potential to transform the lives of not just the lowest-paid directly employed workers in the core public service but also the thousands of contracted workers in government departments: the armies of cleaners, security guards and others.

Residential training was scheduled to ensure that the movement was ready to hold effective forums and the right people were trained to lead them. A national five-day course was again held at Vaughan Park in Auckland. Among the participants was Marlon Drake, a student leader from Victoria University, who would go on to become a leader in the Wellington network and eventually took on my role as the Wellington community organiser. Other participants included Marion Sanson from the Whanganui Quakers, a group from the Rail and Maritime Transport Union, the Tongan Youth Trust and a representative from Aotearoa Resettled Community Coalition – the usual spread of faith, community and unions. The training was once more led by Sister Maribeth Larkin, and this time the final evening action included the issue of housing as well as the living wage. The stories at the action included the heart-wrenching testimony of a young woman from the

Tongan Youth Trust who grew up without a fridge because her parents were minimum-wage workers and unable to provide their family with things that most New Zealanders take for granted.

Election forums were held in Auckland, Hamilton, Wellington and Christchurch. At each, party representatives were challenged to make a commitment to deliver the living wage in the core public service to directly employed workers in the first year following the election, and to contracted workers by the end of the three-year parliamentary term.

The Auckland forum was at Manurewa's Catholic church, St Anne's. The issues of working poverty and housing were two sides of a coin, especially in south Auckland, and the living wage team built into the forum an evidence-based ask on housing. As Annie Newman says:

> The 2017 general election must be seen against the backdrop of a housing crisis where many working New Zealanders were sleeping in cars, unable to find accommodation. The testimony from a young sole parent and full-time worker, who took her children for 'night adventures' in the car until they fell asleep so they did not know they had no home to go to, powerfully illustrated the indivisibility of the multiple issues of working poverty.

At St Anne's, candidates from Labour, the Green Party, the Māori Party (Te Pāti Māori) and New Zealand First all endorsed their commitment to housing and the living wage.

Housing was also an issue in Wellington. In the lead-up to the Wellington forum, Ibrahim Omer, Jenny Dawson and I met with Bishop Justin Duckworth on behalf of Living Wage Wellington to seek his support for a forum at Wellington Cathedral of St Paul. Bishop Duckworth was keen to support the living wage, but his priority was to do something for the elections jointly with the Wellington Catholics. Unfortunately the Anglican bishop's enthusiasm for the living wage was not yet shared by the Wellington Catholic leader, Cardinal John Dew, and the local Catholic Peace and Justice group was adamant that the forum would have a single focus: housing.

We tried to secure agreement that the agenda for a joint forum would include broader poverty issues of income, including the living wage, but although Catholic Bishop Pat Dunn in Auckland had embraced the living wage, Cardinal Dew had not yet done so. Without the endorsement of their leader, Wellington Catholics, with the exception of some individuals, were on the periphery of the local Living Wage Movement. This was eventually remedied in 2022 when the Catholic Archdiocese of Wellington Ecology,

Above: SFWU organiser Fala Haulangi and Sisters of Mercy leader Margaret Martin, and (right), Maria Puaula from Vinnies Youth, speak at a general election forum at St Anne's Catholic Church in Manurewa, Auckland, September 2017.
Photos: Jason Fell

Justice and Peace Commission was welcomed as a Living Wage Movement Aotearoa NZ member organisation, with Cardinal John Dew's support.

For now, however, a Wellington joint Anglican–Catholic forum in St Paul's Cathedral went ahead with housing as the sole issue, accompanied by powerful stories from homeless people and those working with them. Politicians pontificated on the big society and heaped praise on community groups, conveying a clear expectation that they expected stretched community organisations to continue to carry the load. But this forum had no asks or challenges, and therefore no commitments. The people power of 700 participants seemed wasted.

A week later a very different forum took place at St Peter's on Willis, which focused on securing specific commitments to deliver the living wage. St Peter's temporary minister, Reverend Annette Cater, was an enthusiastic host, and the parishioners, who were well used to opening their church to community meetings and providing hospitality, served soup and bread rolls. All parties in Parliament were invited to send representatives to this forum, and Labour, New Zealand First, the Green Party and Te Pāti Māori accepted; National and ACT did not. An empty chair placed beside the other speakers carried a sign that read 'The National Party'. In 2017 ACT was seen as a very minor party and retained just one seat on election night, compared to National's 58.

Labour Party representative Kelvin Davis was not well prepared: he arrived at St Peter's and asked how long he had to speak. John Ryall explained that his role at the forum was to listen to the voice of the community and respond to clear asks. Davis had been emailed a detailed background paper and he repaired to a small room to read this and consider his response. Better organised were Jan Logie from the Green Party and Mei Reedy-Taare from Te Pāti Māori, who both said yes enthusiastically to all the asks. Long-time supporter Tracey Martin from New Zealand First not only said yes but also declared that the minimum wage should be the living wage. Faced with 350 people and the force of compelling personal stories, Kelvin Davis also said yes to all the asks. All four candidates then signed commitment forms, recording their agreement.

A Christchurch election forum was held with Unions Canterbury at Addington Showgrounds. Unions Canterbury convenor Karena Brown organised for the living wage to be part of the forum, which was attended by around 200 union members. Representatives of Labour, New Zealand First and the Green Party attended; National and ACT declined the invitation. Unions Canterbury gave up the last part of the forum to the signing of a living wage pledge. Labour MP Ruth Dyson and Green Party MPs Eugenie Sage and Mojo Mathers signed; a couple of New Zealand First candidates were happy to sign in support of the directly employed, but crossed out the line extending the living wage to contractors. Karena was delighted with the outcome: 'All in all it was a good result. We felt quite excited.'

We made plenty of effort to persuade the National Party to send representatives to the forums, with little success. One representative came to a

St Peter's on Willis, the venue for Living Wage Wellington's 2017 general election forum. Photo: Sam Gribben

small Hamilton forum, but the local MP, David Bennett, was clear: no living wage commitment would be on his party's agenda.

With commitments received from Labour, New Zealand First, the Green Party and Te Pāti Māori, the movement had done well. Polls, however, suggested National would secure the largest proportion of the vote, and there was a widespread assumption that National would win the election. In that case, the movement would have no commitments, an unsympathetic government, and another three years without progress for workers in the core public service.

The election outcome was a surprise. Six weeks out from polling day the Labour Party had a change of leadership and the party's fortunes changed. When Jacinda Ardern became Labour's leader, a mood of positivity gripped the campaign with the slogan 'Let's do this'. After protracted negotiations with New Zealand First, Jacinda Ardern emerged as New Zealand's new prime minister in a coalition government with New Zealand First and support on confidence and supply from the Green Party. This was good news for the Living Wage Movement, which had the hard-copy evidence of Labour, New Zealand First and the Green Party's commitments to the living wage in the core public service.

Something to celebrate

Soon after the new government was sworn in, Living Wage Movement Aotearoa NZ invited government MPs to celebrate outside Parliament. Around 60 supporters arrived in a festive mood with a large living wage banner. We were joined by a group of politicians, including new Labour MP and former trade unionist Michael Wood and Green Party co-leader Marama Davidson, both of whom addressed the crowd and reiterated their commitment to the living wage. E tū member Avei Toaitiiti, a contracted security guard at the Reserve Bank, spoke about her long hours working for just over $16 an hour.[10] 'Minimum wage for me is going to work in the dark and coming home in the dark. As a parent, it's heartbreaking when your child comes up and tells you she hardly sees you anymore because of your long working hours. The living wage for me would mean fewer hours working and more time with my daughter and loved ones.' She told the crowd she would be supporting the government to honour its living wage pledge, saying, 'As our lovely prime minister would say: Let's do this!' A cheer also went up for two Labour MPs, Tamati Coffey of the Ponsonby Road Lounge Bar in Rotorua and Jo Luxton of Headstart Early Learning Centre in Timaru, the first fully accredited Living Wage Employers to enter Parliament.

There was something else to celebrate. In November, after years of waiting for corporate employers to come on board, the first major firm was finally accredited: the electrical lines company, Vector. Annie Newman described this development as momentous, as it included Vector's cleaners and other low-paid contracted workers. 'The movement has contacted many of the top New Zealand firms to invite them to be living wage and Vector is the first to embrace the concept. We hope it is just the beginning.' Vector's chief executive Simon McKenzie said pledging to pay their workers $20.20 and above was a way to help address the inequality of living standards.[11]

It would be more than a year before the next large corporate employer became accredited, but this was a start. It demonstrated that corporates, which had no problem with affordability, could easily sort out issues around contractors.

Living Wage Movement national convenor Annie Newman addresses MPs from the newly formed Labour-led government at a rally on Parliament's steps, November 2017.
Photo: Sam Gribben

With the new government in place, it wasn't long before there was progress on the commitment to deliver the living wage in the core public service. Just before Christmas 2017, Parliament's Speaker Trevor Mallard, who had regularly supported living wage events as the MP for the Hutt South electorate and later as a list MP, announced the staged implementation of the living wage for all cleaners, security guards and hospitality workers at Parliament.

Living Wage Wellington was invited to bring 20 people to the Speaker's announcement in the Labour Party caucus room. The delegation gathered outside the Beehive with an air of excitement. The Living Wage Movement's speaker, Reverend Hiueni Nuku, was resplendent in a black shirt, dog collar and large gold cross, his wife Tongi beside him. Inside Parliament, Hiueni's speech began with the words from Psalm 118: 'This is the day the Lord has made. Let us rejoice and be glad in it.' There was certainly rejoicing. This announcement had been a long time coming. Parliamentary cleaner and E tū member Eseta Ailoa was the worker speaker on the day: she said receiving the living wage meant she could at last take her family on a holiday.

The directly employed workforce across the core public service moved to a minimum rate of the living wage in 2018. But although the government was setting an example to other employers, the three-year term was unexpectedly frustrating and the Labour-led government did not deliver on the full commitment made at forums. It certainly didn't help to have the handbrake of New Zealand First in government, and officials also dragged the chain. Annie Newman recalls:

> Labour delivered on the ask of establishing an ongoing relationship with the movement through a committee to monitor progress toward contracted workers in the core public service receiving no less than the living wage, but this was four years in the making as the new government re-organised public procurement processes … Astonishingly, it seemed the system was so decentralised ministers had no information on who was impacted or what the cost was. All we wanted was a commitment to every agency contract, including rates that were at least the living wage, but political will seemed to be defeated at every turn by the impediments of bureaucracy.

It was the eve of the 2020 election before Ministry of Social Development security guards became the first group of contracted workers in a government department to move to the living wage; and not until the 2020 election campaign did Labour make an unequivocal commitment to deliver the living wage for all contracted workers in the public service.

The new government did move quickly on one important issue, however. One of the main barriers to lifting contracted workers in local councils to the living wage was the insistence of council legal officers that this was in contravention of the Local Government Act 2002. The 2002 Act included provision for councils to play a broad role in promoting the social, economic, environmental and cultural wellbeing of their communities. In 2012 the National government had removed these 'four wellbeings' from the Act. The Labour government now moved to reinstate them.

In December 2017 John Ryall passed on a letter to Hutt City Council officers from Associate Local Government Minister Meka Whaitiri, confirming that the government intended to restore the wellbeings to the Local Government Act as soon as possible. Living Wage Hutt Valley spelt it out to the officers: this would mean that any perceived legal barriers to extending the living wage to contracted workers were now irrelevant.

Community leaders gather at Parliament to celebrate the announcement that parliamentary cleaners, hospitality workers and security guards would move to the living wage, December 2017. Photo: Sam Gribben

Changes to the Local Government Act 2002 were introduced to Parliament in April 2018 and reinstated local councils' focus on the wellbeing of communities. The clause of the Act that living wage opponents relied on, and which described one purpose of local government as 'to meet the current and future needs of communities for good-quality local infrastructure, local public services, and performance of regulatory functions in a way that is most cost-effective for households and businesses', was gone. In its place was 'to promote the social, economic, environmental and cultural wellbeing of communities in the present and for the future'. Local Government New Zealand said the changes acknowledged 'that local authorities have a broader role in fostering liveable communities than simply providing core services'.[12] The legislation change demolished the barrier to paying the living wage to contracted workers in councils – although if Wellington City Council could implement the living wage for contracted workers despite the clause, then others could have too. They just chose not to.

By the end of 2017, with the government's commitment made, the council campaigns in strong momentum and a major corporate business on board, the work of the movement was having a tangible impact on the industrial and social landscape of Aotearoa.

Before the year ended there was one more election forum. Wellington City Councillor Paul Eagle had won the seat of Rongotai in the general election, necessitating a local council by-election in the Paekawakawa Southern Ward. Living Wage Wellington decided to hold a forum to ensure that the living wage was visible on the city's agenda and to seek commitments from candidates.

The forum was at the Assembly of God Church in Rintoul Street, Newtown, a big old building with a Pacific congregation and a supportive pastor, Sonny Taimalelagi. Like others in the local Sāmoan ministers' group, Pastor Sonny had a humble background. He was used to struggling on the minimum wage and had a good understanding of in-work poverty among his congregation. Pastor Sonny happily opened his church, which was visibly in need of repair and sparsely furnished. There was a lot of aroha in that building and in the forum.

Most Southern Ward candidates attended, and over 100 people filled the church to hear from community leaders and workers. Mike Butler from St Peter's on Willis threw himself into a roll-call of member organisations. The pinners, trade unionist Gina Lockyer from NZEI Te Riu Roa and student leader Rory Lenihan-Iken, were dynamic. The Assembly of God youth group performed and there were powerful stories from local workers. There was an emphatic yes from almost all of the candidates, including from Fleur Fitzsimons, who won the by-election, became the council's living wage portfolio holder, and was instrumental in the subsequent accreditation of Wellington City Council as New Zealand's first living wage council.

CHAPTER 10

New beginnings: 2018

'I quit my part-time job. I spend more time with my kids. I am going back to university. Living wage has changed my life.'

AHMED DINI, Wellington City Council cleaner

New rate, new roles and new support for an old campaign

The 2018 updated living wage rate announcement took place on 4 April at the Rogue & Vagabond in central Wellington, the first New Zealand craft beer bar to become a Living Wage Employer. Owner Gwilym Waldren provided live music from the Frank Burkitt Band and trays of bubbles for the large crowd, and Mayor Justin Lester announced the new rate. At $20.55 an hour, it was the smallest annual increase since the New Zealand rate was launched in 2013.

The rate followed the first five-yearly review to ensure the living wage remained accurate and fit for purpose. The cost of goods and services on which the calculation was based had been updated, and new research measuring expenses in areas such as energy, health, communication and education was included. As reviewer Charles Waldegrave explained, there had been a significant increase in support for families in the Labour-led government's Families Package, without which the rate would have been $22.45 – a difference of nearly $2.00 an hour.

Around this time there were changes in the community organiser roles. Fala Haulangi returned to her organiser job at E tū and Jocelyn (Jo) Vicente Angeles became the Auckland community organiser. Jo came from a background in community organising in the Philippines. My own position as Wellington community organiser reduced to 20 hours a week to match the Auckland role, and I pulled back from organising the Victoria University campaign. The TEU Victoria University of Wellington branch redirected the allocated funding to support student activist Marlon Drake to play a more prominent role.

The campaign at Wellington City Council had now been running for nearly six years and campaigners were keen for a resolution. Support for the campaign continued to grow and at the living wage stage at the Newtown Festival in March, over 1000 people signed letters applauding the mayor's living wage commitment and calling on the council to become accredited. In May living wage supporters gathered at Newtown Library to present the letters to the mayor and Councillor Fleur Fitzsimons. Library assistant and PSA member Lauryn Hedley shared her story, and Adullahi Mohamed, a Somalian refugee employed by Spotless to clean the library, described how receiving the living wage meant his wife could now stay at home to care for their six children while he worked. Mayor Lester and Councillor Fitzsimons made clear their endorsement of the living wage and their commitment to Wellington City Council becoming a living wage council, but it was time to deliver.

Time to deliver

A new development provided the leverage the Wellington campaign needed. In June 2018 Hutt City Council met to consider three options on the living wage. The first was to do nothing; the second was to stage the implementation by adopting a $20-an-hour rate for directly employed workers and delaying the full living wage for a year; and the third was to adopt the full living wage. The Hutt Valley network planned a big presence at the meeting, and supporters gathered outside for the obligatory photo on a chilly winter's morning. Unfortunately, John Ryall and Muriel Tunoho, who had invested so much in this, were overseas and missed one of the biggest highlights in the Hutt City living wage campaign.

As is so often the case in Aotearoa, Hutt City's deputy mayor, David Bassett, was a friend and neighbour of Charles Waldegrave. Bassett invited Waldegrave to meet with himself, Mayor Ray Wallace and the council's chief executive beforehand to allay any fears the others might have. Wallace was concerned that if the council adopted the living wage as the minimum rate for all directly employed workers, it would have to be applied to the many young workers at the council's swimming pools; the chief executive was worried about cost. Waldegrave explained that, like anyone, young people also needed the living wage to meet rents, student debt and other costs. And he pointed out that research in New Zealand and overseas showed that the costs of implementing the living wage were offset by the benefits of higher motivation, increased productivity, lower staff turnover and reduced absenteeism.

Mayor Wallace was a cautious politician and nervous about recommending option three, the full living wage, because it had attracted just over 50 percent support in community consultation, and Councillor Milne, the 'Man with a Plan' who strongly opposed the living wage, was on the warpath.

I spoke to Charles Waldegrave early on the morning of the council meeting and he referred to the discussion. I said we would push hard for option three, as the mayor had promised the council would introduce the option that received the most community support during the consultation process.

An hour later the Living Wage Hutt Valley delegation filed into the council chambers. Michelle Maguren was the living wage speaker and shared her story of life as a low-paid school secretary in the Hutt Valley. Michelle was a great speaker, down to earth, genuine, and calm and emphatic in her ask. She challenged councillors to deliver on the commitments made and to honour the outcome of the community consultation.

As the day went on it became clear that it would be many hours before the vote took place. The Living Wage Hutt Valley delegation had already shown a strong presence and people needed to return to work and other commitments. I stayed on to hold the fort with Petone resident Betsan Martin from the Methodist Public Issues network. Aware that the mayor was wavering, we knew it was vital to confront him and remind him of his commitment – but he was not answering his phone and the council was in session. Councillor Josh Briggs came to the rescue and organised an impromptu meeting with the mayor. Ray Wallace asked if Living Wage Hutt Valley would support the compromise option. I said no: he had promised he would act on the outcome of the consultation. Without hesitation, Wallace then said he would back option three.

That wasn't quite enough, however. We needed council commitment to continue the work on getting contracted workers across the line, and a timeframe for a report – preferably by December. Wallace said that was fine, but we would have to include Neville Hyde from the Chamber of Commerce in the working group along with council officers, John Ryall and myself. That wasn't a problem – we were used to working with Neville. It was the council's own officers who were the problem.

Wallace kept his word. When the vote came up on the agenda, he moved to lift all directly employed staff to the current living wage rate of $20.55. He also moved that the chief executive continue to work with Living Wage Hutt Valley and the Hutt Valley Chamber of Commerce on the issues around contracted workers and report back in December. The vote eventually took place around 6pm: 10 were in favour, two were against, and one abstained. The community had spoken, and the mayor and councillors had responded.

Once outside in the freezing dark, I was overcome by exhausted relief mixed with elation over the Hutt campaign outcome and the strength of the local movement. I returned to my car and, before heading home, emailed the result to my comrades John and Muriel in the UK. My email was frank:

> Tony [Stallinger, the chief executive] gave quite an odd report about how he doesn't think there is a legal risk any longer, which just made a complete mockery of the whole legal issues thing last time. Chris Milne … asked a whole lot of stupid questions and Margaret Cousins asked a question. Then Michael Lulich gave a really good speech as did Campbell [Barry] and Josh [Briggs], and I thought Ray [Wallace] was actually very good too. He also spoke strongly about the need to do something about contract workers. Glenda [Barratt] also spoke … Chris Milne and Leigh [Sutton] … voted against and Margaret Cousins abstained … Now it's all done.

'There was a round of applause as Hutt City Council voted to pay its lowest-earning staff the living wage,' the *Dominion Post* reported next morning:

> Councillors voted to introduce the living wage for all directly employed staff during a Community Plan Committee meeting on Wednesday night. From July 1 this year, 230 Hutt City Council staff who currently earn below the living wage will have their pay bumped up to $20.55 an hour. The change is understood to affect many staff who work at the council's libraries and pools. The vote passed with nine councillors for the motion, two against and one councillor who abstained. Mayor Ray Wallace voted for the living wage and said his decision was not based on political ideology. 'It's an issue about paying our lowest paid workers and giving them a feeling of self-worth and value.' Councillor Campbell Barry, a big supporter of the living wage, was reported to say that the affirmative vote had been a long time coming. 'This will make a big difference for 230 [council staff] that earn below the living wage. A key thing is we as a council can take a leading role in paying the living wage [in the hope] that other employers will follow suit.'[1]

The Hutt City victory put pressure on the leadership of Wellington City Council. Most Wellingtonians thought their council had adopted the living wage for all directly employed workers long ago – the council's own rhetoric certainly gave that impression. But council officers had in place a barrier that prevented all directly employed council staff from being on the living wage rate or higher – a so-called 'training rate' that kept some directly employed staff on a lower rate. We had repeatedly told council officers that this needed to go. Now was the time, or Hutt City could overtake Wellington in achieving accreditation. We talked to Fleur Fitzsimons, who contacted the council's head of human resources, Nicola Brown, to ask how quickly workers on training rates could be lifted to the full living wage rate, and what it would cost.

As it happened, the cost was small: the idea of keeping workers on the lower rate was driven by the ideology of officers, not cost. Fitzsimons rang the mayor, who agreed it was well past the time to get rid of the training rate and, just like that, political will won over officer determination to maintain control.

Work on implementing the living wage for contracted workers now accelerated rapidly. Wellington City Council moved to fulfil the pledge made by Celia Wade-Brown in August 2012: that Wellington would be New Zealand's first living wage council.

Landmark victories

The movement continued to grow beyond Auckland and Wellington. Te Waipounamu the South Island started to buzz with activity, including the establishment of Living Wage Bluff. This small Southland community has a long history of worker activism. The local Sanford seafood factory employed hundreds of people, many of whom were on very low pay. These workers were E tū members and called on their community to support their bid to win the living wage. They were led by their E tū delegate Linda Bevin (later Fraser) and ably supported by their union organiser, Anna Huffstutler. Sanford was a tough employer. The chief executive lived in the North Island and was out of touch with the workers, who were gutsy and determined.

Up north in the Waikato, a community hub at Go Eco Environment Centre became the engine room for campaign activities in the area.

After directly employed workers in the core public service moved to the living wage in September 2018, the National Library's PSA members put on morning tea for their cleaners, including Mareta Sinoti (left).
Photos: Sam Gribben

Leadership was provided by Rose Black and Anna Casey-Cox from Poverty Action Waikato, former New Zealand Nurses Organisation organiser Jo Wrigley, Sharryn Barton from E tū's rūnanga and others.

Then came September, a month of landmark victories for the movement. On 1 September 2018, all directly employed workers in the core public service moved to a minimum rate of the living wage. Two days later Wellington City Council hosted an event at the Wellington Museum to announce its accreditation as New Zealand's first living wage council.

Wellington City Mayor Justin Lester (right) cuts a cake to celebrate the council's living wage accreditation on 3 September 2018. He is assisted by council workers (left to right): Malcolm Hirini, Ahmed Dini and Eleanor Haggerty-Drummond. Photo: Wellington City Council

The mayor's office organised a gigantic cake, and around 100 community supporters, politicians and council staff attended, including chief executive Kevin Lavery. Emerging local living wage leader Marlon Drake was MC, and three council staff, Malcolm Hirini, Eleanor Haggerty-Drummond and Ahmed Dini, shared their stories.

Malcolm Hirini began work as a council parking warden in 2005 when it was a minimum-wage job. With four daughters, he was working up to 70 hours a week to make ends meet. When the parking wardens moved to the living wage, Malcolm was able to reduce his hours to 40 and reclaim some family time. 'Now my wife and I have date nights. Now I have a life,' he said. Library assistant Eleanor Haggerty-Drummond said winning the living wage meant she felt valued; the extra income had helped her to buy a house with her partner.

Ahmed Dini was a refugee from Somalia with three small children. The only work he could find was cleaning on the minimum wage. To improve his English, he enrolled in a course and worked part time cleaning at the council. In order to feed his family, however, he was forced to drop his studies and work longer hours. When the council cleaners' pay rates increased by over

30 percent, Ahmed said, he was able to quit his part-time job. 'I spend more time with my kids. I am going back to university. Living wage has changed my life.'

Ibrahim Omer, who helped Ahmed translate his speech, soon after saw Ahmed playing with his children in the playground on his day off:

> A lot of the cleaners who got the living wage were refugee background, cleaning council flats and public toilets. Every success was significant, but I was proud of that because a lot of my community members who are very poor and vulnerable benefited. That is what this movement is all about: participation in community, living a dignified life.

A Wellington City Council media release on the accreditation event announced: 'Living Wage Aotearoa today officially confirmed the council has joined the list of more than 100 accredited living wage employers.' Justin Lester said becoming accredited was the right thing to do. 'When I talk with our cleaners and security staff, many of whom work six days a week to make ends meet, they tell me the better wages make a big difference in their families' lives.'[2] Looking back, Lester recalls:

> I was proud of them and how courageous they were to stand up, sometimes against their own employer, to say 'we're standing up for what's right'. I wanted them to be able to go home to their families and feel respected and that we valued their work. I know I did, and the councillors did, and before me Celia did. She set this ball rolling. The most compelling thing for me was that, in order for any of these things to happen … Wellington had to be the stone in the lake that sets this ripple cascading across the rest of the country.

Sarah Free would later say this was Celia Wade-Brown's finest achievement in council: 'We literally faced threats. People were trying to change our minds all the time. Celia never wavered. I was so proud of her leadership, against strong staff advice and in the face of strong advocacy from people who were opposed.'

Mayor Lester gave credit to the Living Wage Movement:

> What made it possible was the strength of the community movement, that had church groups and social groups, the unions together with the workers and an outpouring of community support, because what that led to was public support, with the wider Wellington knowing this was the right thing to do, a good thing to do. It made our jobs easier. The strength of that movement was absolutely critical and it was empowering.

The campaign to lift the wages of Wellington City Council's lowest-paid workers could never have been won through direct bargaining across the table with contractors. Instead, the local network built the necessary power to convince Wellington local body politicians to take action. Hundreds of Wellingtonians were involved as activists. The campaign transformed the lives of many council workers, and the power of the people prevailed over the institutional power of a council chief executive and officials.

The determination of council officials and a small group in the Wellington Chamber of Commerce to prevent the adoption of the living wage can only be explained as ideological. In December 2020 the *Dominion Post* revealed that in 2016 Kevin Lavery, on behalf of Wellington City Council, had taken out membership of the right-wing lobby group and think tank the New Zealand Initiative.[3] The $92,000 membership fee was within his designation. The New Zealand Initiative consistently opposed increases to the minimum wage and was a vehement opponent of the living wage. In March 2020, the new Wellington City Council chief executive, Barbara McKerrow, decided the think tank didn't align with the politics of the current administration and discontinued the membership.

In 2020 I joined New Zealand Initiative chief economist Dr Eric Crampton in a videotaped *National Business Review* debate on the living wage. Crampton was invited after an *NBR* reporter, Fiona Rotherham, contacted me to seek assistance with the story. Rotherham asked for contacts who were Living Wage Employers. That was easy: I sent her to Karma Cola co-founder Matt Morrison and AMP New Zealand Wealth Management chief executive Blair Vernon, both successful business people and strong advocates for the living wage. Rotherham also asked for a contact among the business community who was opposed to the living wage. I was taken aback: it was not the role of the movement to find opponents for the media. It clearly proved difficult to find an employer willing to speak out about why they chose not to pay the living wage, and that left the New Zealand Initiative – who, along with the Taxpayers' Union, was always happy to push its ideologies and champion unidentified business interests – looking rather isolated. During the debate, Crampton's arguments were overwhelmed by the positive first-hand experiences of the real-life business leaders, Matt Morrison and Blair Vernon.

Big steps, small steps, standing still

In Auckland another campaign milestone was achieved with the beginning of the implementation of the living wage for directly employed Auckland Council workers, the sheer scale of which had a huge impact. This was well understood in the Living Wage Movement as step one of a process – the contracted workers would come on board later. Like the IAF, the movement pushed hard for an end result that was often poles apart from where the employer was at the time, then negotiated the steps along the way.

The ability to celebrate every win is a key principle of the movement. Annie recalls a celebration event at which the Auckland movement invited Mayor Phil Goff to speak:

> At the beginning we would not celebrate a win for employed staff in case we then lost the battle for contracted workers, but we soon realised that we would miss an opportunity to acknowledge the hard-earned victories along the way. To use an IAF phrase, we 'polarise' as we drive up the aspirational goal, but we also have to negotiate in the real world of politics and celebrate every win we get.

To supporters like Susan Adams, this Auckland win was positive and exciting. 'It was great to have some wins,' she says. 'It's very easy to wait until you feel as if you've had the big win, but you've got to celebrate these small incremental things on the way through and see the energy that's generated by them as something to build on. You have to celebrate.' Annie recalls that Phil Goff saw it like this: 'Once I've done this first step, I've won the argument. I don't have to argue about whether the living wage is a good concept or whether we should be getting there, because I've done it for directly employed and all it is about is saying "now we're going to extend it".'

This was also the path the Living Wage Hutt Valley network chose with Hutt City Council. The ask of the living wage for the whole workforce – including the contracted workers – was always to the fore, but the implementation was staged. That brought many wins, one at a time. In October 2018 Living Wage Hutt Valley hosted a community event to celebrate achieving the living wage for directly employed workers at Hutt City Council. Held at Avalon Intermediate, it was a great community event with local worker speakers, Sāmoan and Cook Islands dancing, kapa haka and a huge table groaning with food. The purpose was to celebrate the win and to keep pressure on Mayor Wallace to make a public commitment to extend the living wage to the contracted workers. The Hutt City mayor, deputy mayor, a number of councillors and chief executive Tony Stallinger attended. One of the worker speakers was Toreka Tanu, a contracted council cleaner whose husband was also a cleaner. Toreka, who was 54 years old and from a village in Upolu in Sāmoa, told the gathering: 'The living wage would make a big difference to me and my family because then we would be able to support our kids, and be able to live a happier life, knowing that we don't have to stress or struggle anymore.'

Mayor Wallace had to leave early and asked to speak before he went. Seemingly moved by the community presence and his cleaner's story, he announced that the council cleaners would soon be on the living wage.

His public commitment made, it still proved difficult to get Wallace to deliver. A few days later, John Ryall and I were back with the council officers and the Hutt Valley Chamber of Commerce, discussing how to deliver the living wage to contracted workers. The officers wanted to devise a questionnaire for contractors to gather information on their current pay rates and their views on the living wage, and the report to councillors, formally requested months before by a council vote, had not been prepared. Despite the euphoria of the community action and the mayor's emphatic public commitment, the council's contracted workers were forced to wait.

Community leaders stand up

The Porirua network was also struggling to make progress with their council. From 2017, Living Wage Porirua met regularly at Porirua Union and Community Health Service in Cannons Creek and came up with many creative actions and ways to demonstrate community support. In March 2018 network members collected messages in support of the living wage from hundreds of people in the community. Andrew Chick collated these to create the Living Wage Porirua submission on the annual plan, and network leaders came back to council once again to ask the mayor and councillors to listen to the community and take action. A group of leaders from the network met informally with the mayor, Mike Tana, who said he needed support from other councillors and asked the network to lobby them. Although this had already been done in the election campaign, at the next network meeting the group divvied up the councillors and set about seeking their support in individual face-to-face meetings.

One meeting stands out as a clear example of why the IAF principle 'no permanent friends, no permanent enemies' is essential in relationships with political leaders. The general feeling was that Northern Ward councillors Ross Leggett and Anita Baker were right wing and therefore opponents. They were placed low on the list of priority meetings. Hiueni Nuku contacted Ross Leggett and he refused to meet. I offered to meet with Councillor Baker, who was friendly and welcoming. We got to talking about low-wage jobs like cleaning. Far from being removed from the reality of living on a low wage, Anita Baker had direct experience in her own family and was sympathetic to the call for cleaners to be valued. She said she had opposed the living wage for directly employed workers because she thought it was unfair to exclude the lowest-paid workers employed via contractors. She confirmed her support in principle, but added the proviso 'if the budget allows'. That face-to-face meeting revealed common interest between Councillor Baker and the Living Wage Movement that would never have been revealed had she been written off as an opponent.

The individual meetings with Porirua City councillors confirmed that the living wage had majority support; all that was needed was for the mayor to take the lead. This did not happen, however, and the year drifted on.

In August 2018, Porirua's Corinna School became New Zealand's first accredited living wage school. Living Wage Porirua organised a celebration with the cleaners and teacher aides, which Reverend Perema opened. Most of the support staff, cleaners and caretakers lived in the community, and principal Michele Whiting said the school needed to show they were valued with 'a worthy wage for their contribution to the school and to education in this area': 'We try to create an atmosphere of whānau here.'[4]

Mayor Mike Tana attended the celebration and asked to speak. There was only one thing the local network wanted to hear: that the council would follow Corinna School's lead and deliver on the promises already made on the living wage. If this decile one school could do it, then the council could respond to the clearly demonstrated will of the community. But Tana had no progress to report.

Soon after this I met informally with Mike Tana for a coffee on the waterfront. I asked how the local network could help him get things over the line. This time he suggested that a concrete demonstration of support from community leaders might help. I took this challenge back to the network.

We decided to create a 'Fifty Leaders' Letter' to the mayor. Network members would ask leaders in the community – from politicians to sportspeople, faith leaders, academics and employers – to sign the letter, and the local network would present it at a community event. The network was a very connected group of people when it came to their own community, and they welcomed with enthusiasm the idea of assembling some heavy hitters to demonstrate support for the living wage. A list of names compiled on a whiteboard showed the depth of community connections and the range of local stars that the leaders in the Living Wage Porirua network were confident would sign.

Their confidence was justified. The group secured support from over 60 local leaders, including All Black TJ Perenara, current MP Kris Faafoi, past MP and local resident Graham Kelly, health leaders, school principals, academics, and a long list of Pacific ministers from Reverend Perema Leasi's Sāmoan ministers' group.

The 'Dear Mike' letter was a call for action:

> Dear Mayor Mike Tana
> During your election campaign in 2016 you pledged to adopt the Living Wage at Porirua City Council. I personally appreciate that commitment – thank you. I strongly support the living wage and I want to see my council lead the way on this issue in our city. You are now over halfway through your first term as mayor. I and many others want to see you make progress on the living wage. I will support you and your council to take the next step forward. We are here to back you to do the right thing for our community.

In 2018 the Living Wage Movement national training took the form of a one-day course with local trainers and a two-day course with Sister Maribeth. During a break in the training, Andrew Chick and I talked about the Porirua plan and I rang the mayor to suggest the idea of assembling the community leaders to deliver the letter at a public event.

The 5 November gathering, once again in Reverend Perema's Cannons Creek church, was a powerful statement from the local community. Ngāti Toa leader Dr Taku Parai attended, lending the support of mana whenua. Filmmaker and Living Wage Employer Tony Sutorius and community leader Caroline Mareko spoke, and the letters of support were presented to Mayor Tana. Reverend Jenny Dawson challenged Tana to make a firm commitment; he eventually responded, saying he would ensure there was action at Porirua City Council.

Breaking the low-wage barrier

In the deep south of Te Waipounamu, Living Wage Bluff was launched formally on 18 November at the local rugby club. More than 70 people attended, including Sanford workers and representatives from St Anne's Catholic Basilica, Awarua Social and Health Services, local unions and businesses. Sanford worker Tabitha Jessiman told supporters:

> I can't participate in the community because I don't have the funds, I can't repair my house, my daughter can't play softball. You are trying to be a grown-up, be an adult and you can't do it. You are ashamed because you have to ask your mum and dad for money and yet you are working a 40-hour-a-week job, but you can't stand on your own feet.[5]

With their campaign underway, the next step for the movement's newest network was to challenge Sanford chief executive Volker Kuntzsc, who remained impervious to the connection between profits and the poverty wages of workers. Like the Bluff community itself, however, the local network was tough and new ways of organising to lift low wages were sorely needed in small towns. The southernmost Living Wage Movement united the community around this goal. Annie Newman reported to the living wage governance board: 'It is a vibrant group and an exciting new way of raising the living wage profile in small New Zealand towns that are suffering greatly from poor local economies and low wages.'[6]

Another year of significant victories had transformed the lives of thousands of workers and their families. The movement had demonstrated that community organising can break the barrier of low wages for contract workers, and now a new development had emerged. Living Wage Movement Aotearoa NZ committed to supporting the creation of an organisation called Te Ohu Whakawhanaunga, to be based in Tāmaki Makaurau Auckland and funded by the Peter McKenzie Project, an initiative of the JR McKenzie Trust. Living Wage Auckland would be just one of a number of organisations sponsoring the development of this new alliance, which had the same commitment to building community power as the Living Wage Movement but targeted a range of issues as identified by communities.

In 2017, at the living wage general election forum at St Anne's in Manurewa in South Auckland, commitments to deliver on both the living wage and housing had been secured from candidates. But despite efforts by activists within the local Living Wage Movement, only the living wage got

At the Living Wage Bluff launch on 18 November 2018 (left to right): Father Pat McGillian, Joanne Geeson, Anne Diamond, Carl Stapleton, Kerrie Brett, Linda Fraser, Corinna Johnson, Satya Ram and Tabitha Jessiman. Photo: Annie Newman

traction after the election. 'Our movement was built on a commitment to lift workers out of poverty. It was not built to solve the housing crisis,' says Annie Newman. 'No matter how real and important the issue, we did not have the organisation or the resources to run a parallel campaign of accountability on housing. The initiation of Te Ohu Whakawhanaunga meant that housing as a human right could become a fully-fledged campaign within a broad-based community alliance.' The IAF principles that the Living Wage Movement had used in New Zealand to win wage increases for workers would also be at the heart of Te Ohu Whakawhanaunga.

The effectiveness of community organising had been proven. It united diverse communities in creative, positive campaigns that led to real change. There was still much to do in living wage campaigns to lift low wages, but now it was also time to take on new issues, develop new leaders and work with new communities.

CHAPTER 11

No permanent friends, no permanent enemies: 2019

> 'Three years ago I came to the living wage forum and said no …
> This time I'm saying yes.'
> **ANDY FOSTER**, Wellington mayoral candidate

The big banking win

In February 2019 Westpac announced its accreditation as a Living Wage Employer, the first bank in New Zealand to do so. It was big news, and the TV3 breakfast programme, the *NZ Herald* and Radio New Zealand's *Nine to Noon* gave the announcement extensive coverage. The Living Wage Movement, from the outset, had identified wealthy corporates as primary targets, so this accreditation was significant.

FIRST Union represented the directly employed workers and had secured the living wage for them in collective agreement negotiations some months before. Now, for the hundreds of contracted cleaners, security guards and those working in the bank's cafés and gardens, Westpac's accreditation meant a big pay rise.

Former National Party cabinet minister Simon Power fronted for Westpac as the company's corporate affairs manager. As a committed advocate of the living wage he had plenty to say:

> This change will mean a weekly pay rise of more than $100 in the hand for the roughly 500 workers who provide these services to Westpac. We believe this will improve their financial wellbeing and reduce pressure on their households – it might mean working one day less a week, allowing more time with family, being able to afford a new pair of school shoes for their kids, or being able to save for a holiday.[1]

FIRST Union was a member organisation of the Living Wage Movement, and this victory uncovered the first tension between the movement as a whole and a union member organisation. The union's national secretary, Dennis Maga, was unhappy that he had not been advised of the accreditation in advance. A FIRST staff member was informed but had not passed the information on, probably because the accreditation did not affect FIRST Union's own members. FIRST felt they should have received recognition for the achievement as the lead union in the finance sector, but in fact celebrations in the movement were intentionally owned by the whole community movement that underpinned every success.

The incident highlighted differences between the way unions work and how the broad-based community alliance worked. Unions are focused primarily on achieving wins for their own members; the Living Wage Movement is underpinned by the principle of no workers being left behind.

Within the Living Wage Movement there was a commitment to finding a resolution to this conflict, and the governance board agreed that the Council of Trade Unions living wage steering group would consider options to address the issue. As a result, a protocol was put in place that stipulated notice time for any union affected by an employer announcing living wage accreditation. This was in effect when the rest of the finance sector came on board over the next 18 months.

Given Dennis Maga's commitment to social unionism and working with community, it is not surprising that the issues were resolved. Dennis brought that commitment with him from the Philippines. In his home country he had been a secretary-general of one of the union federations, a role he took over from his mentor, a former member of parliament who was imprisoned by the government. Dennis was his mentor's face outside the prison cell, and in this role he engaged with international trade unions and Philippines solidarity groups overseas. In 2007 he was invited to New Zealand to take part in a protest during a visit by the Philippines' president. At the centre of the parliamentary protest was Dennis, inside a cage, representing the plight of his people. Images of his stunt attracted international media coverage, and on his return Dennis found himself in the sights of the government, which was pursuing a legal case against him. He returned to New Zealand before he could be charged and has been unable to return to the Philippines ever since.

In Aotearoa Dennis worked for the SFWU and the NZCTU. He took an organising job with the Northern Distribution Union, which became FIRST Union after an amalgamation with Finsec, the finance sector union. In 2017 Dennis was elected general secretary of FIRST Union and brought with him principles of social movement unionism. 'We as trade unions, we don't live just among trade unionists, we should actually be living with trade unions and community organisations,' he later reflected. 'We are no longer in a situation where we are the most dominant institution and we can maximise opportunities out there, especially with the community strand, in order to push for the interests of the working class.'

Dennis brought a commitment to the principles of educate, organise and mobilise, and his first few years as general secretary were dominated by strike action and campaigns to lift the low pay of FIRST Union's members. The union was searching for a rate to campaign for, and Dennis was familiar with the living wage concept. 'The CPI at that time was low. Inflation was also low,' he recalls:

> These are narratives that you cannot use in your bargaining. When the living wage was introduced and the Living Wage Movement was established, we started using that narrative. Instead of minimum wage, there is a living wage. That helped us a lot in terms of what target we should be aiming for, especially for low-paid workers.

An antidote to hatred

Living wage campaigns continued across the country. Another living wage stage at the Newtown Festival took place in early March, the Whanganui group organised a community workshop, and a living wage delegation met with the Victoria University of Wellington senior leadership team. The latter was one of many frustrating meetings: Vice-Chancellor Grant Guilford cried poor, but while he was on a salary of $750,000, the institution's cleaners were on the minimum wage.

New funding from the JR McKenzie Trust enabled the movement to employ Chas Muir as a community organiser in Christchurch, where he set to work building stronger relationships with community organisations and faith groups, including the Muslim community. Chas was a parishioner at the Christchurch Transitional Cathedral (the Cardboard Cathedral) and a member of the living wage national governance board. His role took on a different meaning after 15 March 2019, when 51 Muslims were massacred at the Al Noor Mosque and the Linwood Islamic Centre. After the terror attack, living wage activists in Christchurch met with a range of refugee, multicultural and interfaith groups associated with the Muslim community. Chas recalls: 'We subsequently hosted two events … in the Cardboard

Cathedral and a local body election forum. At both events we had a significant Muslim presence, including the presence of Gamal Fouda, the Imam of Al Noor Mosque, which only a few months earlier had seen the worst attack imaginable.'

Ibrahim Omer was also a member of the national living wage board and chair of ChangeMakers Resettlement Forum, the Wellington-based advocacy group for former refugees. The terror attack moved him into the public role of addressing a crowd of thousands at Wellington's Basin Reserve on behalf of ChangeMakers and the Muslim community. At the time, the communal sense of horror in the wake of such targeted violence brought New Zealanders together, and Ibrahim's speech reflected this mood of unity and solidarity. There was an outpouring of support across Aotearoa and from around the world.

The events of 15 March were evidence of some deep divisions in our society but also showed how we can reach out across diversity and form alliances. Those of us in the Living Wage Movement were grateful to have established connections with refugee and migrant groups, including many Muslims. For a number of us, the Living Wage Movement had opened our lives to include Muslims for the first time. Ibrahim was certainly my first Muslim friend, and he introduced me to many others. 'I had never met Muslim people except through the living wage,' recalls Rebecca Matthews, 'and I think that's the real antidote to the hatred and xenophobia in the world today – to have good and deep connections with people that you would never normally encounter in your daily life, who live a completely different life, have a completely different belief system.'

Largely through Ibrahim's organising, many low-paid Muslims were active in the Living Wage Movement in the Wellington region. Refugees from Somalia, Eritrea, Ethiopia, the Middle East and South East Asia worked as cleaners, security guards and in other low-paid and mainly contracted jobs that were the focus of the campaigns. Many were employed in the large cleaning workforce at Victoria University, Wellington City Council and elsewhere in the private sector around the city. Unions possibly considered these groups of workers hard to organise; for Ibrahim, who spoke six languages, attended Friday prayers at the Kilbirnie Mosque and shared the experience of escape from a totalitarian regime with other refugee-background workers, organising them was an act of love.

Seizing opportunities everywhere

In 2019 a living wage network emerged in South Canterbury. One of the local instigators, Timaru resident Julian Maze, recalls, 'South Island unions decided to encourage community action in support of the living wage. An initial meeting showed promise.' A dedicated group formed and met monthly. Along with Julian, it included Timaru locals like Ruth Swale, who was active in social justice issues; Anglican priest Indrea Alexander from a parish in Waimate, who later moved to another parish in Ashburton; Jon Henning, a PSA organiser based in Dunedin; and Don Swan, a retired long-time union figure living in Timaru and well known to his former colleagues in the SFWU.

The group targeted the South Canterbury district councils of Timaru, Waimate and Mackenzie, none of which was paying the living wage. The plan was to achieve the living wage in local bodies, and then promote them in the community as employers to emulate. 'Our group set itself realistic goals that were within its capacity to achieve,' says Julian. They gathered data, engaged with councils, attended public forums and election meetings and worked to build a media strategy. 'That remains our model,' he says. 'Beyond the three district councils, Living Wage South Canterbury has advocated to ECAN [Environment Canterbury] and the South Canterbury District Health Board, approached supermarket chains in the area and other local employers and met with the local Chamber of Commerce to explore common ground.'

This small local network enjoyed some success, as both Timaru and Waimate district councils adopted the living wage for directly employed staff. The network went on to encourage them to become accredited and worked to increase the number of Living Wage Employers in the region. It also provided support to a new Living Wage Waitaki network based in Ōamaru and to other South Island groups interested in establishing a living wage community.

By now the Living Wage Movement was geared up to ensure that, every year, the local networks seized the opportunity of council annual plan consultations. Having achieved the goal of accreditation, a delegation making a submission to Wellington City Council advocated for Wellington to become New Zealand's first living wage city. The delegation's spokesperson, Gina Lockyer, was a great presenter, full of life and with a big smile. When she told councillors she had chosen Zealandia as the venue for her wedding because it was a Living Wage Employer, everyone in the council chamber smiled too.

The 2019 rate announcement took place in April at Seashore Cabaret in Petone, Hutt City. Media took a strong interest in the rate launches, and the 2019 event was an opportunity to showcase a successful hospitality business. Matt Wilson and Freya Atkinson, owners of Seashore Cabaret, Good Fortune Coffee and a new café, Miss Fortune's, had set the goal of achieving the living wage across their businesses three years earlier. Wilson is the son of former CTU president Ross Wilson and had operated cafés in Wellington for over 25 years.

Stuff carried a story on the rate announcement that focused on this business with 52 employees. Wilson told Stuff that valuing workers was one of the keys to running a successful business in hospitality. 'The minimum wage is just too low for any sort of decent existence. Especially in Wellington, with the massive costs of rentals and stuff, I don't see how people can get by. We can afford to do it, so we've done it and we're very proud of it,' he said. 'If you're really good to staff and pay better, they want to work with you for longer, which is invaluable. We want to keep staff turnover low because hiring and training new staff is expensive and time consuming.' Wilson felt that many businesses in the industry focused too much on the bottom line: 'Everyone wants to cut their wage costs at 30 percent. We're a little more philosophical; we focus on the staff, produce and café environment. If you get those three things perfect, then the bottom line takes care of itself.' The business had not completely ignored profits: 'We've been profitable since day one.'[2]

National Party MP for Hutt South Chris Bishop was present, the first National MP to attend a living wage event in the Wellington region. Perhaps the concept was becoming mainstream? Mayor Ray Wallace and his deputy David Bassett also attended. When Matt Wilson addressed the crowd, he directed a challenge to the city's leaders. He wanted his council to follow Seashore's lead and become a living wage council, extending the living wage to the contracted workers. If a medium-sized business in the tough hospitality sector could achieve this, surely the council could too.

In March Living Wage Porirua organised another community submission on the council's annual plan. It was the last chance for Porirua City Council to take action on the living wage before the end of the council term. Leaders in the local movement approached Mayor Mike Tana again and

The announcement of the updated New Zealand living wage rate at Seashore Cabaret, Petone, Lower Hutt, April 2019. Photo: Ehsan Hazaveh

asked him to meet a small group of us at Peppermill Delicatessen café. The meeting was led by Stella Teariki from the PSA, and Reverend Jenny Dawson and Hiueni Nuku were also present. Stella was frank: she challenged the mayor to deliver on his promises. He agreed to do this. The network leaders warned him that it was getting very close to the time when they would need to approach other councillors who were prepared to actively champion the living wage.

This time Mike Tana did act, but the election was not far away and there were rumours of other mayoral hopefuls. Councillor Ana Coffey was ready to declare her candidacy. When Tana finally told his chief executive Wendy Walker that he had the numbers to support a resolution to adopt the living wage, he was shafted. Walker handed the resolution to the finance committee, which was chaired by Ana Coffey. This put Councillor Coffey in a position to put the resolution, and Councillor Izzy Ford seconded it. As a result, Mayor Tana would not be credited with the long-anticipated living wage victory at Porirua City Council. In May 2019 Porirua City Council finally voted to move directly employed workers to the living wage with a strong majority: eight to three.

The voice of the community had been heard, but Living Wage Porirua continued to call on elected representatives to deliver on the commitments made to contracted workers.

Hometown victory

Then came a major development at Hutt City Council. In June 2019, another day with a chilly southerly blowing through the Hutt Valley, a hardy group of Living Wage Hutt Valley supporters assembled to present to Hutt City Council. The chamber was packed to overflowing, and when the Taxpayers' Union's Jordan Williams arrived there was space only in the foyer. Muriel Tunoho delivered Living Wage Hutt Valley's presentation and shared the story of one of the council's cleaners. She called on the mayor to make good his commitment of the previous year, when he had promised the cleaners would move to the living wage. It was time for Hutt City: there was no doubt the community backed the living wage. But once again the mayor was wavering. Instead of the promised action, he intended to propose further community consultation on extending the living wage to contracted workers. When public speaking time was over there was a long wait before the living wage debate and the all-important vote would come before councillors. Living Wage supporters returned to work and other commitments, and Muriel Tunoho and I settled in at an adjacent café. Attempts to ring or text the mayor to set up an eleventh-hour meeting were unsuccessful, and we were not sure how we could call him to account.

At the lunch break we returned to the council chamber, having heard that the living wage would soon return to the agenda. In a déjà vu moment that mirrored the previous year's encounter, we ran into Ray Wallace outside his office. Muriel and I seized the opportunity to challenge him to deliver on the commitment he had made at the living wage celebration at Avalon Intermediate. Wallace asked if Living Wage Hutt Valley would be happy if council just moved the cleaners to the living wage. We responded that it was time to fulfil his commitment to all the council's contracted workers; however, it would be a step forward to ensure that the cleaners got their promised pay rise. He agreed to do this.

The meeting resumed. When the mayor proposed that the council's cleaners move to the living wage, the opponents were stunned. Councillors Chris Milne and Leigh Sutton protested vigorously. But it was too late: with the mayor's support the vote passed easily. This paved the way for the rest of the council's contracted workers. The living wage for the low-paid Hutt City Council cleaners was won through the work of the local network, the leadership of local activists, consistent community pressure and the voices of workers. But why did every living wage event in the Hutt Valley come with a southerly storm?

Please explain

After persistent campaigning by Living Wage for Vic, there appeared to be movement in the university leadership. Chancellor Neil Paviour-Smith had become involved and seemed supportive of lifting cleaners' wages. In May there was another Living Wage Day at the hub, largely organised by the students and led by Marlon Drake. They coordinated a creative action in which students left thank-you notes to cleaners in various locations around the university. The notes were then collated into a book to present to cleaners at the event.

Along with fellow cleaner Ema Leo, Rebecca Nyakuong Kuach shared her story once again. Ibrahim Omer had arranged with OCS management (the cleaning contractor) for the two workers to speak and their manager had agreed, but once again Rebecca's courage had negative repercussions.

The Victoria University of Wellington student newspaper, *Salient*, reported on the forum and quoted Rebecca's call for the living wage for the university's cleaners. A few days later I received a phone call from Ibrahim, who sought advice on a response to a letter he had received from Rebecca's manager at OCS, who warned that she could again face disciplinary action. I asked Ibrahim to forward me the letter. What I saw was an email thread that had originated from someone in the university's communications team, who had forwarded a link to the *Salient* story to the facilities manager who oversaw the university's cleaning. It could only be interpreted as a 'please explain'.

The phone number of the staff member who sent the original email was contained in the signature, so I rang and spelt out the problem her action had caused for Rebecca. She was adamant it was nothing to do with her or the university as Rebecca was employed by OCS. I reminded her of the university's growing support for the living wage concept, right up to the level of the chancellor, Neil Paviour-Smith. I left her in no doubt about what would happen if Rebecca was sacked: Living Wage Wellington would do everything it could to highlight this injustice through the media. They would assemble large numbers of supporters in front of the Hunter Building at the university and remain there until they had certainty that Rebecca would not lose her job. Ibrahim sent a letter to OCS explaining that Rebecca was reflecting the university's own support for the living wage and had every right to ask for the living wage in public. No action was taken; Rebecca kept her job.

My Life To Live

In June our campaigning took a new approach in Wellington. Ibrahim had been a champion for the living wage in his own refugee-background community since 2013. At the end of 2018 he and I met at the Change-Makers office to share ideas about what we could do to highlight some of the issues this community faced and the connection with the living wage. Auckland-based photographer Nando Azevedo had produced an exhibition for the Aotearoa Resettled Community Coalition, which was hosted by ChangeMakers on World Refugee Day 2018 at the New Zealand Portrait Gallery in Wellington. *The Resettlement Portraits* highlighted the cultural heritage that people of refugee backgrounds and from asylum-seeker and family unification programmes bring to Aotearoa. We decided to do something similar for World Refugee Day 2019.

Our photo project was a collaboration between Living Wage Wellington and ChangeMakers Refugee Forum (now ChangeMakers Resettlement Forum), and told of refugee-background workers who were either struggling on low pay or experiencing the transformative power of the living wage. The exhibition, called *My Life To Live*, included personal stories of life on a low wage from cleaners like Rebecca Nyakuong Kuach and security guards like Alexandra Guevara, and told of the difference the living wage had made to the lives of workers like cleaner Suleman Salih from Eritrea and community support worker Niguisse Fenja from Ethiopia.

It was an ambitious project, but many were keen to participate. Eshan Hazaveh, an Iranian PhD student at Victoria University of Wellington, spent many hours photographing the six workers in the exhibition – at work, with their families and in their communities. Historian Dr Cybèle Locke conducted interviews with participants, and local author Elizabeth

Victoria University of Wellington cleaner Rebecca Nyakuong Kuach featured in the photo exhibition *My Life To Live* in June 2019. Photos: Ehsan Hazaveh

Wellington City Council cleaner Suleman Salih featured in the photo exhibition *My Life To Live* in June 2019. Photos: Ehsan Hazaveh

NO PERMANENT FRIENDS, NO PERMANENT ENEMIES: 2019

Security guard Alexandra Guevara on the cover of a booklet produced for the exhibition *My Life To Live*. Design: Eleanor McIntyre, photo: Ehsan Hazaveh

Knox converted the interview transcripts to 700-word stories. Eleanor McIntyre from Pixel Boom provided design expertise, living wage printer Pivotal produced an exhibition booklet, and AMP NZ, now also an accredited Living Wage Employer, gave financial support. Wellington City Council also made a financial contribution and made available the New Zealand Portrait Gallery. Karma Cola, Garage Project, Tuatara, Archangel and Six Barrel Soda provided refreshments for the opening, the Anglican Diocese paid for the food, and Wellington Chocolate Factory also contributed.

The exhibition booklet described the message we wished to share:

> Refugee-background New Zealanders come with nothing but hopes and dreams. They are filled with determination to build new lives and support

Prime Minister Jacinda Ardern meets Suleman Salih and his children at the exhibition *My Life To Live*, watched by Ehsan Hazaveh and Ibrahim Omer. Photo: Mohammad Barzegar

their families. They are hard-working and bring skills and potential to their new home. But often the only jobs available are the lowest paid – in sectors like cleaning, hospitality and security.[3]

We invited Prime Minister Jacinda Ardern to open the exhibition on World Refugee Day, 20 June 2019, but as she was unable to attend she asked instead to meet with the participants and their families in the morning. Ardern accompanied the workers and their families around the exhibition, listening intently as they shared their stories with her. A capacity crowd of 400 attended in the evening when the exhibition was opened by local MP Grant Robertson. Wellington mayor Justin Lester spoke, as did Blair Vernon, chief executive of AMP New Zealand Wealth Management.

One worker's story was particularly moving. Pau Gershom attended the launch with his wife, brother and daughter. A small man, when he came forward in his national dress it was soon clear that he was a compelling speaker. Pau grew up in a village in Myanmar where soldiers would come to the house and take cows and pigs and chickens: 'It was the most dangerous place. We couldn't stay there.' In 2004 Pau left Myanmar for Malaysia without a passport and eventually arrived in Wellington as a refugee with his wife and daughter: 'The city was beautiful. And when we got to the house, everything was here, food in the fridge, everything. It felt like a paradise.' The only work Pau could find was a minimum-wage kitchenhand job from midnight to 3am. 'There was no bus at night. I walked home. Sometimes in winter, in the middle of the night, it's raining, cold and scary.' He got a job in a hotel, cleaning and making the beds. As a supervisor he received a higher rate, but his wife, who also worked at the hotel, was on the minimum wage. Pau had dreams. He wanted to get a degree: 'If my workplace became a Living Wage Employer that would be enough for us to spend time with the family and help my parents, who are very old now … My goal is to be a social worker. Because I came here as a refugee, my desire is to help people.'

After a 10-day showing at the New Zealand Portrait Gallery, the exhibition moved to the Anglican Cathedral in Molesworth Street, where Kate Day from the Anglican Diocese organised an event for Anglicans to hear these stories of refugee-background workers. Some months later the photo project travelled to Auckland, where AMP sponsored the opening and exhibition. It was a new way of sharing the living wage story and inspiring local communities to action.

Dunedin done and dusted

In September the Living Wage Employers for 2019 were announced and included Dunedin City Council, the second council to become an accredited Living Wage Employer. The move was something of a surprise, but the PSA had been campaigning, Mayor Dave Cull was supportive and Councillor Jim O'Malley had an interest in OCHO, a chocolate manufacturing company and Ōtepoti Dunedin's first Living Wage Employer. Councillor Aaron Hawkins had long been a supporter and had interviewed me for student radio some years earlier when I visited Dunedin to speak at the city's first living wage public meeting. On accreditation, a celebration was held with council workers and union and Living Wage Movement representatives. Over a thousand directly employed and contracted workers were affected. PSA national secretary Glenn Barclay told Stuff:

> Low pay for anyone is not only morally unacceptable, it also puts downward pressure on pay and conditions for everyone. When low-paid workers get a pay rise, the money goes directly into local businesses

and stimulates the local economy. This is good for everyone, and we look forward to seeing Dunedin reap the benefits of a living wage city council.[4]

Throughout Aotearoa there were now almost 160 accredited employers, large and small, in the private, public and NGO sectors. Joining the 2019 list were AMP Capital Investors and Western Springs College, New Zealand's first accredited secondary school. Smaller businesses included Scout Hair (the first hairdresser) and Mai Day Spa (the first massage therapist). 'The commitment to paying the living wage has, for some time, been led by small- to medium-sized businesses, who felt strongly that this was the right thing to do,' said Living Wage Movement's accreditation coordinator, Felicia Scherrer. 'Through their leadership and the success of these businesses, we now have larger organisations and corporations also committing to paying the living wage. They too have realised investing in their workers is an investment in their business.'[5]

Changing of the guard

Residential training for the year was held in Auckland and Wellington, led for the final time by Sister Maribeth Larkin, who was leaving her work with IAF to lead her order, the Sisters of Social Service, based in Encino, Los Angeles. Tributes flowed to this wonderful woman who had made a significant contribution to Living Wage Movement Aotearoa NZ and to all our lives. For me, Maribeth was a valued friend and mentor, a wise and inspiring activist and thinker who had enriched my organising and my life.

Another local body election was due in October 2019, and hundreds of supporters attended forums in Auckland, Hutt, Porirua, Wellington, Christchurch and Invercargill. In Auckland Phil Goff was seeking a return to office. He was the front-runner, and it was vital that Living Wage Auckland secure his commitment to concluding the living wage implementation. This time he did commit to taking the first step for contractors by moving the council's cleaners to a living wage. Mayoral candidates in Christchurch, Hutt and Porirua cities also made the commitment to move contracted workers to a living wage.

A dramatic outcome at the Wellington forum demonstrated exactly why the IAF principle of 'no permanent friends, no permanent enemies' was so effective. Many in Wellington thought Justin Lester would be returned as mayor. He had played a big role in achieving the living wage in the capital

Co-chairs Sandra Grey from the TEU and Motekiai Fakatou from the Wesley Methodist Church at a living wage election forum at St Peter's on Willis, 19 September 2019. Photo: Ehsan Hazaveh

Below: Reverend Susan Adams at a local body election forum at St Matthew-in-the-City, September 2019. Photo: Jason Fell

city and had ushered in Wellington's accreditation. He recognised the movement, was easy to work with and a real ally. Lester had competition, however. Councillor Andy Foster threw his hat in the ring with the backing of filmmaker Peter Jackson, who launched Foster's campaign. Evidence of Jackson's funding could be seen in the massive billboards promoting Foster's campaign across the city. This was a development Living Wage Wellington had not expected; not once since the first living wage election forum in 2013 had Foster supported the living wage. He had been a vocal opponent

'Pinners' Gina Lockyer and Ibrahim Omer at a living wage election forum at St Peter's on Willis, 19 September 2019. Photo: Ehsan Hazaveh

in council and had consistently voted against living wage remits. Still, the movement had engaged with him, as with all councillors and candidates, and he was not antagonistic. Before rejecting all the asks at the 2016 living wage election forum, he had made a point of acknowledging Living Wage Wellington, saying he was impressed with how the movement worked. Now, Andy Foster agreed to attend the 2019 forum at St Peter's on Willis, where a large number of candidates would be in attendance.

The organising group had decided to call all mayoral candidates up to the front together and to challenge them to commit to each ask individually. The church was full and Living Wage Wellington had a large floor team working to ensure the forum went smoothly. It was my job to coordinate the candidates, and I was positioned nearby in order to shepherd them to the front promptly, as time was short. Immediately prior to the forum Councillor Foster texted to say he would be late. The announcement of this created a disapproving buzz. Maybe he would be a no-show? The time came for the mayoral candidates to move forward, and there was still no sign of him. I texted him: hundreds of Wellingtonians were waiting to hear where the candidates stood on the living wage, and where was he? Foster arrived at that moment and made his way to the front.

Mayoral candidate Councillor Andy Foster addresses the asks at St Peter's on Willis, 19 September 2019. Photo: Ehsan Hazaveh

The other mayoral candidates agreed to the living wage asks, although Diane Calvert expressed a small reservation. Justin Lester was wholeheartedly committed and received resounding applause. Then it was Foster's turn. He took the microphone. The pinner, Gina Lockyer, asked him: 'Councillor Foster, if you are elected as mayor of Wellington, will you commit to maintaining accreditation as a Living Wage Employer?' There was silence as supporters waited for a negative response. Foster started by saying: 'Three years ago I attended the living wage forum and said no.' There was a murmur of disapproval. This was not supposed to happen at living wage forums, where the practice was to applaud positive responses and ignore a negative response. Then he held up his hand to silence the crowd: 'No, wait. This time I'm saying yes.' Foster went on to say yes to all the asks: to develop a plan to adopt the living wage in all council venues, events and projects; to champion the living wage among local employers; to support Living Wage Employers in council's procurement processes; and to work with Living Wage Wellington to create a living wage city.

Andy Foster won the election by a narrow margin; the Living Wage Movement had won the commitment that mattered. The successful mayoral candidate and a majority of councillors backed the living wage. At the

2019 local body elections for Wellington City Council, living wage activist Rebecca Matthews was elected to represent the Wharangi Ward and became the living wage portfolio holder on council.

Soon after the election a Living Wage Wellington delegation met with the new mayor. We ran into Sarah Free, the new deputy mayor in the foyer. When we told her we were there to talk with the mayor about the living wage, her response was immediate. She had always backed the living wage and still remembered her visit to our first residential training as a newly elected councillor in late 2013. Relationships matter, establishing shared interest and common ground matters, consistently demonstrating community support matters, and recognition from those in power matters. Mayor Foster confirmed at the meeting that he would keep his public commitments and continue to support and progress the living wage.

A dramatic changing of the guard in Hutt City, too, accelerated the progress of the living wage campaign there. Mayor Ray Wallace was unable to attend the Living Wage Hutt Valley election forum, and as there were only two mayoral candidates in Hutt City there was some feeling that it might be a waste of time to hold the forum without the front-runner present. It went ahead anyway, and was a very grassroots community affair. The pinners, Dina Awarau from Hutt Union and Community Health Service and Drew Mayhem from the New Zealand Nurses Organisation, were theatrical and wildly energetic. Muriel was MC, and the worker speaker was again Toreka Tanu. Avalon Intermediate School hall was packed and full of community spirit. There was near-unanimous support from candidates for the asks. Councillor Campbell Barry, a long-time living wage supporter, made an emphatic commitment and, in the election, took the mayoralty from Ray Wallace. Shortly afterwards, the new mayor met with living wage leaders and promised to act quickly. Councillor Josh Briggs, a strong and consistent supporter, became the living wage portfolio holder. Living Wage Hutt Valley would see the council head towards accreditation at last.

In Porirua, Mike Tana was struggling to hold on to the mayoralty. Again, the local movement had taken the 'no permanent friends, no permanent enemies' approach and invited all candidates to the forum, held once more at Reverend Perema's church. The 2019 Porirua election forum was an electrifying community event. Stella Teariki suggested a Zumba session, led by Pastor Terrance Tauira, as entertainment. It was an unusual choice, but Pastor Tauira had the whole hall, candidates and community alike, on their feet. The place was rocking. What a way to set the scene to challenge the candidates! A Porirua City council cleaner, Salota Sami, was the worker speaker; she had to stand on a box to reach the lectern and microphone but had a big and inspiring story.

It was fortunate that the relationship with Councillor Anita Baker was in place because she couldn't attend the Porirua event. She made her commitment to the living wage by email and this was shared at the forum. Mike Tana again declared his support enthusiastically, as did mayoral candidates Izzy Ford and Ana Coffey. After a bitter and controversial campaign, Anita Baker was elected mayor. She had made a commitment. No permanent friends, no permanent enemies.

In each of the Wellington cities where the movement had active networks and campaigns, there was a change of mayor. In all three, a declaration of support for the living wage was secured from successful candidates prior to election day.

Challenge to government

With the local body elections over, the movement marked Living Wage Week around the country. This year there was a focus on central government's delay in delivering the living wage to contracted workers in the core public service. Representatives of the movement had been meeting with government MPs for some time, but MBIE officials dragged the chain and meetings were frustrating due to their lack of progress. Core government contracts continued to be tendered with no sign of any adopting the living wage. The movement issued a challenge to the Labour-led government, calling for the delivery on the commitments made to contracted workers. As Annie Newman would later say:

> These workers are public servants, paid by the government, even if their pay cheques come from private contractors. It's time we stopped the cycle of competitive tendering, where government agencies save money while private businesses make huge profits off the backs of the most vulnerable in society. It is a false economy, because ultimately everyone suffers from the poverty wages paid to these workers.

As part of Living Wage Week, E tū coordinated with local living wage networks to take groups of low-paid cleaners and security guards to electorate offices to talk with local MPs. I joined a group of security guards visiting the Taita office of their local MP, Chris Hipkins, who was also Minister of State Services. The workers, from Taita, Stokes Valley and elsewhere in the electorate, shared their stories of hardship on low pay. They were accompanied by supporters from Hutt Union and Community Health Service and local resident Awak Apiak, one of the Victoria University of Wellington cleaners. Awak, a refugee-background single mother from South Sudan, had two cleaning jobs in Wellington. One was in parliament. Thanks to the many determined years of campaigning by SFWU, E tū and the Living Wage Movement, the contracted parliamentary cleaners were now paid the living wage after the Speaker of the House Trevor Mallard had ensured that the Parliamentary Services' budget provided for this in 2017. At the university, cleaners were still on the minimum wage.

ANZ announced its accreditation during Living Wage Week. Another big bank was over the line, benefiting hundreds of contracted cleaners, security guards and other workers. In Wellington, Westpac hosted a get-together of local businesses to talk about the living wage. This was a collaboration between the Sustainable Business Network (an accredited Living Wage Employer) and Living Wage Wellington. At the event was Roger Beaumont, chief executive of the New Zealand Banking Association, who would soon play a leadership role in bringing the entire banking sector on board with the living wage.

The strategy of building community power for wage justice was working. For too long, chief executives, senior managers, council officials, council lawyers, MBIE and other government officials had claimed the power to decide who was elevated and who was relegated to a life on low pay. Through adopting the strategy of building power through community organising, the Living Wage Movement was challenging that power in corporations, councils and in the core public service and finding that, when united communities stand up to institutional power, we could win.

CHAPTER 12

Mā te wā: 2020 and on

'Mā te wā.'
MURIEL TUNOHO, E tū

Covid times

In early February 2020 local networks began meeting to plan for the year ahead. With a general election in September, residential training was scheduled and forum venues booked. Before the election, however, the movement's leaders were determined to get delivery on the pledges made three years before at the last general election. Pressure was on to make the government move at least some groups of contracted workers in the core public service to the living wage before the election and to secure a firm commitment at the forums for the next term.

On 20 February, Rebecca Matthews, now a Wellington City councillor and the council's living wage portfolio holder, accompanied me to meet with Dr Ganesh Nana, who, at the time, was research director of Business and Economic Research Limited (BERL). A long-time supporter, Nana was keen to undertake research into the business case for the living wage. Our conversation ranged from the upcoming increase in the minimum wage to the Covid-19 virus that was spreading throughout the world. The first case of the virus would be identified in New Zealand just eight days later.

It was a busy time for the Living Wage Movement. The movement's original goal – to target wealthy corporates – was bearing fruit. One by one, the big banks were taking up accreditation and changing the lives of thousands of contracted workers. The year began with the accreditation of the Co-operative Bank, and on 2 March ASB Bank announced theirs.

Aotearoa Artists for a Living Wage once again organised the living wage stage at Newtown Festival on 6 March. Doubtful Sounds choral group and the Te Aro School kapa haka group opened, conducted vigorously by broadcaster Bryan Crump in a living wage T-shirt, and musician Don McGlashan generously gave his time and support. The stage supported the call for Wellington City Council to make Wellington New Zealand's first living wage city. There was always strong union support for the living wage stage. The driving force behind the performances this year came from Ross Teppett of the Council of Trade Unions and Robert Ibell from E tū, and a large team of volunteers collected signatures from Wellingtonians in support of a living wage city.

I was set to leave my living wage community organiser job in April, and Marlon Drake was keen to step into the role. Marlon and I planned to meet with Anca Popoviciu, human resources manager of the Wellington craft brewery Garage Project, to talk through plans for this newly accredited business to host the 2020 updated living wage rate announcement in their bar, the Tap Room. Garage Project represented the modern face of business in Aotearoa: innovative, successful and ethical. Before the meeting Marlon and I enjoyed a coffee and discussed the coming event. Feeling excited, we headed to Garage Project's head office.

But things were changing rapidly in Aotearoa and throughout the world. On my car radio I heard the minister of finance announcing a $12 billion economic package in response to Covid-19. The number of cases in Aotearoa was growing.

On 21 March Prime Minister Jacinda Ardern held a media conference, which was broadcast on all major media outlets. In response to the virus, New Zealand would move to a four-level process of restrictions. Level two took effect immediately, and a few days later the country was in level three. The border closed, businesses were shut down. On 25 March New Zealand moved to level four with significant restrictions. The number of cases accelerated, and meetings and events across the country were cancelled abruptly. In the new Covid world, there could be no event to celebrate the announcement of the rate. Living Wage Movement's newsletter described a 'scary and uncertain time, especially for those struggling with the many issues that the vulnerable face in this unprecedented situation'.[1]

The movement's community organisations and faith groups took on the challenge of staying connected and supporting people. They stepped up to keep health services open, house the homeless and support refugee communities. Porirua Union and Community Health Service, under Hiueni Nuku's leadership, was one of the first to take Covid-19 testing into the carpark. Marlon Drake became a leader in Victoria University of Wellington's student

Reb Fountain performs at a forum at St Matthew-in-the-City in 2016. Photo: Jason Fell

Don McGlashan on the living wage stage at the Newtown Festival in Wellington, March 2020. Photo: Lyndy McIntyre

volunteer army, which was set up to support isolated people. Faith groups, unable to open their churches and gather their people together, connected to their communities by Zoom and social media. The values of relationship and community were more important than ever.

Low-paid workers faced growing uncertainty around their jobs and incomes, and unions organised around the clock to save jobs and ensure workers were protected. Their organisers dealt with widespread exploitation as some employers failed to hand over government wage subsidies and laid off workers in large numbers. Small Living Wage Employers faced the challenge of staying afloat while remaining committed to doing the right thing by their staff and demonstrating the values that motivated them to become accredited. Stories came in of Living Wage Employers extending generosity towards their workers, other businesses and the community. One thing was obvious. The arrival of Covid-19 must not be a reason to step backwards. The movement was determined that the future would be fairer for workers.

The crisis brought recognition of the low-paid workers in essential services who were keeping the country going. The movement's newsletter summed up the growing sense of solidarity:

> Over the past few days, we have seen huge public support for supermarket workers and others such as cleaners and security guards who have long been on rates close to the minimum wage. These workers are finally being recognised for their huge value to our society and we all owe them thanks. But we need to not just thank these workers, but ensure that the future includes them being paid the living wage.[2]

The updated living wage rate of $22.10 was the most substantial rise since the rate was first announced in 2013, and was due to be announced on 1 April. As it was every year, the update was based on the average movement in wages in the 12 months prior to the previous June; this time, wages had moved by 4 percent. The new rate was a justified catch up, but some were nervous. In a conference call, the living wage rate reference group discussed the challenges of announcing a rate increase when businesses were struggling and when New Zealand, along with the rest of the world, faced economic uncertainty and a possible global recession. I joined Charles Waldegrave, the small group of economic advisors and John Ryall and Annie Newman on this call. There were concerns about the economy, the timing and the ability of businesses to pay. It was necessary to update the rate to keep up with historical pay increases, but wages could stagnate or even go down; small businesses were likely to struggle to survive. At the same time, and more than ever, workers needed a rate on which they could live in dignity and participate in society. John advocated strongly for the necessity of the lowest-paid workers getting their pay rise.

It was important to know what Living Wage Employers thought about this, especially the smaller employers, and we took to our phones to sound them out. Although responses were generally positive, some advocated for a delay or a smaller increase. There was no way an independently identified rate could simply be shifted down, and it was updated as planned and small businesses were offered the opportunity to request an extension until 2021 to adjust their pay rates while retaining their accreditation status.

Meanwhile, public and union pressure increased for the work of essential staff to be recognised. Around the world, these workers were thanked for putting themselves at risk for the benefit of others. In her daily media conferences, Prime Minster Jacinda Ardern established a custom of offering gratitude to those who were keeping our essential services running during the lockdown. Ardern singled out supermarket workers, who were on the frontline of maintaining a vital service. As we queued outside supermarkets in our masks and maintained physical distancing at the checkout, every New Zealander came face-to-face with the courage of the checkout operators, who were all too often subjected to the anger of customers, to say nothing of the risk of contracting the virus. These workers were widely applauded. Less visible were others, such as security guards and cleaners, including those on the minimum wage cleaning high-risk areas such as hospitals and aged care facilities.

In one media conference Ardern thanked cleaners and made special mention of Rose Kavapalu, who worked 13-hour days at Ōtāhuhu Police Station: 'These are our essential workers and I hope we continue to recognise them as that long after this pandemic has passed. Thank you for keeping us safe.'[3] Rose Kavapalu was an activist member of E tū and well aware of the campaign for the living wage. She responded to the prime minister's thanks by asking for something more tangible: 'I'd rather not be at work as I have many family commitments, but the police officers really need us to keep the place clean and free from Covid-19. So, I am happy to do the work, but honestly, I deserve more than the bare minimum.'[4]

Cleaners, care workers, security guards, rubbish collectors and supermarket staff struggled to feed their families and pay their bills before the pandemic, and it seemed even more unfair that it took a global health crisis to recognise them as 'essential'. Calls for a different society and a different economy gained momentum. As supermarket workers became increasingly high profile, FIRST Union secured a much-needed increase to the living wage rate for them, but cynical employers dropped it at the end of the first lockdown. What was needed was permanent recognition of the value of the low-paid workers, and secure pay rises for them.

The new normal

Although various levels of restriction would remain for nearly two years, in April 2020 New Zealand moved out of lockdown. The border remained closed but businesses resumed their work in the 'new normal'. The Living Wage Movement slowly returned to face-to-face events and meetings. Marlon Drake took up the role of Wellington's community organiser, and in Auckland Jo Vincente-Angeles moved to work for Te Ohu Whakawhanaunga while Teisa Unga, who had attended residential training a few years earlier, took on the community organising role there.

Major changes lay ahead. At the AGM in July, convenor Annie Newman stood down after leading the movement for eight years. Throughout that time her passion, drive and determination in the fight to lift the wages of low-paid workers had provided the leadership required for the Living Wage Movement to become established and successful. Annie was replaced by Wellington-based Gina Lockyer. The movement was growing in capacity and long-standing campaign goals were being achieved. Living Wage Movement Aotearoa NZ was moving into a new era.

Heartland Bank and Kiwibank both became accredited and, in July, the accreditation of the New Zealand Banking Association (NZBA) ensured that all 17 members of NZBA were on board – including the BNZ, Aotearoa's largest bank. Banking was now a living wage sector. NZBA's own research had shown that almost 80 percent of New Zealanders thought it important that the banking industry should pay the living wage. In a media release, NZBA chief executive Roger Beaumont announced, 'As one of the largest industries in the country, we are showing leadership by committing to paying the living wage. New Zealanders clearly want their businesses to step up and pay a fair and decent wage. It's the right thing to do.'[5]

Contractors over the line

In August 2020 came another long-awaited announcement: Ministry of Social Development (MSD) security guards would move to the living wage. Community supporters joined E tū security guard members at the Labour Party caucus room to hear the formal announcement from former union secretary and now Workplace Relations and Safety Minister Andrew Little and Carmel Sepuloni, the minister responsible for MSD. E tū organiser Yvette Taylor described this as 'a significant milestone in the campaign for the living wage. This is the first government cleaning or security contract to be delivered at the living wage, and it has finally happened.'[6]

E tū delegate Robert (Dusty) Duston, who had been a security guard for 13 years and worked at MSD in Naenae, told supporters that guards in low-income families would no longer have to suffer as he had. He smiled as he told the crowd that he looked forward to waking up every morning

Robert (Dusty) Duston speaks at the announcement at Parliament of the living wage for MSD security guards, August 2020. Photo: E tū archives

Security guards, politicians and members of the Living Wage Movement at the announcement of the living wage for MSD security guards, August 2020. Photo: E tū archives

knowing he was being paid what he was worth and able to save for a holiday for his fiftieth birthday. Standing beside the living wage stand-up banner, Alexandra Guevara, a refugee-background security guard from Colombia, pointed to the line: 'Queros vivir, no solamente existir: We want to live, not just exist.'

Andrew Little said front-line security guards should be properly rewarded for their work standing outside MSD offices: 'We want to see all government departments making sure that not just the core staff, but those who contract to government departments, are getting at least the living wage.'[7] His message was exactly what the movement wanted to hear: a firm commitment from the Labour Party before the election forum. At the online forum, however, although the Green Party and Te Pāti Māori gave a solid endorsement of the living wage in the core public service, Little did not have final sign-off on behalf of his party. The long-awaited commitment came eventually, but it was dangerously close to election day.

Landslide with a mandate

The October 2020 election was a landslide victory for Labour, which became the first party to achieve the votes necessary to govern alone since New Zealand had adopted the MMP voting system in 1996, which provided for representation in Parliament of every political party that achieved more than 5 percent of the vote. The new government had a strong mandate to enact the Labour Party's commitments, including the implementation of the living wage across the core public service. However, with an army of sceptical MBIE officials charged with ensuring delivery on the government's promise, the nagging voice of the movement was still necessary.

In November E tū delegates gathered in Auckland for the union's national conference. With a Labour government in place, the mood was positive. At the top of the union's agenda were the living wage, fair pay agreements, and the extension to security guards of the protections for vulnerable workers afforded by Part 6a of the Employment Relations Act 2000. On the first day of the conference, Muriel Tunoho shared with delegates the news that Hutt City Council waste workers would move to the living wage – another win for the power of community in her hometown and mine.

Prime Minister Ardern addressed the conference on the second day, telling delegates the government would implement the living wage successively for workers employed by contractors in the core public service. In her role as union president, Muriel chaired the session. She thanked the prime minister, and said the union wanted a speedy pace in the implementation of the living wage for workers employed by contractors, and that it was disappointing that the Ministry of Health contract, which had just been re-tendered, did not include the living wage. In her respectful but determined way, Muriel told Ardern the movement would watch closely to make sure the promised progress happened. 'Mā te wā,' said Muriel: 'See you later.'

Employers step up

On 13 November 2020 a new milestone was achieved with the formation of a council of Living Wage Employers.

When Diana Yukich connected with London's Living Wage Foundation in 2012, two things stood out: corporate Living Wage Employers in the UK took leadership in encouraging other businesses to adopt the living wage, and they put money into the movement. Annie Newman had long wanted to find a way for accredited living wage corporates and organisations in New Zealand to contribute more and support the expansion of the movement. As the banks came on board, income from accreditation fees grew significantly, enabling the accreditation coordinator to increase her hours to cope with the increased complexity of applications from employers with multiple contracting arrangements.

But Annie had something more ambitious in mind: a partnership of committed employers similar to the UK model. She talked it over with Blair Vernon, chief executive of AMP New Zealand Wealth Management. An enthusiastic living wage advocate, Vernon had already been promoting the concept of corporates contributing more to the movement. Discussions between the pair continued, and the Principal Partners Council was the result.

The idea of corporate employers taking leadership on the living wage fitted well with Vernon's values. He found the profit-driven narrative of the corporate world disappointing, preferring to ask: 'How can we celebrate

AMP NZ's Blair Vernon.
Photo: Jason Fell

Below: Mother and daughter Lippy and Jesse Chalmers from Tonzu at the launch of the first New Zealand living wage rate, 14 February 2013.
Photo: SFWU archives

being a successful business if the people coming to clean our premises aren't even being paid the living wage and we don't know if they're able to make ends meet?' Vernon grew up in a home where values revolved around public service. His father served in the police force for over 40 years:

> Public service to me is a core part of how a community fits together and, while my career choice went slightly differently, that doesn't mean that being in the corporate world needs to divorce you from a sense of what's right in terms of the community around you, and what your role needs to be.

Vernon embarked on his banking career in the 1990s, initially folding bank statements in the National Bank. By 2017 he was managing director of AMP New Zealand Wealth Management. In an industry where his peers are fixated on a mantra of 'you should save more', he says, 'It's all great to talk about budgets and saving for retirement, but that's completely irrelevant if you're not able even to put food on the table.'

Vernon came across the living wage concept through UK businessman Sir Clive Cawdry, a long-time advocate and supporter of the UK movement. Vernon contacted the New Zealand movement and began the process of AMP's accreditation. The cost impact for the company was not on the base payroll but on contracts:

> That's where corporates will face the challenge because it requires, not simply changing the contract, but changing behavioural attitudes. I could see the challenge for us wasn't going to be our own business, as we had only a fraction of staff who fell below the living wage. It was the supply contracts. That was interesting, because procurement people in corporates were rewarded for smashing people in contracting, screwing everyone for the lowest cleaning contract, lowest everything. That's an interesting behavioural challenge to remap.

Vernon observed that there was little corporate involvement in the movement, something he noted was 'a big gap relative to the UK'. He recalls that living wage conversations in the corporate environment were 'a bit like you're a radical left-wing person', and says: 'I'm just interested in wellbeing and equity for people in the community. I don't believe it has to be right or left. It just has to be fair and equitable and how would we like people to be treated.'

So the Principal Partners Council came together. Living wage accreditation coordinator Felicia Scherrer describes this as a response to businesses wanting to do more to grow the movement for decent wages in New Zealand – not only corporates but also small- to medium-sized enterprises that had experienced a tough time in the 2020 Covid year, like Wiri Licensing Trust in Auckland and Rogue & Vagabond bar in Wellington, both in the challenging hospitality industry. 'We are excited that so many of our Living Wage Employers have embraced this, from not-for-profits like Auckland City Mission to social enterprise Downlights, and our big corporate supporters like Westpac, AMP, Vector and Kiwibank,' said Felicia.[8] A long-time advocate for higher pay rates in hospitality, Rogue & Vagabond's Gwilym Waldren said, 'I love the living wage, but it can't remain a niche thing. An island of well-paid employees is a hindrance to an industry and individual businesses.'[9]

It soon became evident that the additional income from the Principal Partners Council would make a difference. The number of paid organisers in Auckland increased from one to two, and Hamilton and Christchurch each received one.

The living wage transformation

On 26 November 2020 the former refugee, cleaner, and union and living wage activist Ibrahim Omer delivered his maiden speech in Parliament. There was a sense of hope and excitement as groups from the refugee-background community, E tū and other unions, and the three streams of our movement gathered in Parliament's foyer. Ibrahim told his story of transformation to a packed chamber:

> Ten years ago, I was cleaning at Te Herenga Waka, Victoria University of Wellington. I worked with some of the hardest-working people I know. Some of them are here today: Rebecca, Awak, and Ema. All I did was clean, clean, clean, day and night. I didn't have a life. I didn't meet people. I wasn't active in the community. I didn't have the time to think or even dream.

Ibrahim described how the living wage had transformed to his life, and acknowledged workers like Rebecca Nyakuong Kuach and Awak Apiak, who were still on the lowest wages. 'They work very hard and very long hours and yet they still struggle to provide three meals for their kids, and after 10 years of working hard they are still poor. It shouldn't be like that,' he said. 'My vision is for all workers to lead decent lives and participate in society with dignity and respect.' He spoke of his pride when E tū members who are MSD security guards won the living wage, saying: '[I] told them that we will win the living wage if we all stand up together. After we won, I rang up all of them and told them that this is what it means to be in the union. This is what it means to be active in the living wage movement. This did not come from nothing; it's our victory.'[10]

The year of delivery

It was almost 10 years since John Ryall had the idea that led to the formation of Aotearoa's Living Wage Movement, and the movement and its impact on workers' lives was very much a reality. The year 2020 had been a challenging one of change; 2021 was to be a year of delivery for many of the movement's long-held campaign goals.

On 1 April 2021, for the first time, the announcement of the updated living wage rate – $22.75 – took place in a corporate setting, AMP Capital's upmarket premises in Wellington. In his capacity as the MP for Wellington Central, Minister of Finance Grant Robertson was one of the speakers. He noted the trajectory of the various rate announcements over the years and compared AMP Capital's slick surroundings to earlier venues like Pivotal's print factory floor and the down-market Rogue & Vagabond bar. While waiting to speak, he had crunched the numbers on how the minimum wage had closed in on the living wage. The steady increases in the minimum wage since Labour came to power in 2017 were bringing the minimum wage and living wage rates closer together.

April also brought the announcement of the living wage for Auckland Council's cleaners. It was the realisation of one of the first goals of the movement, 10 years after Jen Natoli and Fala Haulangi were first tasked with organising these workers, many of whom had told their stories in support of the council campaign. There had been countless delegations to local boards and council meetings, organising and actions, election forums to secure commitments, and subsequent meetings with politicians to call them to account. For the movement it was vital to get the Auckland Council cleaners over the line, and at last it was happening.

Mayor Phil Goff was proud to shepherd this step forward for Auckland Council:

> I didn't make a lot of promises in 2016, but that was one of the very clear promises that I did make because it was a personal commitment. To achieve that and to work collaboratively with a number of councillors who didn't vote for it the first time, to persuade and encourage them to vote for it, I was very proud we were able to do that. If you want to be a more inclusive community and society, let's make sure that our lowest-paid workers were paid more, and by the same token, our highest-paid workers at the chief executive level aren't getting the pay that their predecessors used to get.

Goff's values were driven by his early experiences. His paternal grandparents emigrated to New Zealand from the UK after World War I. His grandfather died young, at the height of the Depression, leaving behind a widow who was unable to keep up payments on their home. The house was lost, and Goff's father left school at a young age to take up a railway apprenticeship. Goff himself left home at 16 while still at school:

> Just trying to get through my last half year at school and then through university without any family support in those days was pretty tough. I worked in the freezing works during the holidays and a cleaner's job at night, so I got a bit of a gut feeling for how it is for people that are struggling to make ends meet.

As mayor, Phil Goff walked the talk on reducing higher salaries. By the end of his term, he estimated his chief executive was paid around $200,000 a year less than the amalgamated Auckland Council's first chief executive in 2010. 'It was just an idea that, okay, let's lift the bottom and let's say at the top, if you're in a public service job, we want good people, but if you're on a salary of over $600,000, life isn't too tough,' he reflects:

> I keep getting these strategic pay unit reviews saying, 'When you appoint this chief executive the pay range is usually close to seven figures, if not above seven figures.' And I say, 'No, that's bull. This is public service and we need to pay our people well to reflect their responsibility, but let's try and just keep our pay differentials in a more reasonable scale. So, lift the bottom and be conservative at the top.'

Other wins came in 2021 too. After seven years, the campaign for the living wage for Victoria University of Wellington's cleaners was inching towards a win. Student activist Una Dubbelt-Leitch, a regular at living wage actions, took up the campaign coordinator role at the university and worked closely with Marlon Drake, again with funding from TEU. Marlon recalls, 'She planned out a campaign to get students involved, start talking to E tū and TEU and have an event like we do every year. We thought: let's just get this thing locked in.'

The student campaigners bought 16 metres of calico, painted banners with messages of thanks to the cleaners, and began to collect hundreds of signatures across all the university's campuses. One of the volunteers spotted Vice-Chancellor Grant Guilford discreetly adding a heart and a tick to a banner – a good sign. Marlon talked with the chancellor, Neil Paviour-Smith, about the need to get a university decision-maker to the Living Wage Day event, which would be a living wage-style forum. The university's chief operating officer was Mark Loveard, the son of an East London caretaker, who had long ago expressed support for the cleaners. He told Marlon the university was already planning to implement the living wage for the cleaners and last year had put in an extra $150,000 to lift their wages.

Prior to the forum, Marlon became aware that the university was about to announce the living wage for the cleaners. It grated that the announcement was made in the university's internal newsletter, a week before the forum, yet omitted to mention the high-profile six-year campaign. The campaign leaders conferred. Should the forum go ahead? They decided it should: a public commitment to the living wage in front of the cleaners and supporters was required.

Close to 200 people showed up, and Marlon recalls a pair of commanding speakers: student president Michael Turnbull and Tu Williams, a TEU member working in Campus Care:

> [Tu] gets up and gives a really solid speech about the cleaners and the role they play at the university being bigger than just cleaning. There's a point where he talks about how the university's got the power to pay them the living wage and he looks at Mark Loveard and he says, 'Eh, Mark?' It created that tension that we want from a forum, but in a sort of affectionate way.

Ema Leo, the cleaner who had shared her story alongside Rebecca Nyakuong Kuach the previous year, spoke. 'She gets up and just kills it,' Marlon says:

> Her husband's a cleaner at Vic as well, both on the minimum wage. She wants to take her kids back to Sāmoa and see where she's from, and wants to be able to afford basics like food and bills. Most of all she wants to be able to work less, because currently it's her husband and her both working all these hours. All the other cleaners are there as well, up the front.

The time came to challenge Loveard to commit. Marlon remembers everyone clapping: 'We're stoked because we finally get the commitment.' That evening he got a tip that after the forum the university's procurement team received an email asking them to put a requirement for the living wage in proposals for maintenance contracts the following week. 'You couldn't have asked for better,' says Marlon. The commitment to the cleaners was a

Left to right: John Ryall and Muriel Tunoho with Hutt City Mayor Campbell Barry, Deputy Mayor Josh Briggs and chief executive Jo Miller at an event to mark Hutt City Council's accreditation, November 2021. Photo: Hutt City Council

staged one, however, and campaigning would continue until the full living wage rate was paid to all the university's contracted workers.

In another 2021 campaign win, six years after the campaign for Hutt City Council was launched, Mayor Campbell Barry announced the successful vote for the council to seek accreditation. Once again Muriel Tunoho had led a delegation to address her council, in May 2021. In July, Hutt City Council presented Muriel with an award for her role as the convenor of the Living Wage Hutt Valley network and 20 years as chair of Hutt Union and Community Health Service.

The Porirua City Council campaign was also close to a win in 2021. In May a large group of supporters presented to the council, including some locals who had been around since the beginning of the campaign: Reverend Jenny Dawson, Cybèle Locke, Bella Pardoe, Hiueni Nuku, Andrew Chick and the former national secretary of the PSA, Glenn Barclay. With them was Eleanor Haggerty-Drummond, who had spoken at one of the earliest Wellington City Council delegations as a library assistant, and Mareta Sinoti, the Cannons Creek cleaner whose home I had visited with the *Campbell*

Live team in 2013. In June a young Labour councillor, Josh Trlin, put up a proposal that the council extend the living wage to contracted workers and seek accreditation. Porirua City Council finally voted yes to paying their contracted workers the living wage.

In August, after eight years of local activists campaigning, presenting and submitting to Christchurch City Council, councillors there voted 12:3 to require the council's contractors to pay the living wage and for the council to start the accreditation process. Said Deputy Mayor Andrew Turner: 'This is about self-worth, respect, the way we value people, equity, just reward, meaningful pay and the kind of city we want Ōtautahi Christchurch to be.'[11] When Christchurch City Council's cleaners finally moved to the living wage in October, the council's *Newsline* reported: 'OCS and the council have recently renegotiated their contract and for the first time it includes a requirement that the 82 cleaners working across the council's facilities must be paid a Living Wage.'[12]

Ten years on

In August 2021 a community case of Covid-19 was discovered in Auckland and the country moved back into lockdown. On 1 September the new living wage rate of $22.75 would become effective. This time the milestone was achieved during the lockdown with no kickback. Seventy-five new employers were announced, among them the international corporate Ricoh.

Although this lockdown was relatively short-lived for most of the country, when Living Wage Week arrived in November Covid restrictions in Auckland meant a planned South Auckland fair was postponed. But community organiser Teisa Unga was busy in her community, coordinating young people to support Tongan mass vaccination events. Elsewhere in the country, living wage leaders were doing the same. Muriel Tunoho was at Hutt Union and Community Health Service supporting her community to vaccinate hard-to-reach Māori; Hiueni Nuku was leading Porirua Union and Community Health Service in a drive to increase vaccination rates among the Pacific community.

One event that was able to proceed in the 2021 Living Wage Week in November was the community celebration of Hutt City Council's long-awaited accreditation, alongside the announcement of the accreditation of New Zealand's first tertiary institution, Open Polytechnic in the Hutt Valley.

Coincidentally, the 300th fully accredited Living Wage Employer, Team Naenae, happened to be a community trust based in the Hutt Valley. As I sat in the Dowse Art Gallery at this event, jointly hosted by Living Wage Hutt Valley and Hutt City Council, I reflected on my old hometown. The Hutt Valley was no longer the land of milk and honey of my early years. The city was now a place of significant wealth disparity. State houses dominated the suburbs of Naenae, Taita, Pōmare and my first home, Stokes Valley. Living Wage Hutt Valley had challenged this disparity with the call for their city to take a lead in lifting the wages of the working poor.

At the end of Living Wage Week another milestone was achieved, one which would affect many of these workers. The government announced that all security, cleaning and hospitality contracts in the core public service would be concluded on the basis of paying the living wage.[13]

The updated living wage rate of $23.65 was announced in April 2022. In 2023 it would jump to $26, an increase of 9.9 percent on the previous year's rate.

One by one the early campaign goals were realised. In June 2022 Porirua City Council voted to become accredited, a move championed by Councillors Josh Trlin and Geoff Haywood. The resolution was proposed by Mayor Anita Baker and supported by chief executive Wendy Walker. At a celebratory event, Hiueni Nuku once more began with the words: 'This is the day the Lord has made. Let us rejoice and be glad in it.'

Power to win

Living Wage Movement Aotearoa NZ emerged as a response to the problem of poverty pay. In 2011, SFWU had been looking for ways to lift the wages of New Zealand's lowest-paid workers for 20 years. The problem was power. Following the decimation of union density and the other impacts of the ECA, the union lacked the power necessary to pressure employers to pay fair and decent wages. SFWU was not alone in caring about poverty pay. By the time New Zealand's Living Wage Movement was formally launched in 2012, a range of unions, faith groups and community organisations had begun to create an alliance committed to lifting the incomes of the working poor.

Over the next decade the movement won pay increases in the public and private sectors, in small- and medium-sized enterprises and in large corporates. As an outcome of community campaigns, thousands of workers moved to the living wage. For those who had been on the minimum wage, pay increases were sometimes as high as 30 percent.

In 2011, contractors were in a race to the bottom, tendering on the basis of low pay rates in order to secure contracts. By targeting the funder, or client, the movement shone a light on the poverty pay rates of cleaners, security guards, hospitality workers and others employed via contractors. Local and central government, public institutions and large corporates came under pressure to acknowledge that these workers were part of their workforce and needed to be valued and paid accordingly.

The movement went further, gaining a trademark and adopting an accreditation process of licensing genuine Living Wage Employers as a means to ensure that employers cannot hijack the branding to promote themselves unless their living wage commitment extends to their whole workforce, including those employed via contractors. Accreditation ensures no worker is left behind. The determination to win accreditation has been key to winning living wage campaigns in local authorities, the entire finance sector, and other corporates and small-to-medium employers.

The impact of the Living Wage Movement has been greater than the campaign wins. The visibility of the movement and the power of the simple definition – the rate that ensures workers and their families can live in dignity and participate in society – has put upward pressure on the minimum wage. As Charles Waldegrave says,

> The Living Wage has a transparent logic about it. The calculations and final costs are set out logically in the five-year reviews. They provide an empirical basis for arriving at the reasonable costs for the living wage. The minimum wage has no such logic. It neither sets out a budget for key costs nor provides a justification of how it is adequate for those on modest incomes.

The living wage is now routinely used as a fair starting rate. Ten years ago the term was barely used in Aotearoa; now it is firmly established in our lexicon. 'Everyone talks about the living wage now,' says Council of Trade Unions president Richard Wagstaff. 'It hasn't been a union Living Wage Movement, but it's brought a new dimension to unions. It's allowed us to learn a different way of doing things and develop our sense of campaigning. It's been good for unions, good for our profile.'

The living wage rate has been routinely adopted by unions as a rate to campaign around. 'We now have lots of our collective agreements where the bottom rate is above the living wage,' says TEU national secretary Sandra Grey. Tertiary education employers are also adopting the living wage in procurement, although they have been reluctant to sign up for accreditation. But, as with the banking sector, the approach is to win accreditation one institution at a time.

The movement has brought unions together to campaign. From the early days of living wage campaigning, the PSA actively campaigned for low-paid contracted workers in worksites where PSA members are the dominant union. In September 2018, directly employed workers in the core public service moved to the living wage as a minimum rate. Having won the living wage for its own members, the PSA then encouraged members to campaign in solidarity with the low-paid cleaners and other contract workers.

In the private sector, unions have leveraged off public support for the living wage as the acceptable minimum rate for workers in Aotearoa. FIRST Union's 'Worth It' campaign centred on the goal of achieving the living wage for the union's members employed in the retail sector. Based on a strategy of direct action plus workers' stories, the campaign achieved a high profile. Retail workers, particularly in supermarkets, were the face of essential workers during the Covid-19 pandemic and gained a high level of public sympathy. In late 2022 FIRST Union's members in Countdown stores won the living wage for directly employed workers – a first in supermarkets.

Winning depends on power, and the defining issue of the Living Wage Movement is learning how to build power to win. The movement was built to create a new power, moving from the transactional relationships unions are used to – calling in community allies to support actions – to taking time to develop long-term relationships around a common cause. Building power with the community means unions are power-sharing with partners from the faith and community streams. Annie Newman acknowledges this is hard work:

> It is that alliance building that is the secret to winning, the fact that ordinary people can't win without being part of organisations that join together in common cause. It requires years of patient, persistent organisation building, and hundreds of leaders from the grassroots who are dedicated to social change. It takes an absolute belief in the power of democracy to deliver for working people.

The three streams – unions, faith and community – enrich and strengthen the larger movement, and the sum of the three is more powerful than each is alone. 'The thing that makes it work is the involvement of community, spreading out and showing how effective community is,' says E tū member activist Jason Fell. 'It's a lot easier to get gains when you have community support. It's like joining the dots.'

For living wage activists from faith traditions, it is a way to align their actions with their beliefs. Reverend Jenny Dawson's commitment is driven by her faith:

> The faith motivation for me is that God is part of this whole world and people are not meant to be privileged while others are not privileged. There's not meant to be divisions between people and there's not meant to be many opportunities for some and none for others.

While unions have a strong tradition of campaigning, faith groups bring a tradition of contemplation and reflection that enriches gatherings and the wider movement. Faith groups also bring what Reverend Susan Adams sees as moral authority:

> There are still people in society who've grown up with the church in their frame of reference. For those people, if the church as a whole puts its weight behind the Living Wage Movement, that will carry significant authority for them to also consider putting their weight there.

The community stream brings voices from across our many communities. Former student politician Marlon Drake learned from the Living Wage Movement that broad-based organising is the key to winning power for real change:

> First because it is very effective. But more than that, broad-based organising looks at workers as being worth more to the movement than just the labour they provide. It looks at the church they worship at, the community they are a part of. It looks at the whole person.

The Living Wage Movement has forged relationships where none existed and has demonstrated that working in alliance, using the principles of community organising, is a winning strategy. One of those principles is the overriding message of hope; the search for the world as it should be. Sandra Grey says this is the magic energy of the movement:

Living Wage Wellington rallies outside Greater Wellington Regional Council, August 2023. Photo: Finn Cordwell

I think about all those people who've spoken at living wage events. They don't look out in anger. It's what makes the movement successful. It's humans reaching other humans. I've cried at more than one living wage event. I've watched other people cry and it motivates you to get up and do more.

In 2012 the Living Wage Movement's quest to lift the wages of the working poor led the movement to become part of the IAF international community. The links with Australia, London, the US and Canada have brought Living Wage Movement Aotearoa NZ into an internationalist movement in which the same principles result in different campaigns in each country. The support of IAF and the interaction with the international network of alliances has been a vital part of the development of the movement in Aotearoa.

'The IAF provided a lever for activists seeking a new model of community organising that would bring together civil society organisations to win better lives for working people,' says Annie Newman. 'We chose from this model the elements that supported our single-issue campaign.' The New Zealand movement did not follow the IAF methodology based on building relationships first and identifying issues to organise around when the alliance was ready to campaign. 'This was a significant difference,' says Annie:

But IAF leaders were prepared to set it aside. That generosity enabled us to build on our own terms and with the mentoring and support of the IAF. It built a confidence in broad-based organising and an imagination for a new way of working that is now taking root in a genuine broad-based IAF alliance, Te Ohu Whakawhanaunga.

Ten years on, Te Ohu Whakawhanaunga has emerged to take the model and its principles to organise around a range of issues. This new alliance has followed the IAF model closely, establishing a broad-based alliance over four years before launching formally on 7 September 2023. Te Ohu Whakawhanaunga brings together the Aotearoa experience of using the principles of Saul Alinsky and the IAF, the shared experiences of the international movement, and the realities of the search for social justice in Aotearoa.

For Annie Newman, the legacy of the movement in New Zealand is the recognition that the living wage is the baseline for lifting workers out of poverty. 'SFWU started this campaign, but the victory of the movement was that this union stepped back to share power with other organisations that held to the same values,' she says:

> That opened the floodgates of support from all the rich diversity of people and their communities in Aotearoa that want a better, more just world. The job will never be finished. But we can do this. The Living Wage Movement has shown that. Now a city-based alliance in Auckland, Te Ohu Whakawhanaunga o Tāmaki Makaurau, is leading the way to fight for other issues in exactly the same way the living wage was won. The legacy lives on.

There are still challenges. One is a sense that it has all been achieved. Another is the reluctance of social justice organisations, including unions, to replace transactional organising with relational, long-term alliance building. John Ryall says this is the main lesson of the campaign: that uniting with those in the community who share our values builds our power to win real change – change like higher wages. He says it is a lesson that has not yet been realised by some prominent unionists in New Zealand.

But the Living Wage Movement continues to show that it is possible to lift the wages of the lowest-paid workers in Aotearoa by building alliance with others. The idea works. It has changed the way we talk about wages in New Zealand. It has worked for the thousands of workers and their families who have been lifted from in-work poverty. It has worked for those of us who have experienced the power of community organising and will never return to campaigning in silos, be they in unions, faith or community.

The Living Wage Movement used the power of community to win campaigns that seemed unwinnable. This new way of organising revealed a solution to the problem of low pay that faced the SFWU in 2011 and for 20 years before that, following the passage of the Employment Contracts Act 1991. Living Wage Movement Aotearoa NZ united thousands of ordinary people across diversity and around a common cause.

The quest for the power to win just and decent pay rates is as necessary as it was in 2011. As long as thousands of workers and their families still bear the brunt of low wages, this idea, this movement, has work to do.

> Kua tawhiti kē tō haerenga mai, kia kore e haere tonu.
> He nui rawa ō mahi kia kore e mahi tonu.
>
> We have come too far not to go further.
> We have done too much not to do more.
> **SIR JAMES HENARE**

Postscript: February 2024

When the National Party government of the time pushed through its radical industrial relations law, the Employment Contracts Act 1991 (ECA), the impact on Aotearoa's lowest-paid workers was devastating, and the collective organisation of workers in unions was decimated.

Over 30 years later, a Labour government enacted long-promised legislation to return to New Zealand workers and unions the ability to negotiate in a process similar to the award system that was lost with the passage of the ECA. The Fair Pay Agreements Act 2022 (FPA Act) provided a framework to bring together employers and unions advocating for workers to set binding pay and employment terms for all workers within an industry. Retail workers, cleaners, early childhood workers, bus drivers, hospitality staff and security guards could all look forward to the support and protection of guaranteed minimum pay and conditions.

In November 2023 the National Party formed a coalition government with New Zealand First and the ACT Party. High on the list of shared commitments was a pledge to repeal the FPA Act. On 20 December 2023, under urgency, the Act was wiped off the statutes and the promise of fair pay agreements was gone. Leaked cabinet documents showed the impact of cancelling FPAs would hit hardest those on low incomes, particularly those who are 'more likely than other groups to earn low wages', that is, women, Māori, Pacific people and young people.[1]

Wellington security guard Rosey Ngakopu said the FPA that had been proposed for her sector was 'such an important document for us workers because it gives us the ability to bargain to improve conditions, health and safety, our levels of pay. It's supposed to build a future.'[2]

The fight to achieve fair pay agreements goes on. But it is also more important than ever to continue to build the power of civil society to address the problem of poverty pay. It is not new for the Living Wage Movement to be working under a National-led government. The first six years of the movement – building networks, identifying the rate, announcing the first Living Wage Employers, and the early campaigns – all happened under a National-led government. The Living Wage Movement has a record of securing commitments from politicians regardless of their political colours. No permanent friends, no permanent enemies. Gains have been won with decision-makers not seen as left or progressive. Among these are mayors of local authorities who made commitments to the living wage because community power won their support and the movement established relationships across political divides. The Living Wage Movement continues as before: developing relationships, building alliances and uniting communities to build the power to win the living wage.

The week after the 2023 elections I joined others from the Kāpiti Coast at our local council. We'd come to call for our council to become an accredited Living Wage Employer. We wanted to live in a fair community, where our workforce, including the contracted cleaners and security guards, are valued. We came to use our power to ensure that they were valued by receiving the living wage. That community power delivered a vote for 'immediate accreditation'. Jim works at Kāpiti Coast District Council. As a security guard, he is stationed at the door. He's always there with a friendly 'kia ora'. His response to the pay rise to $26 an hour: 'Awesome.' The campaigns in local communities continue regardless of who is in government.

Bill has been a school caretaker in nearby Porirua for many years. His union is E tū, and he was an active supporter of the campaign for his council to become an accredited Living Wage Employer. In August 2023, Bill attended the launch of a new campaign to secure the support of school communities to ensure that the living wage is paid to all workers in their schools, including cleaners and caretakers. The Living Wage Movement's national schools campaign has the backing of the education unions NZEI Te Riu Roa and the PPTA. The campaign continues regardless of who is in government.

Dinah is a security guard and a single mother. She works extra hours as a bouncer at a nightclub to bring much-needed income into her whānau. On 7 September 2023 she shared her story with a 600-strong crowd at the Lesieli Tonga Auditorium, on the grounds of the Free Wesleyan Church of Tonga in Māngere, Auckland. The occasion was the founding of Te Ohu Whakawhanaunga o Tāmaki, the Auckland-based community alliance that, like Living Wage Movement Aotearoa NZ, has become an active member of the global Industrial Areas Foundation. Te Ohu brought to the event the leader of the Labour Party, the co-leader of the Green Party and the deputy leader of the National Party to hear the voices of the community and respond to their asks.

Finding power depends on uniting communities and mobilising those communities to exert pressure on decision-makers, be they corporates or institutions funded with public money. The greater the challenge, the greater the need to focus on the grassroots, build networks, reach across diversity and find common ground. These are the principles that continue to guide the Living Wage Movement and that now guide Te Ohu Whakawhanaunga in taking on other issues, while also supporting the living wage kaupapa. We've seen the power of these principles in action again and again in the Living Wage Movement. We see it in a room full of people and when a worker shares their story. We see it in the diversity of communities united around common cause.

Securing the living wage does not depend on the vagaries of particular governments. In the decades-long search for a solution to low pay after the advent of the ECA, that solution was not found simply in times of left-wing or right-wing governments. The solution was found to lie in a different way of organising, using the principles adopted by successful social justice campaigns in Aotearoa and globally, in people power. At the heart of this search is finding power: the power to win.

APPENDIX

Comparison between New Zealand living wage and minimum wage, 2012–23

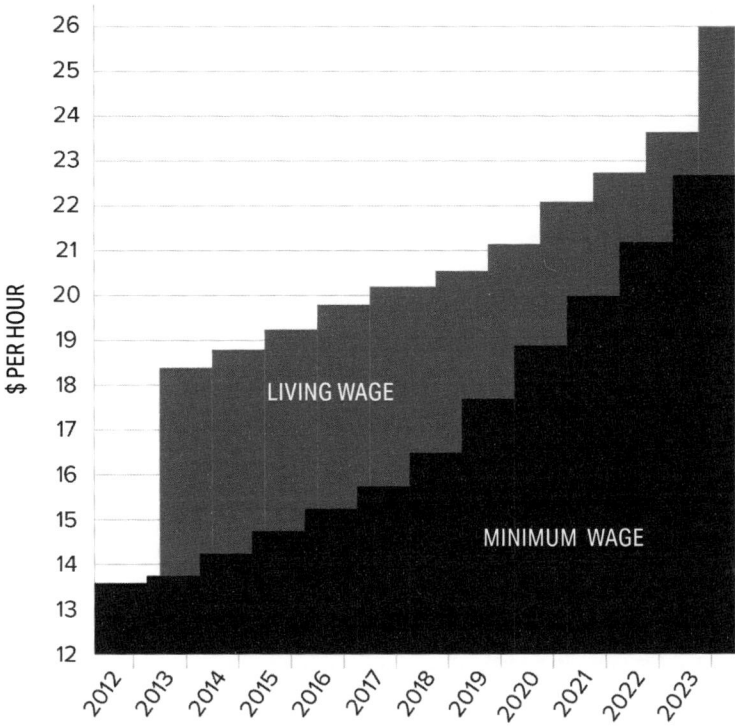

Note: The living wage applies to all workers over 16 years with the exception of trainees undertaking NZQA qualifications to a minimum of Level 3 or above in order to meet the requirements of their job. The trainee rate (90 percent of the full rate) applies only for 12 months or 1040 hours of work, whichever is the lesser.

The living wage rate is updated each year by the average movement in wages as recorded by Stats NZ in the Quarterly Employment Survey. Every five years a full review takes into account changes in the cost of household items, such as rent, transport and food, and levels of government support.

The minimum wage rate shown is the adult rate, which at time of writing applies to employees aged 16 years and over. The minimum wage also includes a lower rate, the criteria for which has varied over the years to include those under 20, 18 and 16, trainees and new starts. (Graph: Eleanor McIntyre)

Timeline

1991
- **14 May** Five of the regionally based Hotel and Hospital Workers unions amalgamate with four regional cleaners unions to become the Service Workers Union of Aotearoa (SWU)
- **15 May** The Employment Contracts Act 1991 becomes law

1997
- The SWU amalgamates with the United Food and Beverage Workers Union to become the Service and Food Workers Union (SFWU)

2005
- John Ryall is elected as SFWU national secretary

2006
- John Ryall and Muriel Tunoho meet London Citizens and experience first-hand the community organising methods of the Industrial Areas Foundation (IAF) in London

2011
- The SFWU national executive endorses John Ryall's proposal for the union to adopt a living wage campaign

2012
- **February** SFWU employs Annie Newman as campaign director, tasked with leading a living wage campaign in partnership with the community
- Annie meets London Living Wage Foundation and New York-based IAF director Mike Gecan
- **23 May** National launch of the living wage campaign/movement in St Stephen's Presbyterian Church hall, Ponsonby, Auckland
- **30 August** Wellington living wage launch at the Wesley Methodist Church, Taranaki Street, Wellington

2013
- **14 February** Announcement of the first NZ living wage rate: $18.40
- **September** First living wage local body election forums
- **30 October** Inaugural Living Wage Movement AGM endorses the name Living Wage Movement Aotearoa NZ

- **November** First annual five-day residential training courses based on the IAF organising model are held in Auckland and Wellington

2014
- **January** 450 directly employed Wellington City Council workers move to the living wage, the first time a large group attains the living wage as a direct outcome of the community campaign
- Living Wage Whānau Day at the Manukau Rugby League Club, Auckland, establishes the community-based events that would characterise the movement
- **February** Launch of the Living Wage Employer accreditation programme and announcement of the first updated living wage rate of $18.80 at O'Sarracino restaurant, Auckland
- **July** Announcement of the first fully accredited Living Wage Employers

2015
- **February** Community organisers employed in Auckland and Wellington
- Updated living wage rate announced: $19.25
- **24 June** Mop March in Wellington
- **July** The first Māori and first corporate Living Wage Employer Tūaropaki Trust achieves accreditation
- **5 August** Selwyn Supporters Coalition holds a public meeting as part of the campaign to win the living wage for workers at Auckland's Selwyn Village care home
- **28 October** Wellington City Council votes to extend the living wage to contracted security guards against the advice of Wellington City Council chief executive
- **November** Inaugural Living Wage Week

2016
- **February** Announcement of the updated living wage rate: $19.80
- **May** Wellington City Council chief executive and chief executive of Wellington Chamber of Commerce reach a secret agreement, limiting the extension of the living wage to workers employed via contractors
- **August** Wellington City Council contracted security guards and the first of the contracted cleaning workforce move to the living wage
- Living Wage Movement Aotearoa NZ formally affiliates to the IAF
- **September** Greater Wellington Regional Council votes to become a living wage council, although the vote to become an accredited Living Wage Employer does not happen until seven years later

2017

- **April** Announcement of the updated living wage rate: $20.20
- **August/September** Inaugural general election living wage forums
- **October** Labour-led government is formed with a commitment to adopting the living wage in the core public service
- **November** Auckland-based lines company Vector becomes first major corporate accredited Living Wage Employer
- **December** Implementation of the living wage announced for parliamentary contracted cleaners, security guards and hospitality workers at a celebration at Parliament

2018

- **April** Announcement of the updated living wage rate following the first five-yearly review: $20.55
- Local Government Act 2002 is amended to remove the perceived barrier to delivering the living wage to contracted workers in local authorities
- **August** Corinna School in Porirua becomes the first living wage school
- **1 September** Directly employed workers in the core public service move to the living wage as the minimum rate
- **3 September** Wellington City Council is the first council to become an accredited Living Wage Employer
- Auckland Council begins implementation of the living wage for directly employed workers

2019

- **February** Westpac New Zealand is first bank to achieve accreditation as a Living Wage Employer
- **April** Announcement of the updated living wage rate: $21.15
- **20 June** World Refugee Day exhibition *My Life To Live* opens at Wellington's New Zealand Portrait Gallery
- **September** Dunedin City Council announces its accreditation as a Living Wage Employer

2020

- **March** New Zealand enters Covid-19 restrictions
- **April** Announcement of the updated living wage rate: $22.10
- **July** The New Zealand Banking Association becomes accredited, establishing banking as the first living wage sector
- **August** Minister of Social Development announces that contracted MSD security guards will move to the living wage

- **13 November** Formation of Principal Partners Council of Living Wage Employers

2021
- **1 April** Announcement of the updated living wage rate: $22.75
- Announcement that Auckland Council cleaners will move to the living wage
- **May** Victoria University of Wellington begins staged implementation of the living wage for contracted cleaners
- **August** Christchurch City Council votes to require the council's contractors to pay the living wage and to begin the accreditation process
- **November** Hutt City Council becomes an accredited Living Wage Employer
- The first tertiary institution, Open Polytechnic, achieves accreditation

2022
- **April** Announcement of the updated living wage rate: $23.65
- **June** Porirua City Council votes to become an accredited Living Wage Employer

2023
- **April** Announcement of the updated living wage rate: $26.00
- **7 September** Founding launch of Te Ohu Whakawhanaunga

Acronyms

AUS Association of University Staff of New Zealand
AUT Auckland University of Technology
BERL Business and Economic Research Limited
CPI Consumers Price Index
CSU Community Services Union
ECA Employment Contracts Act 1991
EPMU Engineering, Printing and Manufacturing Union
Finsec Finance Sector Union
FIRST Union Finance, Industrial (Textile and Wood) Retail, Stores and Transport Union
GLA Greater London Authority
HART Halt All Racist Tours
HHWU Hotel and Hospital Workers Union
IAF Industrial Areas Foundation
LCWC London Citizens Workers Centre
LHMU Liquor, Hospitality and Miscellaneous Union
MBIE Ministry of Business, Innovation and Employment
MMP Mixed Member Proportional
MSD Ministry of Social Development
NZCTU New Zealand Council of Trade Unions Te Kauae Kaimahi
NZEI New Zealand Educational Institute Te Riu Roa
OECD Organisation for Economic Co-operation and Development
UNO United Neighborhoods Organization
PSA Public Service Association Te Pūkenga Here Tikanga Mahi
PUCHS Porirua Union and Community Health Service
SFWU Service and Food Workers Union
SWU Service Workers Union of Aotearoa
TELCO The East London Communities Organisation
TEU Tertiary Education Union – Te Hautū Kahurangi
VUWSA Victoria University of Wellington Students' Association

Interviews

The following people were interviewed by the author for this book.

Reverend Dr Susan Adams	Rebecca Matthews
Paul Barber	Julian Maze
Glenn Barclay	Leonie Morris
Karena Brown	Chas Muir
Brian Dawson	Jen Natoli
Reverend Jenny Dawson	Annie Newman
Marlon Drake	Reverend Hiueni Nuku
Jason Fell	Rebecca Nyakuong Kuach
Phil Goff	Ibrahim Omer
Sandra Grey	Bella Pardoe
Sam Gribben	Andrea Rushton
David Hall	John Ryall
Fala Haulangi	Felicia Scherrer
Iain Hines	Yvette Taylor
Prue Hyman	Muriel Tunoho
Sue Kedgley	Blair Vernon
Reverend Stephen King	Celia Wade-Brown
Lemo Lemo	Richard Wagstaff
Justin Lester	Charles Waldegrave
Deborah Littman	Nicki Wilford
Dennis Maga	Diana Yukich

Notes

PREFACE
1. Max Rashbrooke, 'Understand Inequality': www.inequality.org.nz/understand/
2. Danya Levy, 'Parliament's cleaners seek a pay rise', Stuff, 16 August 2012: www.stuff.co.nz/business/industries/7486644/Parliaments-cleaners-seek-pay-rise

CHAPTER 1
1. The Service and Food Workers Union, Property Council New Zealand and the Building Service Contractors of New Zealand, joint media statement, 'Historic Property Services Agreement Signed', Scoop, 28 March 2008: https://m.scoop.co.nz/stories/PO0803/S00270/historic-property-services-agreement-signed.htm
2. John Ryall, 'Union investment through the Victory Fund in 2012: Options to consider', paper for the SFWU National Executive, September 2011, author's archive.
3. John Ryall, 'Campaigning for a Living Wage in 2012', paper for the SFWU national management team, October 2011, author's archive.
4. Ibid.
5. Annie Newman, 'Living Wage Aotearoa New Zealand 2013 campaign strategy', March 2012, author's archive.
6. TVNZ, *Campbell Live*, 11–14 February 2012, notes from the author's archive.
7. Ibid.
8. Ibid.
9. Chris Trotter, 'Low-paid staff need solidarity', *Press*, 19 February 2013: www.stuff.co.nz/the-press/opinion/columnists/8320836/Low-paid-staff-need-solidarity

CHAPTER 2
1. Jaziel Crossley, 'Family struggles daily to live on minimum wage', *Dominion Post*, 30 August 2012, author's archive.
2. Max Rashbrooke, 'How a living wage increases opportunities – not just fairness', Pacific Scoop, 12 September 2012: https://pacific.scoop.co.nz/2012/09/how-a-living-wage-increases-opportunity-not-just-fairness
3. Auckland Council, *The Auckland Council Plan 2012*, p.151: www.aucklandcouncil.govt.nz/plans-projects-policies-reports-bylaws/our-plans-strategies/Documents/auckland-plan-2012-full-document.pdf

CHAPTER 3
1. Simon Collins, 'Battle for a living wage: The pay you need to survive', *NZ Herald*, 11 February 2013: www.nzherald.co.nz/nz/battle-for-a-living-wage-the-pay-you-need-to-survive/ITPOWM23IZ7ICAQSLM4WDDSHOY/

2. Ibid.
3. Katie Chapman, 'Mayor pushes to give hundreds of staff a pay increase', *Dominion Post*, 12 February 2013: www.stuff.co.nz/dominion-post/8289717/Mayor-pushes-to-give-hundreds-a-pay-increase
4. Ibid.
5. Editorial, 'Tough choices in quest for a living wage', *Dominion Post*, 15 February 2013: www.stuff.co.nz/dominion-post/comment/editorials/8305146/Editorial-Tough-choices-in-quest-for-a-living-wage
6. Kate Shuttleworth, 'Battle for a living wage: Ghosts in corridors of power highlight disparities in pay', *NZ Herald*, 13 February 2013: www.nzherald.co.nz/nz/battle-for-a-living-wage-ghosts-in-corridors-of-power-highlight-disparities-in-pay/GJTRK2KJSOUMAEYAUUMT6QPD5E
7. Simon Collins, 'Battle for a living wage: Hard working poor families desperate for a living wage', *NZ Herald*, 14 February 2013: www.nzherald.co.nz/nz/battle-for-a-living-wage-hard-working-poor-families-desperate-for-a-living-wage/MEZ2IEVDQKGB3GYU2ISTO3Q6RA/
8. Ibid.
9. Rod Oram, 'A living wage is an investment in the future', *Sunday Star-Times*, 25 February 2013: www.stuff.co.nz/business/opinion-analysis/8308981/Oram-A-living-wage-is-an-investment-in-the-future
10. Ibid.
11. Ibid.
12. Brian Scott, 'A review into the basis for a living wage rate in New Zealand': www.nzcpr.com/wp-content/uploads/2014/03/A-Review-into-the-Basis-for-a-Living-Wage-Rate-in-New-Zealand-by-Brian-Scott.pdf
13. Charles Waldegrave, 'Response to Brian Scott's critique: A review into a living wage rate in New Zealand', 29 January 2014: https://d3n8a8pro7vhmx.cloudfront.net/nzlivingwage/pages/129/attachments/original/1434872264/Scott_response_to_LW_critique_1_14.pdf
14. David Farrar, 'A damning critique of the so-called Living Wage', Kiwiblog, 3 January 2014: www.kiwiblog.co.nz/2014/01/a_damning_critique_of_the_so_called_living_wage.html
15. The Treasury, Living Wage Information Release, 30 September 2013: www.treasury.govt.nz/publications/information-release/living-wage-information-release
16. Minister of Finance Bill English, 'Advice shows "living wage" would not work', media release, 2 November 2013: www.beehive.govt.nz/release/advice-shows-"living-wage"-would-not-work
17. Wellington City Council Strategy and Policy Committee, minutes, 11–13 June 2013, author's archive.
18. Paul Eagle, email to the author, 12 June 2013, author's archive.

19. Katie Chapman, 'Wellington leads the way with living wage policy', *Dominion Post*, 13 June 2013: www.pressreader.com/new-zealand/the-dominion-post/20130613/281724087108075

CHAPTER 4
1. Anna Turner, 'Struggling mum backs living wage call', *Press*, 7 August 2013: www.stuff.co.nz/the-press/9010494/Struggling-mum-backs-living-wage-call
2. Bernard Hickey, 'Living wage is good for everyone', *NZ Herald*, 12 October 2014: www.nzherald.co.nz/nz/bernard-hickey-living-wage-is-good-for-everyone/2Z6NBGDZVK6CK7XUEAUI4MVG3U/
3. Kerrie McBride, 'Cleaners upstage the candidates', *Dominion Post*, 26 September 2013, A5.
4. Living Wage Movement Aotearoa NZ, 'Annual Report 23 April–31 October 2013', author's archive.
5. Ibid.
6. Ibid.
7. Ibrahim Omer, maiden speech to Parliament, New Zealand House of Representatives, *Parliamentary Debates (Hansard)*, 26 November 2020: www.parliament.nz/en/pb/hansard-debates/rhr/document/HansS_20201126_051600000/omer-ibrahim

CHAPTER 5
1. Annie Newman, 'Living Wage Update February 2014', internal email to SFWU and living wage groups and individuals, 9 March 2014, author's archive.
2. Lyndy McIntyre, email to Celia Wade-Brown, Justin Lester, Iona Pannett, Brian Dawson, Annie Newman, 18 February 2014, author's archive.
3. Wellington City Council Government, Finance & Planning Committee, Report 1, 'Mayor's Introduction to the 2014/15 Annual Plan', (4.1) Key issues raised in consultation, (4.1.2) Living Wage, 15 April 2014, author's archive.
4. Tessa Johnstone, 'Protest rallies against inequity in schools', *Dominion Post*, 29 March 2014: www.stuff.co.nz/dominion-post/news/9883562/Protest-rallies-against-inequity-in-schools
5. Katie Chapman, 'Parking wardens new "ambassadors"', *Dominion Post*, 18 December 2013: www.stuff.co.nz/dominion-post/news/9528593/Parking-wardens-new-ambassadors
6. Ibid.
7. Jim Rose, 'Living wage policies: The best of intentions but the worst of results', 20 February 2017: www.taxpayers.org.nz/living_wage
8. Sam Gribben, 'Parking warden "living" on the living wage', *Our Voice*, May 2017, author's archive.
9. Simon Collins, 'Restaurant serves up living wage', *NZ Herald*, 18 February 2014: www.nzherald.co.nz/nz/restaurant-serves-up-living-/7OJ6AAGEDXT4NPU7CYNCIYTSLQ/

10. Annie Newman, 'Community organisers for a broad-based alliance', application to the J R McKenzie Trust, 10 August 2014, author's archive.

CHAPTER 6
1. John Milford, letter to Wellington City mayor and councillors, 25 May 2015, author's archive.
2. Taxpayers' Union, 'Taxpayers' Union back legal challenge', media release, 29 May 2015, Scoop: www.scoop.co.nz/stories/PO1505/S00396/taxpayers-union-back-legal-challenge.htm
3. TVNZ, 'Tuaropaki becomes first living wage accredited Māori trust', *Te Karere*, 2 July 2015: www.youtube.com/watch?v=H9Y3EueC134

CHAPTER 7
1. Simon Collins, 'Selwyn Village targeted by living wage campaign', *NZ Herald*, 4 August 2015: www.nzherald.co.nz/nz/selwyn-village-targeted-by-living-wage-campaign/4BNCAXUZ4MI6TYMBUGFYLJR5LM/
2. Virginia Fallon, 'Reverend Perema Leasi remembered as a leader and champion of Porirua City', *Dominion Post*, 8 November 2019: www.stuff.co.nz/dominion-post/news/wellington/117206746/reverend-perema-leasi-remembered-as-a-leader-and-champion-of-porirua-city
3. Living Wage Movement Aotearoa NZ, 'Annual Report Living Wage Movement Aotearoa NZ, 1 April 2014–30 March 2015', author's archive.
4. Lyndy McIntyre, letter to Wellington City Council Chief Executive Kevin Lavery, Mayor Celia Wade-Brown and Deputy Mayor Justin Lester (cc'd to Paul Barber, John Ryall and Brian Dawson), 2 December 2015, author's archive.
5. Max Rashbrooke, 'High council salaries give lie to wage fears', *Dominion Post*, 28 October 2015, A11. Rashbrooke's further comment: www.inequality.org.nz/wellington-city-council-highest-earners-calculations/
6. Editorial, 'City council move on living wage is modest and sensible', *Dominion Post*, 29 October 2015: www.stuff.co.nz/dominion-post/comment/editorials/73505057/city-council-move-on-living-wage-is-modest-and-sensible
7. Editorial, 'Living wage the right thing to do', *Dominion Post*, 30 October 2015, author's archive.
8. Michael Forbes, 'Wellington City Council pays more staff a living wage, costing ratepayers $1.7m', Stuff, 29 October 2015: www.stuff.co.nz/business/73450003/wellington-city-council-pays-more-staff-a-living-wage-costing-ratepayers-17m
9. David Farrar, 'Wellington City council does the "big FU" to ratepayers', *National Business Review*, 29 October 2015: www.nbr.co.nz/wellington-city-council-does-the-big-fu-to-ratepayers/
10. Collette Devlin and Michael Forbes, 'Wellington City Council will have to defend its living wage policy in court': *Dominion Post*, 6 November 2015:

www.stuff.co.nz/business/73778014/wellington-city-council-will-have-to-defend-its-living-wage-policy-in-court
11. Ibid.
12. Ibid.
13. Chen Palmer Partners, 'Living wage litigation', media release, Scoop, 19 November 2015: www.scoop.co.nz/stories/PO1511/S00308/living-wage-litigation.htm

CHAPTER 8
1. Collette Devlin, 'New Zealand living wage rate of $19.80 to kick in July 1', Stuff, 29 February 2016: www.stuff.co.nz/business/money/77378686/new-zealand-living-wage-rate-expected-to-increase
2. Ministry of Education, 'A school's decile measures the extent to which the school's students live in low socio-economic or poorer communities. Decile 1 schools are the 10% of schools with the highest proportion of students from low socio-economic communities': https://parents.education.govt.nz/secondary-school/secondary-schooling-in-nz/deciles. Note: The decile system was replaced by the Equity Index in 2023.
3. Paul Barber, 'Let's make sure Wellington is a people-centered city. Living wage proposal for the 2016/17 Annual Plan', submission on the 2016/17 Wellington City Council Annual Plan, author's archive.
4. Editorial, 'Council churlish on living wage', *Dominion Post*, 4 March 2016: www.stuff.co.nz/dominion-post/comment/editorials/77574202/editorial-council-churlish-on-living-wage
5. Katie Chapman and Olivia Wannan, 'Living wage voted in despite criticism', *Dominion Post*, 11 December 2013: www.stuff.co.nz/dominion-post/9506386/Living-wage-voted-in-despite-criticism
6. Shane Cowlishaw, 'Living wage very much on the menu', Stuff, 24 July 2014: www.stuff.co.nz/dominion-post/news/10303217/Living-wage-very-much-on-the-menu
7. Agreement between Wellington Employers' Chamber of Commerce and Wellington City Council, 'Terms of Mutually Acceptable Position', 11 May 2016, author's archive.
8. Ibid.
9. 'Wellington Chamber of Commerce does U-turn on legal action living wage stance', Stuff, 16 March 2016, author's archive.
10. Ibid.
11. Collette Devlin, 'Wellington City council cleaners still waiting on the living wage', Stuff, 1 July 2016: www.stuff.co.nz/business/81629254/wellington-city-council-cleaners-still-waiting-on-living-wage

NOTES

12. Nicola Middlemiss, 'Full list of Living Wage employers revealed', 1 July 2016: www.hcamag.com/nz/news/general/full-list-of-living-wage-employers-revealed/146218
13. Living Wage Movement Aotearoa NZ, 'Living Wage Movement Aotearoa NZ Annual Report 1 April 2015–30 March 2016', author's archive.
14. Ibid.
15. Todd Niall, 'Goff vows to restore public faith in Auckland Council', RNZ news, 8 October 2016: www.rnz.co.nz/news/national/315185/goff-vows-to-restore-public-faith-in-auckland-council
16. Annie Newman, 'Living Wage Briefing', paper prepared for Auckland Council Mayor Phil Goff, 21 November 2016, author's archive.
17. Ibid.
18. 'Wellington Regional Council votes to become a living wage employer', Stuff, 28 September 2016: www.stuff.co.nz/business/84749899/wellington-regional-council-votes-to-become-a-living-wage-employer
19. Ibid.
20. Erin Gourley, 'Councillors embarrassed, irritated by delay in living wage', Post, 25 August 2023: www.thepost.co.nz/a/nz-news/350060441/councillors-embarrassed-irritated-delay-living-wage

CHAPTER 9

1. Auckland Council Living Wage Advisory Group, 'Record of Actions', 16 January 2017, author's archive.
2. Auckland Council officers' draft report prepared for Auckland Council's 2017/18 annual budget public consultation document, author's archive.
3. 'Wellington council cleaners get a living wage', NZ Herald, April 2017: www.nzherald.co.nz/business/exclusive-wellington-council-cleaners-get-a-living-wage/63E7T6LLDPMQC677VH7CA6C2J4/
4. Ibid.
5. Simpson Grierson, legal opinion prepared by Jonathan Salter and Matthew Hill for Hutt City Council, 27 April 2017, author's archive.
6. 'Summary of Hutt Chamber of Commerce business survey', attachment to a letter from president of Hutt Valley Chamber of Commerce Neville Hyde to Divisional Manager Human Resources Hutt City Council Jo Beck, 6 October 2017, author's archive.
7. Rebecca Nyakuong Kuach, My Life To Live, photo exhibition booklet, May 2019, author's archive.
8. Nick Truebridge, 'Christchurch City Council adopts living wage for staff', Press, 3 August 2017: www.stuff.co.nz/the-press/news/95412858/christchurch-city-council-adopts-living-wage-for-staff
9. Ibid.

10. *E tū and You*, December 2017: https://etu.nz/?s=Avei+Toaitiiti
11. Living Wage Movement Aotearoa NZ, 'Vector comes on-board as accredited Living Wage Employer', media release, Scoop, 6 November 2017: www.scoop.co.nz/stories/BU1711/S00142/vector-comes-on-board-as-accredited-living-wage-employer.htm
12. Local Government NZ President Dave Cull, 'Four well-beings restored to local communities', media release, 6 April 2018: www.lgnz.co.nz/news-and-media/2018-media-releases/four-well-beings-restored-to-local-communities/

CHAPTER 10

1. Matthew Tso, 'Hutt City Council votes to pay staff the living wage', Stuff, 6 June 2018:www.stuff.co.nz/business/104516677/hutt-city-council-votes-to-pay-staff-the-living-wage
2. Wellington City Council, 'Wellington City Council gets Living Wage accreditation', media release, 3 September 2018, author's archive.
3. Tom Hunt, 'Ratepayers pay $92,000 for membership of libertarian think tank', Stuff, 22 December 2020: www.stuff.co.nz/dominion-post/news/wellington/123768322/ratepayers-pay-92000-for-membership-of-libertarian-thinktank
4. Jared Nicholl, 'Meet the Porirua people working at New Zealand's first living wage primary school', Stuff, 24 August 2018: www.stuff.co.nz/national/106536924/meet-the-porirua-people-working-at-new-zealands-first-living-wage-primary-school
5. Sam Gribben, 'Workers want Bluff to be a Living Wage town': https://etu.nz/articles/living-wage-2/
6. Annie Newman, 'National Convenor's Report', Living Wage Governance Board meeting, 21 February 2019, author's archive.

CHAPTER 11

1. Simon Power, opinion piece, Interest.co.nz, 1 February 2019: www.interest.co.nz/opinion/97883/westpacs-simon-power-explains-why-bank-extending-living-wage-key-contractors
2. Anuja Nadkarni, 'Wellington cafe Seashore Cabaret pays all 52 staff living wage', Stuff, 4 April 2019: www.stuff.co.nz/business/111733582/wellington-cafe-seashore-cabaret-pays-all-52-staff-living-wage
3. *My Life To Live,* photo exhibition booklet, May 2019, author's archive.
4. Hamish McNeilly, 'Dunedin City Council workers to earn living wage', Stuff, 2 September 2019: www.stuff.co.nz/national/115461508/dunedin-city-council-employees-to-earn-living-wage
5. Living Wage Movement Aotearoa NZ, 'Dunedin becomes second Living Wage city in NZ', media release, September 2019: www.livingwage.org.nz/dunedin_becomes_second_living_wage_city_in_nz

CHAPTER 12

1. Living Wage Movement Aotearoa NZ, 'A Message to our Living Wage Community', newsletter: www.livingwage.org.nz/a_message_to_our_living_wage_community
2. Ibid.
3. Nick Hirst, 'Essential workers deserve a Living Wage': www.livingwage.org.nz/essential_workers_deserve_a_living_wage
4. Ibid.
5. New Zealand Banking Association, 'Banking becomes first living wage accredited industry', media release, 27 July 2020: www.nzba.org.nz/2020/07/27/banking-becomes-first-living-wage-accredited-industry/
6. RNZ, 'Govt announces living wage for MSD security guards', *RNZ news*, 10 August 2020: www.rnz.co.nz/news/political/423160/govt-announces-living-wage-for-msd-security-guards
7. Ibid.
8. Living Wage Movement Aotearoa NZ, 'Living Wage movement announces new employer council', 'News': www.livingwage.org.nz/living_wage_movement_announces_new_employer_council
9. Ibid.
10. Ibrahim Omer, maiden speech to Parliament, New Zealand House of Representatives, *Parliamentary Debates (Hansard)*, 26 November 2020: www.parliament.nz/en/pb/hansard-debates/rhr/document/HansS_20201126_051600000/omer-ibrahim
11. Christchurch City Council, 'Council suppliers will need to be Living Wage employers', *Newsline*, 13 August 2021: newsline.ccc.govt.nz/news/story/council-to-require-suppliers-to-be-living-wage-employers
12. Christchurch City Council, 'Cleaners to get Living Wage', *Newsline*, 20 October 2021: newsline.ccc.govt.nz/news/story/cleaners-to-get-living-wage
13. RNZ, 'Living wage guaranteed to public service contractors', *RNZ news*, 10 November 2021: www.rnz.co.nz/news/political/455359/living-wage-guaranteed-to-public-service-contractors

POSTSCRIPT

1. Thomas Coughlan, NZ Herald, 5 December 2023: www.nzherald.co.nz/nz/politics/government-shaken-by-leak-of-cabinet-paper-criticising-urgent-repeal-of-law-to-lift-wages-conditions-of-low-paid-workers/IKBGVHVLGRB4HOMIL53UN2QCL4/
2. Morning Report, Radio New Zealand, 30 November 2023: www.rnz.co.nz/national/programmes/morningreport/audio/2018917490/security-guards-unhappy-over-scrapping-of-fair-pay-agreement

Acknowledgements

In March 2020 I left my job as a community organiser for Living Wage Movement Aotearoa NZ after five years in the role. That job had followed a long life in the trade union movement. A few days later I was walking on the beach when the national coordinator of the Living Wage Movement rang. Annie Newman asked if I would like to document the story of our movement. What a good idea we agreed. Four years later, I have Annie to thank for throwing me into the life of a book. There are many others to thank for being part of this.

Every worker who stood up, spoke out and shared their story in the quest for better lives for their whānau and other workers, thank you. To the 42 people who participated in interviews and shared their stories, memories and reflections and to John Ryall and Muriel Tunoho for being there from beginning to end, always ready to read, advise and support, thank you.

Sue Wootton of Otago University Press, thank you for taking on the living wage story with calm and confidence and blessing me with an editor like Imogen Coxhead, the brilliant team of Fiona Moffat, Mel Stevens and Meg Hamilton and the indexer Lee Slater.

Thank you Jason Fell and Simon Oosterman Beckers for your photographs, and Sam Gribben and Maria McMillan for lifesaving technical advice.

Thank you to the JR McKenzie Trust for the support of a grant of $15,000, to the Labour History Project for a grant of $2000, and to Living Wage Movement Aotearoa NZ for the ongoing support.

For patient reading, for wise counsel and, most of all, for your friendship: Tilly Lloyd, Rebecca MacFie and Jenny Davies. For neglecting your southern hemisphere holiday to read and comment, Scarlett Thomas.

To whānau, including my perfect sisters, Susan Edwards and Stephanie McIntyre, and wonderful daughters, Gabriel Thomas and Eleanor McIntyre. And my partner Marion Edmond for sharing the life of the movement and the book, for turning the pages late into the night and braving the frank conversations. For keeping the fires burning and the garden growing and for always believing. Thank you, more than I can say.

ACKNOWLEDGEMENTS

To all those in faith groups and community organisations who stand up for the living wage, and to Aotearoa's trade union movement for a lifetime lived alongside workers standing together for a fairer world. A heartfelt thank you.

> E tū kahikatea
> Hei whakapae ururoa
> Awhi mai awhi atu
> Tātou tātou e
>
> Stand like the kahikatea tree
> To brave the storms
> Embrace and receive each other
> We are one together
>
> (From the waiata by Hirini Melbourne)

Index

Bold denotes illustrations.
I, II, III, IV etc. refer to page numbers in colour section.

accreditation, Living Wage Employer 65–66, 76, 82, 84, 95, 102, 140, 216, 226
ACT New Zealand 162, 232
Acts *see* legislation
Adams, Susan 38, 96–97, 103, 104, 110, 123, 178, **201**, 228
Advance Pasifika (march) 33
aged care sector *see* caregivers
agreements/contracts
   arbitration 13
   collective bargaining/agreements 14, 15, 19, 50–51, 100, 185, 227
   fair pay agreements 215–16, 232
   individual bargaining/agreements 10, 108, 125
   national agreements/awards 13, 14
Ailoa, Eseta 10, 165–66
Alinsky, Saul 21, 86, 230
alliance building 230–31
   communities, faith groups and unions, between 22, 48–51, 61, 62, 83, 85–87, 96–97, 111–12, 187, 225, 227–28
amalgamation of unions 8, 14, 75, 124, 186
AMP New Zealand 177, 198, 200, 216, **217**, 218, 220
Anderson, Bruce 50, 70
Angeles, Jocelyn (Jo) Vicente 169
Anglican Church/organisations
   Anglican Action 94
   Anglican Advocacy 74, **75**
   Anglican Care 74, 76
   Anglican–Catholic forum 160–61, **161**
   Living Wage Movement, support for 38
   Selwyn Village 121–23, **122**
   Social Justice Council 45
   St Matthew-in-the-City (Anglican church) 38, 131–32, **131**, **142**, **201**, **209**
   St Peter's on Willis (Anglican Church) 70, 80, 81, 141, 162, **163**, **201**, **202**, **203**
   training, living wage 88
   Wellington Cathedral of St Paul 102, 112–13, 160, 161, 199
   see also Adams, Susan; Dawson, Brian; Dawson, Jenny; Duckworth, Justin; Hall, David
Anglican–Catholic forum 160–61
anti-apartheid movement 16, 18, 139
Aotearoa Artists for a Living Wage 103, 207
Aotearoa Resettled Community Coalition 50, 103, 159, 194
Apiak, Awak 206, 219, **VII**
arbitration 13
Ardern, Jacinda 163, **198**, 208, 211, 216
ASB Bank 207
Assembly of God Church (Newtown) 168
Association of University Staff of New Zealand 44
Atkinson, Freya 190

INDEX

Auckland Action Against Poverty 26, 49, 65
Auckland City Mission 218
Auckland Council
  Brown, Len 63–64, 82
  cleaners 220
  contractors/contracted workers 142, 220
  Goff, Phil 142, **143**, 144, 147–48, 152, 178, 200, 220–21
  living wage campaign for council workers 47–48, 63, 97, 111, 142–43, 148, 151–52, 178, 220
  living wage implementation 151–52, 178
Auckland (Tāmaki Makaurau)
  Living Wage Auckland 148, 151–52, 182, 200
  living wage networks 33, 37–39, 98–99, 103
  Māngere 39, 93, 111, 133, 233–34
  Ōtara 28, 59
  Pacific people march 33
  Parnell 38
  Point Chevalier 121
  Ponsonby 27, 140
  South Auckland 39, 93, 99, 104, 111, 133, 152–53, 182, 233–34
  Te Ohu Whakawhanaunga (community alliance) 230
  West Auckland 33, 78, 98–99, 111, 142
  Whānau Day 93, 99, 113, **IV**
Auckland University 53, 94, 108
Auckland University of Technology (AUT) 26–27, 54, 56, **57**, 104, 108, 109
Auckland Women's Centre 45, 50, 65, 110
Australia 28, 118
Awarau, Dina 134, **135**, 204
award system 13, 14, 44, 232
Azevedo, Nando 194

Baddeley, Tamara 109
Baker, Anita 180, 205, 225
banks/banking 119, 185, 206, 207, 212–13, 216, 218
Barber, Paul 35, 39, 40, 50, 73, 77, 85, 90, 136, 139, 149
Barclay, Glenn 199–200, 223
Barry, Campbell 172, 204, **223**
Bartlett, Kristine 17
Barton, Sharryn **58**, 118, 174
Bassett, David 170, 190
Beaumont, Roger 206, 212–13
Belcher, Kelly 30
Bennett, David 163
Best of Intentions, Worst of Results (Taxpayers' Union report) 100–101
billboards/posters **131**, 201, **I–VIII**
Bill (Porirua caretaker) 233
Birch, Tina **135**
Bishop, Chris 190
Bishop, Marianne **69**
Black, Rose 103, 174
Bleakley, Raewyn 137
Blue, Jackie 94
Bragg, Billy 95
brand/branding, Living Wage Movement 65, 76, 226, **I**
branding/trademark, Living Wage Employers' 65, 66, 76, 226, **I**
Brass Razoo Solidarity Band 109, 113, 116, **117**
Brett, Kerrie **183**
Briggs, Josh 171, 172, 204, **223**
Brown, Eileen **69**
Brown, Karena 74, 75, 76, 88, 144, 159, 162
Brown, Len 63–64, 82
Burns, Gerry **69**
Business and Economic Research Limited 207
Butler, Mike 168

'Campaigning for a Living Wage in 2012' (Ryall) 23

253

campaigns, living wage
  Auckland Council 47–48, 63, 97, 111, 142–43, 148, 151–52, 178, 220
  Christchurch/Christchurch City Council 74–76, **75**, 144, 159, 224
  Great Britain 19, 21, 35–36, 218
  Greater Wellington Regional Council (GWRC) 148–50, **229**
  Hamilton City Council 66, 76, 160, 163
  Hutt City Council 136, 155, 156–57, 178–79, 192–93
  Living Wage Bluff 182
  living wage city campaign (Wellington) 67, 68, 72, 97, 147, 189, 203, 208, **III**
  Living Wage for Vic 102, 103, 104, 108, 109, 124, 132, 134, 187, 193, 221
  local body election forums 77–78
  Porirua City Council 110, 123–24, 132, 139, 140, 145–47, 155, 179–81, 190–91, 192, 223
  schools 233
  Selwyn Village 121–23
  Service and Food Workers Union (SFWU) 15, 22–23, 24, 25–26, 27, 100, 108, 121, 206, 225
  tertiary education institutions 66
  United States of America (USA) 36
  Wellington City Council (campaign) 41, 42–43, 44, 66–68, **69**, 70–72, 73–74, 97–98
  Wellington City Council (implementation/delay) 73–74, 77, 85, 91, 93, 97, 113–16, 125–31, 140, 153–54, 170, 173, 174, 201
  'Worth It' 227
  see also contractors/contracted workers; *individual Living Wage networks*
Campbell, John 32
Campbell Live (TV programme) 10, 11, 30, 223–24

Cannons Creek 10, 40, 102, 123, **146**, 181
caregivers 15, 17, 123, 145, 211
Carlyon, Stevan 101
Carols for Our Cleaners 90, 150, **I**
Casey-Cox, Anna 174
Cater, Annette 162
Catholic Archdiocese of Wellington Ecology, Justice and Peace Commission 160–61
Catholic Church/Catholicism 16, 26, 62, 63–64, 140, 160–61, **161**, 182
Cawdry, Clive 218
Chalmers, Jesse 56, **217**
Chalmers, Lippy **217**
Chamber of Commerce *see* Hutt Valley Chamber of Commerce; Wellington Chamber of Commerce
Chand, Bernie 121, **122**
ChangeMakers Resettlement Forum 50, 73, 188, 194
Chick, Andrew 102, 103, 105, 139, 143, 146, 147, 179, 181, 223
chief executive salaries 76, 221
child poverty 10, 47, 50, 98, 110, 160
children 8, 10, 29, 30, 40
Chrastil, Joe 103, 118
Christchurch City Council
  Dalziel, Lianne 76, 144
  elections/election forums 144, 160, 162, 200
  living wage for Christchurch City Council workers 74–76, **75**, 144, 159, 224
Christchurch (Ōtautahi)
  2019 mosque attacks 187–88
  election forum 162
  living wage network 103
  public meeting 94
  Transitional Cathedral 140, 187
churches/cathedrals
  Assembly of God Church (Newtown) 168
  Christchurch Transitional Cathedral 140, 187–88

INDEX

Holy Trinity Cathedral 140
interfaith unity 49, 65, 187–88
Methodist Church 38, 39, 41, 50, 65, 70, 116, **117**, 143, **201**
Pacific Islanders' Presbyterian Church (Cannons Creek) 40, 123, **146, 181**
Pacific Islanders' Presbyterian Church (Newtown) 40, 81
principles/teachings 112–23
relationships between communities, faith groups and unions 22, 48–51, 61, 62, 83, 85–87, 96–97, 111–12, 187, 225, 227–28
St Andrew's on The Terrace (Presbyterian church) 39–40, 50, 83
St Anne's Catholic Church (Manurewa) 160, **161**, 182
St Matthew-in-the-City (Anglican church) 38, 131–32, **131**, **142**, **201**, **209**
St Peter's on Willis (Anglican Church) 70, 80, 81, 141, 162, **163**, **201, 202, 203**
St Stephen's (Presbyterian church) 27, 33
Unitarian Church 45
Wellington Cathedral of St Paul 102, 112–13, 160, 161, 199
Wesley Methodist Church 40, 41, 50, 70, 116, **117**, 143, **201**
Church, Kevin 64, 65, 102
cleaners/cleaning industry
 Auckland Council 220
 Carols for Our Cleaners 90, 150
 contracted workers/contractor power 14, 15, 21, 59, 60, 97–98, 145, 158, 193–94, 220–21, 224
 Covid-19 pandemic 211–12
 Living Wage Week 205–06
 Fresh Desk (company) 133
 OCS (company) 158, 193–94, 224
 Parliament, New Zealand 8–10, **9**, 59, 165–66
 pay rates/poverty 8–10, 13, 14, 30, 42, 59, 60, 141, 145
 Service and Food Workers Union (SFWU) 8–10
 Spotless (company) 59, 140, 154, 170
 stories, workers' 8–10, **9**, 42, 68–70, 75–76, 80, 132, **142**, 158, 179, 193, 194, 219, 222
 union membership levels 13, 14
 university cleaners 7, 48, 108, 151, 158, 193, 195, 206, 219, 221
 Wellington City Council 153–54, 169, **196**
 working hours/conditions 8, 10, 30, 41–42, 154, 175–76, 222
 see also individual people
Clearwater, Phil 75, 76
Co-operative Bank 207
Coffey, Ana 191, 205
Coffey, Tamati 140, 164
collective bargaining/agreements 14, 15, 19, 50–51, 100, 185, 227
 see also individual bargaining/agreements
collectivism 17, 22, 48, 232
 see also alliance building; community organisations
Collins, Simon 55, 56, 59
community forums 85, 113–14
community organisations
 Aotearoa Resettled Community Coalition 50, 103, 159, 194
 Auckland Action Against Poverty 26, 49, 65
 Auckland City Mission 218
 Auckland Women's Centre 45, 50, 65, 110
 ChangeMakers Resettlement Forum 50, 73, 188, 194
 Covid-19 pandemic response 208–10
 Downtown Community Ministry 143

255

East London Communities Organisation (TELCO) 19, 21
Hutt Union and Community Health Service 21, 134, **135**, 204, 206, 223, 224
Inequality Network 50
London Citizens 19–20, 21, 22–23, 24, 35, 77
London Citizens Workers Centre (LCWC) 19–20
Migrant Action Trust 50, **122**
Porirua Union and Community Health Service 102–03, 104, 105, 179, 208, 224
Poverty Action Waikato 174
relationships between communities, faith groups and unions 22, 48–51, 61, 62, 83, 85–87, 96–97, 111–12, 187, 225, 227–28
Selwyn Supporters Coalition 121–23, **122**
student associations 45, 49, 80, 84, 103
Te Ohu Whakawhanaunga (community alliance) 182–83, 212, 230, 233–34
Tongan Youth Trust 159–60
United Neighborhoods Organization 87
see also forums
community organisers 19, 20, 21, 27–28, 49, 78, 105–06, 107–08, 110, 152–53, 159, 169, 187, 208, 224
community power 44, 63, 76, 86, 91, 93, 111, 114, 131, 134–36, 206, 227
Community Services Union 18–19
compulsory unionism 23, 44, 108
Consumers Price Index (CPI) 82, 126, 187
contractors/contracted workers
 Auckland Council 142, 220
 banks/corporates 218
 Christchurch City Council 224

cleaners/cleaning industry 14, 15, 21, 59, 60, 97–98, 145, 158, 193–94, 220–21, 224
funder/contractor relationship 59, 60, 226
Great Britain 20
Hutt City Council 156–57, 178–79
Labour Government (2017–2023) 205
living wage campaigns 93, 97–98, 126
living wage, receiving 213–14, **213**, **214–15**
parking services 99–100
pay rates, effect on 14
Porirua City Council 224
public service (general) 166, 213–16, **213**, **214–15**
security guards 128–29, 130, 136, 138, 140–41, 160, 166, 213–14, **213**, **214–15**
tendering process 15
Wellington City Council 73–74, 97–98, 99–100, 114–16, 127, 129, 144, 154, 178
contracts *see* agreements/contracts
Conway, Peter 45, **69**, 82–83
Coomber, Sophie **157**, 158
Cooper, Linda 78, 79, 94
Corinna School 180
corporate businesses/employers 48, 96, 101, 105, 119, 164, 167, 185, 206, 207, 216–18, 224, 225–26
cost of living 13, 42, 76, 152
Council of Trade Unions *see* New Zealand Council of Trade Unions Te Kauae Kaimahi (NZCTU)
Countdown (supermarket) 227
Covid-19 pandemic 207, 208–10, 211–12, 218, 224, 227
Crampton, Eric 177
Cranney, Peter 17, 121, 128
Crosby, Michael 23, 62
Cull, Dave 199
Cunliffe, David 99

INDEX

Dalziel, Lianne 76, 144
Davidson, Marama 164
Davis, Kelvin 162
Dawson, Brian **69**, 70, 81, 90, 97, 114, 118, 130, 138
Dawson, Jenny 139–40, **146**, 160, 181, 223, 228
Day, Kate 75, 83, 199
democracy 77–78, 85, 93, 97, 105–06, 128, 149, 227
Dew, John 160–61
Diamond, Anne **183**
dignity 19, 25, 46, 124, 159, 176, 211, 219, 226
Dini, Ahmed 169, 174–75, **175**
Diocesan School for Girls 59–60
Dominion Post (newspaper) 42, 56, 59, 71, 80, 91, 99–100, 127, 129–30, 136–37, 138–39, 153, 172, 177
Doubtful Sounds (choral group) 207
Downlights (social enterprise) 218
Downtown Community Ministry 143
Drake, Marlon 169, 175, 193, 208–10, 212, 221, 228
Dubbelt-Leitch, Una 221
Duckworth, Justin 94, 102, 110, 116, 144, 160
Dunedin City Council 199–200
Dunn, Pat 160
Duston, Robert (Dusty) 213–14, **213**

Eagle, Paul 71, 81, 136–37, 150, 168
early childhood education 44, 134
East London Communities Organisation (TELCO) 19, 21
elections, general
  2014 84
  2017 153, 159–60, **161**, 162–63, **163**, 168, 182–83
  2020 166, 207, 215
  forums 159–63, **161**, **163**, 166, 182, 207, 214, **VIII**
elections, local body/mayoral
  2013 47, 77–78
  2016 125, 141–48
  2019 191, 200–204
  by-elections 43, 168
  forums 76, 77–82, **79**, 118, 140, 141–48, **142**, **146**, 151, 168, 185, 188, 200, 201–03, **201**, **202**, **203**, 204–05, **209**, 220
Employment Contracts Act 1991
  contractors/contracting 14
  Employment Relations Act 2000, replacement by 15
  introduction of legislation 14, 232
  pay rates/working conditions, effect on 14, 15, 53, 108, 232
  unions, effect on 14–15, 74–75, 108–09, 225
Employment Relations Act 2000 15, 215–16
Endermann, Emma 30, **57**
Engineering, Printing and Manufacturing Union (EPMU) 74, 75, 76, 103, 124
  see also E tū (union); Service and Food Workers Union (SFWU)
English, Bill 62, 159
equal pay/women's rights 17, 23, 50, 78, 94, 232
essential workers/services, Covid-19 pandemic 210, 211–12, 227
E tū (union)
  delegates/organisers **122**, 153, 158, 173
  formation 75, 124
  Living Wage for Vic campaign 134
  Living Wage Week 205
  Living Wage Wellington 165–66
  national conference 215–16
  Parliament, New Zealand 206
  Sanford (seafood company) 173
  security guards 8, 205–06, 213–14, **214–15**, 219
  Wellington City Council 125, 154
  see also Engineering, Printing and Manufacturing Union (EPMU);

257

Service and Food Workers Union (SFWU)
Evans, Darryl 28, 39
events, living wage 110
   announcements/accreditations 101, 109–10, 133, 169, 174–75, **175**, 176, 190, 206, **223**, 224–25
   artists' and performers' support 95, 113, 207–08
   Carols for Our Cleaners 90, 150
   council long-term plans 111
   Covid-19 pandemic, effect of 208
   Festival of the Elements 110, 134
   Grey, Sandra 228–29
   Living Wage Day 157–58, **157**, 193, 222, **VII**
   Living Wage for Vic 132
   Living Wage Hutt Valley 178–79
   Living Wage Porirua 110
   Living Wage Wellington 102, 113
   My Life To Live (exhibition) 194–99, **195–96**, **197**, **198**
   Newtown Festival 103, 134, 170, 187, 207–08, **209**
   training course 89
   Victoria University of Wellington Te Herenga Waka 222
   West Fest for a Living Wage 99
   Whānau Day 93, 99, 113
   see also forums; launches; marches; protests; rallies

Fafoi, Kris 181
Fair Pay Agreements Act 2022 232
faith groups
   Anglican Action 94
   Anglican Advocacy 74, **75**
   Anglican Care 74, 76
   Anglican–Catholic forum 160–61, **161**
   Catholic Archdiocese of Wellington Ecology, Justice and Peace Commission 160–61
   Covid-19 pandemic response 210
   interfaith unity 49, 65, 187–88
   Methodist City Action 94
   Muslim groups/involvement 118, 187–88
   principles/teachings 112–23
   relationships between communities, faith groups and unions 22, 48–51, 61, 62, 83, 85–87, 96–97, 111–12, 187, 225, 227–28
   Social Justice Council 45
   see also churches
Fakatou, Motekiai 116, **201**
Family Centre Social Policy Research Unit 46
Farrar, David 61, 85, 130
Fataua, Moli 75–76
Fell, Jason 53–54, 228
Festival of the Elements 110, 134
Finance Sector Union (Finsec) 43, 44, 114, 186
Finance, Industrial (Textile and Wood) Retail, Stores and Transport Union *see* FIRST Union
FIRST Union 44, 45, 97, 185–87, 212, 227
Fitzsimons, Fleur 168, 170, 173
Forbes, Michael 129
Ford, Izzy 191
forums
   community 85, 113–14, 222
   general election 159–63, **161**, **163**, 166, 182, 207, 214, **VIII**
   forums, local body election 76, 77–82, **79**, 118, 140, 141–48, **142**, **146**, 151, 168, 185, 188, 200, 201–03, **201**, **202**, **203**, 204–05, **209**, 220
   London 21
   Victoria University of Wellington Te Herenga Waka 118, 193, 222
Foster, Andy 72, 185, 201–04, **203**
Fouda, Gamal 188
Fountain, Reb 95, **209**
Frank Burkitt Band 169
Fraser, Linda 173, **183**
Free, Sarah 89, 176, 204

INDEX

Garage Project (brewery) 197, 208
Gecan, Mike 36–37
Geeson, Joanne **183**
Gershom, Pau 198–99
Go Eco Environment Centre 173–74
Goff, Phil 142, **143**, 144, 147–48, 152, 178, 200, 220–21
Good Fortune Coffee 190
Granada, Agnes 45, 50, **122**
Great Britain
 campaigns, living wage 19, 21, 35–36, 218
 contractors/contracted workers 20
 corporate involvement in living wage movements 218
 East London Communities Organisation (TELCO) 19, 21
 living wage campaigns/movements 19, 21, 35–36, 218
 Living Wage Foundation 35, 65, 216
 London Citizens 19–20, 21, 22–23, 24, 35, 77
 London Citizens Workers Centre (LCWC) 19–20
 London visit by John Ryall and Muriel Tunoho 19–20
 Newman, Annie (visit to London) 35–36
 pay rate increase 21
 public hospital tendering 19
 Transport and General Workers Union 20
 unionism 35–36
 UNISON (public sector union) 19–20, 35
Greater London Authority 21, 55
Greater Wellington Regional Council (GWRC) 148–50, **229**
Green Party of Aotearoa New Zealand 27, 160, 163–64, 233
Grey, Sandra 48, 108–09, **201**, 227, 228–29
Gribben, Sam 80, 81, 82, 83
Growcott, Cath 102, 139

Guevara, Alexandra 194, **197**, 214
Guilford, Grant 132, 187, 221

Haggerty-Drummond, Eleanor **69**, 70, **175**, 223
Hall, David 38, 45, 64, 84, 88, 103
Halt All Racist Tours (HART) 16, 18, 139
Hamilton living wage network 66, 76, 94, 103, 160, 163, 219
Harré, Laila 95
Haulangi, Fala 24, 26, 32, 33, 38, 47, 94, 152–53, **161**, 169
Haywood, Geoff 225
Hazaveh, Eshan 194, **198**
Headstart Early Learning Centre 164
health/health service 21, 49, 78, 102–03, 104, 105, 179, 208, 224
Henare, James 231
Henning, Jon 189
Herbert, Bill **69**
Heremaia, Alicia **79**, 93
Hiko, Ika 30–32
Hines, Iain 107
Hipkins, Chris 206
Hirini, Malcolm **175**
Holgate, Jane 35–36
Holy Trinity Cathedral 140
hospitality sector/workers 23, 165, **167**, 190, 218–19
Hotel and Hospital Workers Union 16, 17, 23, 110
hours, working *see* working hours
Household Incomes in New Zealand (MSD report) 47
housing costs/issues 7, 30, 46, 59, 153, 160, 161, 183
Huffstutler, Anna 173
Hutt City Council
 contractors/contracted workers 156–57, 178–79
 elections 144–46, 204
 Living Wage Employer accreditation 204, **223**, 224

259

Living Wage Hutt Valley campaign 136, 155, 156–57, 166, 170–73, 178–79, 192–93
  Wallace, Ray 145, 157, 170–72, 178–79, 190, 192, 204
Hutt News (newspaper) 136
Hutt Union and Community Health Service 21, 134, **135**, 204, 206, 223, 224
Hutt Valley
  Living Wage Hutt Valley 121, 134–36, **135**, 145, 156–57, 166, 171–72, 178, 192, 204, 223, 225
  living wage network 104
  Lower Hutt 16, 18, 46, 101, 190, **191**
  Petone 16, 18, 190, **191**
  Pōmare 121, 134–36, **135**
  Stokes Valley 7, 8, 206
Hutt Valley Chamber of Commerce 156–57, 171, 172, 179
Hyde, Neville 156, 171
Hyman, Prue 46, **69**, 82, 118

Ibell, Robert 208
Ika (café) 95
Ikurere, Jaine 8–10
individual bargaining/agreements 10, 108, 125
industrial action 15, 17, 61, 81, 187
Industrial Areas Foundation (IAF)
  Alinsky, Saul 21, 86, 230
  assemblies 78
  Littman, Deborah 21
  Living Wage Movement Aotearoa NZ (relationship/influence) 36–37, 86–87, 94, 105, 106, 111, 178, 183, 229–30
  organisers 21, 87
  organising model 86–87
  principles/models of operation 21, 36–37, 81, 86–87, 94, 112, 152–53, 178, 180, 183, 200–201
  training 118
  United Power for Action and Justice 36

Industrial Relations Foundation 19, 22
inequality 8, 38, 42, 45, 89, 164
  see also poverty
Inequality Network 50
inflation 13, 61–62, 100, 187
interviewees list, *Power to Win* 242

Jackson, Peter 201
Jessiman, Tabitha 182, **183**
job security 15, 16, 68, 215
  see also contractors/contracted workers
Johanson, Yani 75, 76
John, Margaret **135**
Johnson, Corinna **183**
Jones, Warwick 103
J R McKenzie Trust 83, 105, 107, 182, 187

Kāpiti Coast District Council 233
Kauwau, Awhina 155–56
Kavapalu, Rose 211
Kedgley, Sue 148, 149
Kelly, Graham 181
Kelly, Helen **29**, 55, 116
Kelly, Nick **69**
Kelly, Pat 16
Keown, Aaron 159
Kerr, Archie **135**
Key, John 56
King, Peter 46
King, Stephen 49
Knox, Elizabeth 194–97
Kokanovic, Marina 83–84
'Kristine Bartlett' case 17
Kuach, Rebecca Nyakuong 151, **157**, 158, 193, 194, **195**, 219, 222

Labour Governments
  Employment Relations Act 2000 15, 215–16
  Fair Pay Agreements Act 2022 232
  fifth Labour Government (1999–2008) 15

INDEX

fourth Labour Government (1984–1990) 13
sixth Labour Government (2017–2023) 163–67, 169, 205, 215–16, 232
see also individual politicians
Labour Party, New Zealand 27, 62, 99, 160, 162, 163, 165, 214, 233
Lagi, Malia **142**
Lamm, Felicity 54, 82
Larkin, Maribeth 61, 87–88, 90, 107, 110, 118, 131, 159, 200
launches, living wage
  Auckland University 54
  Living Wage Bluff 182, **183**
  Living Wage Employer accreditation 95, 102
  Living Wage for Vic 132
  Living Wage Hutt Valley 134–36, **135**
  Living Wage Movement Aotearoa NZ (Auckland) 26, 27–33, **28, 29, 31**, 40
  Living Wage Movement Aotearoa NZ (Wellington) 40–42
  Living Wage Porirua 123–24
  Living Wage Wellington 41–43
  living wage rate 56, 60, 217
  My Life To Live (exhibition) 198–99
  schools campaign 233
Lavery, Kevin 73–74, 82, 127, 128, 129, 130, 136, 137, 138, 175, 177
Leasi, Perema 40, 49, 123–24, 181
legal cases 16–17
Leggett, Nick 124, 132, 140, 144
legislation
  Employment Relations Act 2000 15, 215–16
  Fair Pay Agreements Act 2022 232
  Local Government Act 2002 74, 115, 128, 166–67
  see also Employment Contracts Act 1991
Lemo, Lemo 7–8
Lenihan-Iken, Rory 168, **VII**
Leo, Ema 193, 219, 222
Lester, Justin 71

election, mayoral (2016) 144, 147
election, mayoral (2019) 200–201
living wage for council workers 71, 126–27, 128, 129, 137, 147, **175**, 176, 200–201
Living Wage Rate announcement 169
My Life To Live (exhibition) 198
parking services 99
library workers 67, 70, 170, **174**, 175
Little, Andrew 213, 214
Littman, Deborah 19, 21, 22–23, 53, 54, 55, **57**, 59, 67, 86, 141
Living Wage Auckland 148, 151–52, 182, 200
Living Wage Bluff 173, 182, **183**
living wage city 67, 68, 72, 97, 147, 189, 203, 208, **III**
Living Wage Day 157–58, **157**, 193, 222, **VII**
living wage, definition/meaning of 24, 25–26, 46–47, 112–23
Living Wage Employers 140
  accreditation scheme 65–66, 76, 82, 84, 95, 102, 140, 216, 226
  AMP New Zealand 177, 198, 200, 216, **217**, 218, 220
  ANZ 206
  ASB Bank 207
  Auckland City Mission 218
  brand/branding 65, 76, 226, **V**
  Commonsense Organics 113
  Co-operative Bank 207
  Corinna School 180
  Covid-19 pandemic 210
  Downlights (social enterprise) 218
  Dunedin City Council 199–200
  Fresh Desk (cleaning company) 133
  Garage Project (brewery) 197, 208
  Good Fortune Coffee 190
  Greater Wellington Regional Council (GWRC) 149
  Headstart Early Learning Centre 164

Heartland Bank 212
Hutt City Council 204
Ika (café) 95
Karma Kola (drink company) 177
Kiwibank 212, 218
La Boca Loca (restaurant) 108
Living Wage Rate updates 211
Mai Day Spa 200
misrepresentation as 76–77
Miss Fortune's (café) 190
New Zealand Banking Association 212–13
Nice Blocks 101, 102
OCHO (chocolate company) 199
Opticmix 64, 65, 101–02
Pivotal (previously Pivotal Thames, Thames Publications) 68–70, 133, 197, 220
Ponsonby Road Lounge Bar 140, 164
Porirua Union and Community Health Service 102–03, 104, 105, 179, 208, 224
Principal Partners Council 216–19
Rogue & Vagabond (bar) 169, 218–19, 220
Seashore Cabaret (café) 190, **191**
Sustainable Business Network 206
Tūaropaki Trust 118
Tonzu (food manufacturers) 56, **217**
Vector (power company) 164, 218
Wellington City Council 118, 168, 174–75, **175**, 176, 200–201
Western Springs College 200
Westpac 185, 206, 218
Zealandia (wildlife sanctuary) 189–90
Living Wage for Learning 98, **II**
Living Wage for Vic 102, 103, 104, 108, 109, 124, 132, 134, 193, 221
Living Wage Foundation 35, 65, 216
Living Wage Hutt Valley 121, 134–36, **135**, 145, 156–57, 166, 171–72, 178, 192, 204, 223, 225

Living Wage Movement Aotearoa NZ
alliance/relationships between communities, faith groups and unions 22, 48–51, 61, 62, 83, 85–87, 96–97, 111–12, 187, 225, 227–28
annual general meetings (AGMs)/annual reports 83–84, 103, 212
Auckland meetings 47, 64–65
Auckland network establishment 33
brand/branding 24, 25, 27
community representation 47, 49–50
faith stream/group 38, 45, 49; *see also* churches; faith groups
election, general (2017) 164
establishment 82–83
forums, community 85, 113–14, 222
forums, general election 159–63, **161**, **163**, 166, 182, 207, 214, **VIII**
forums, local body election 76, 77–82, **79**, 118, 140, 141–48, **142**, **146**, 151, 168, 185, 188, 200, 201–03, **201**, **202**, **203**, 204–05, **209**, 220
funding 83–84
governance board 84, 95, 96–97, 103, 104, 111, 186
Industrial Areas Foundation (IAF), influence/relationship 36–37, 86–87, 94, 105, 106, 111, 178, 183, 229–30
launch/incorporation 27–33, **28**, **29**, **31**, 64
living wage movement, genesis of 13, 22–26
local boards, lobbying/meetings 47, 63, 74, 84, 94, 220
local government, targeting of 47–48; *see also individual councils*
national governance board 49, 95, 96, 103, 104, 110–11, 187
national movement, establishment/building of 45–46, 82
newsletter 208, 210
non-party political stance 27, 39, 81, 94, 107, 111, 180, 200–201, 204, 234

principles 83
Te Ohu Whakawhanaunga, support for 182–83
training courses 73, 88–90, 103, 118, 159–60
Wellington network establishment 39–40
see also McIntyre, Lyndy; Newman, Annie
Living Wage Porirua 110, 123–24, 132, 139, 140, 145–47, 155–56, 179–81, 190–91, 192, 223–24
living wage rate
  amount 56, 95, 109, 125, 133, 153, 154, 169, 172, 210, 220, 224, 225, **235**
  announcements 55, 56–59, **57–58**, 83, 95, 109–10, 133, 153, 169, 190, **191**, **217**, 220
  calculation/identification 46–47, 55, 56, 61, 115, 156, 169, 210, 226, **235**
  minimum wage, versus 220, **235**
  reviews/updates 82, 109–10, 125–26, 133, 169, 210–11, 220, 226, 235
  standard of living, effect on 59
  trainee rate **235**
  unions, use by 227
Living Wage South Canterbury 189
Living Wage Waitaki 189
Living Wage Week **131**, 205–06, 224, 225, **III**
Living Wage Wellington
  delegation to Parliament 165–66
  election, mayoral (2019) 201–02
  establishment 39–40
  events 102, 113
  forum, general election 160–62, **163**
  forum, local body election 201–03, 204
  launch/incorporation 41–43
  living wage city campaign 67, 68, 72, 97, 147, 189, 203, 208
  marches/rallies 116, **117**, **229**
  meetings 44, 47

Pacific communities, support from 40
second birthday party 102
submissions 68, 97, 112, 114, 136, 140, 189
Sustainable Business Network collaboration 206
Wellington City Council (campaign) 41, 42–43, 44, 66–68, **69**, 70–72, 73–74, 97–98
Wellington City Council living wage implementation/delay 73–74, 77, 85, 91, 93, 97, 113–16, 125–31, 140, 153–54, 170, 173, 174, 201
Living Wage Whanganui 103, 153, 187
Livingstone, Ken 21
lobbying 85, 94, 111, 177, 179–80
local boards, lobbying/meetings 47, 63, 74, 84, 94, 220
local body elections *see* elections, local body/mayoral
Local Government Act 2002 74, 115, 128, 166–67
Locke, Cybèle 110, 194, 223
Lockyer, Gina 168, 189–90, **202**, 203, 212
London Citizens 19–20, 21, 22–23, 24, 35, 77
London Citizens Workers Centre (LCWC) 19–20
Lower Hutt 16, 18, 46, 101, 190, **191**
Luxton, Jo 164

Maga, Dennis 185–87
Maguren, Michelle 134, 171
Mai Day Spa 200
Malcolm, Robyn 95, 99
Mallard, Trevor 165, 206
Malolo, Ana **57**, 59
Māori
  Covid-19 pandemic 224
  Fair Pay Agreements Act 2022 232
  J R McKenzie Trust 107
  Living Wage Employer 118–19

Parnell 38
Service and Food Workers Union (SFWU) 25
Te Karere (Māori television programme) 118
Te Pāti Māori (Māori Party) 160, 162, 163, 214
Tūaropaki Trust 118–19
union members 19
workers 8, 124, 232
see also individual people
Marama, Teau 103, 105
Mareko, Caroline 124, 181
Marsh, Simon 71–72
Martin, Betsan 134, 171
Martin, Margaret **161**
Martin, Thomas **157**
Martin, Tracey 63, 162
Masoe, Sosefina 41–42
Matthews, Rebecca 43, **69**, 90, 98, 188, 204, 207
Maxwell, Bronwynn 148, 151
Mayman, Margaret 28, 39, 40, 45, 68, 70, 72, 83
Maynard, John 113
Mayrick, Marama **69**
Maze, Julian 189
McCormack, Derek 104
McCormick, Gary 95
McCourt, Rory 45, 49, 80, 88
McGillian, Pat **183**
McGlashan, Don 95, 207–08, **209**
McIntyre, Lyndy 10
  annual general meetings 83
  Campbell Live (TV programme) 10
  community organiser 107, 169
  early union career 17
  forum, general election 160
  Garage Project (brewery) 208
  Hutt City Council 155, 156, 171, 172, 192
  Kāpiti Coast District Council 233
  Littman, Deborah 55
  Living Wage Wellington establishment/launch 39–40, 41
  National Business Review debate 177
  OCS (cleaning company) 193–94
  Porirua City Council 146–47
  Service and Food Workers Union (SFWU) 8, 18, 67
  Stokes Valley, living in 7
  training courses, living wage 88, 118
  Wellington City Council living wage implementation 73
McIntyre, Stephanie **69**
McKenzie, Simon 164
McKerrow, Barbara 177
McRae, Heather 60
media coverage
  Dominion Post (newspaper) 42, 56, 59, 71, 80, 91, 99–100, 127, 129–30, 136–37, 138–39, 153, 172, 177
  National Business Review (online publication) 130, 177
  NZ Herald (newspaper) 55, 56, 59, 76–77, 123, 185
  Post (newspaper) 149
  Press (newspaper) 32–33, 75, 76, 159
  radio 56, 70, 142–43, 185
  Salient (student newspaper) 193
  Stuff (media company) 140, 190, 199–200
  Sunday Star-Times (newspaper) 60
  television 10, 11, 30–32, 110, 185, 223–24
Melian Dialogue, The (Thucydides) 88, 89
Methodist Church 38, 39, 41, 50, 65, 70, 116, **117**, 143, **201**
  see also Nuku, Hiueni
Migrant Action Trust 45, 50, **122**
migrant workers/groups 19, 20, 40, 43, 50–51, 73, 78, 103, 159, 188, 194
  see also refugees/refugee-background workers
Milford, John 115, 130, 137, 138
Miller, Jo **223**

Miller, Katy 124
Milne, Chris 156, 171, 172, 192
minimum wage 190
    Australian figure 28
    caregivers 17
    cleaners 10, 13, 30, 41–42, 59, 121
    living wage, versus 134, 162, 220, 226, **235**
    migrant/refugee-background workers 50, 68, 158
    New Zealand figure 28, 42, 56
    New Zealand Initiative 177
    parking wardens 91, 99–100
    security guard 164
    women 50
Ministry for Business, Innovation and Employment (MBIE) 46, 205, 215
Ministry of Health 216
Ministry of Social Development (MSD) 47, 166, 213–14, **213**, **214–15**, 219
Miss Fortune's (café) 190
Mixed Member Proportional (MMP) 44, 215
Mohamed, Adullahi 170
Monaghan, Kieran 103, 113
Moore, Rhys 65
Mop March 116, **117**, **VI**
Morris, Leonie 45, 50, 103, 110, 151
Morrison, John 72, 81
Mortera, Orquidea Tamayo **79**
Moss, Alana 154
Muir, Chas 74, 75, 159, 187–88
Muslim groups/involvement 118, 187–88
My Life To Live (exhibition) 194–99, **195–96**, **197**, **198**

Nana, Ganesh 207
national awards 13, 14
National Business Review (online publication) 130, 177
National Governments
    fifth National Government (2008–2017) 166
    fourth National Government (1990–1999) 14, 232
    sixth National Government (2023–present) 232
    third National Government (1975–1984) 13
    see also Employment Contracts Act 1991; *individual politicians*
National Library 10, **174**
National Party, New Zealand 94, 162–63, 190, 232, 234
Natoli, Jen 24–25, 26, 38–39
Nelson, Clay 45, 111
Newman, Annie
    alliance building 227
    annual general meetings/annual reports 83, 84
    Auckland Council 147–48, 151, 152, 178
    Auckland living wage network 37–38
    background 23
    campaigns 23–24, 25–26, 27
    community representation/organisers 47, 78, 105–06, 107
    early union career 23–24
    election forums 78, 82, 160
    housing issues 160, 183
    Industrial Areas Foundation (IAF) 87, 229–30
    Labour Government (2017–2023) 166, 205
    Living Wage Bluff 182
    Living Wage Employers 77, 140, 164, 216
    Living Wage Movement, establishment/incorporation of 45, 64
    Living Wage Movement legacy 93
    living wage rate 54, **58**, **59**
    living wage workshop (SFWU) 25–26
    London, visit to 35–36
    New York, visit to 36
    non-party political stance 27

265

organising model, union 26
Palmerston North public meeting 93–94
partnership model 96
rally at Parliament **165**
standing down as Living Wage Movement leader 212
training course, living wage 88
'transfer of undertakings' (SFWU campaign) 15
unionism and the living wage movement 62
Newsline (online Christchurch City Council newsletter) 224
Newtown 40, 81, 113, 168, 170
Newtown Festival 103, 134, 170, 187, 207–08, **209**
New Zealand Banking Association 206, 212–13
New Zealand Clerical Workers Union 75
New Zealand Council of Trade Unions Te Kauae Kaimahi (NZCTU) **28**, 45, 82–83, 186, 226
New Zealand Educational Institute *see* NZEI Te Riu Roa (New Zealand Educational Institute)
New Zealand First 27, 99, 160, 162, 163–64, 166, 232
New Zealand Initiative 177
New Zealand Nurses Organisation 113, 174, 204
New Zealand Portrait Gallery 194, 197, 199
Ngakopu, Rosey 232
Nice Blocks 101, 102
Nine to Noon (radio programme) 56
non-party political stance 27, 39, 81, 94, 107, 111, 180, 200–201, 204, 234
'no permanent friends, no permanent enemies' (IAF mantra) 81, 180, 200, 204, 205, 233
Northern Hotel and Hospital Workers Union 8, 17, 110

see also E tū; Service and Food Workers Union; Service Workers Union of Aotearoa
Nuku, Hiueni 102–03, 103–04, 139, 165, 180, 191, 223, 224, 225
NZEI Te Riu Roa (New Zealand Educational Institute) 19, 44, 98, 134, 234
NZ Herald (newspaper) 55, 56, 59, 63, 76–77, 123, 154, 185

OCHO (chocolate company) 199
OCS (cleaning company) 158, 193–94, 224
Omer, Ibrahim
  Christchurch 2019 mosque attacks 188
  community forum, council-organised 114
  Dini, Ahmed 176
  election forums 80, 160, **202**
  E tū union organiser 158
  Living Wage Day 193
  living wage rate announcement 109
  living wage training course 73, 88, 90
  marches 116
  My Life To Live (exhibition) **198**
  OCS (cleaning company) 193
  Parliament maiden speech 90, 219
opposition to living wage
  ACT New Zealand 162
  Foster, Andy 201–02
  Hutt Valley Chamber of Commerce/council officials 156–57, 171
  National Party/Government 56, 62, 162–63
  New Zealand Initiative 177
  Taxpayers' Union 85–86, 100–101, 115, 130–31, 137, 177, 192
  Treasury New Zealand 61–62
  unionists 62
  Wellington Chamber of Commerce 72, 85, 115, 125, 130–31, 137, 138–39, 177

INDEX

Wellington City Council officials 71–72, 73–74, 85, 97, 98, 125, 126, 128, 130–39, 177
Opticmix 64, 65, 101–02
Oram, Rod 60
Orchard, Sam **131**
Organisation for Economic Co-operation and Development (OECD) 8, 47
organisers
community organisers 19, 20, 21, 27–28, 49, 78, 105–06, 107–08, 110, 152–53, 159, 169, 187, 208, 224
Industrial Area Foundation (IAF) 21, 87
paid organisers 24, 49, 80, 219
union organisers 19, 24, 62, 80, 110, 114, 125, 134, 158, **161**, 210
organising model, union 14, 22, 26, 62, 48, 86
see also relational approach; relationships between communities, faith groups and unions
Osten, Fiona 39, **69**
Ōtāhuhu Police Station 211
Ōtautahi *see* Christchurch (Ōtautahi)

Pacific Islanders' Presbyterian Church (Cannons Creek) 40, 123, **146**, 181
Pacific Islanders' Presbyterian Church (Newtown) 40, 81
Pacific people/communities
activism 24
Advance Pasifika (march) 33
causes 39, 41, 47, 49, 107, 152
cleaners 8, 24, 32, 124
Covid-19 pandemic 224
Fair Pay Agreements Act 2022 232
J R McKenzie Trust 107
Kiribati 99
Living Wage Porirua 123
marches 33

Pacific Islanders' Presbyterian Church (Cannons Creek) 40, 123, **146, 181**
Pacific Islanders' Presbyterian Church (Newtown) 40, 81
Pacific Peoples Advisory Panel 39
Sāmoa 7, 49, 124, 168, 179, 181
support for Living Wage Movement 40
Tonga 103, 159–60, 224, 233
Tuvalu 24, 78
Wellington Samoan Faifeau (Church Ministers) Group 49
women's groups 50
Pacific Peoples Advisory Panel 39
Palmerston North public 93–94
Pannett, Iona 81, 129, 138
Parai, Taku 181
Pardoe, Bella 19, 223
parking wardens 91, 97–98, 99–100, 101, 105, 124, 154, 175
Parliament, New Zealand 11
cleaners 8–10, **9**, 59, 165–66
living wage commitment/ announcement 165–66, **167**
Living Wage Wellington delegation 165–66
Omer, Ibrahim (maiden speech) 90, 219
Parliamentary Services 59, 206
security guards **167**, 213–14, **213, 214–15**
partnership model 22, 48–51, 62, 83, 85–87, 96–97, 111–12
Pattison, Christine **135**
pay equity *see* equal pay/women's rights
pay rates/wage levels
caregivers 17
chief executive, council 76, 221
cleaners 8–10, 13, 14, 30, 42, 59, 60, 141, 145
contractors/contracting, effect of 14, 15

267

Employment Contracts Act 1991,
  effect of 14, 53, 232
 gardener 53
 increases (Great Britain) 21
 increases (New Zealand) 18, 100,
  151, 153, 156, 185, 226, 233
 parking wardens 100
 security guards 141, 164, 233
 see also campaigns, living wage;
  Living Wage Rate; minimum wage
penal rates 8, 13, 108
People's Choice (political group) 76
Peter McKenzie Project 182
Peters, Winston 99
Petone 16, 18, 190, **191**
Pilott, Brenda 45, 84
Pivotal (previously Pivotal Thames,
  Thames Publications) 68–70, 133,
  197, 220
Poluleuligaga, Sanele 153
Pōmare School 134–36, **135**
Ponsonby Road Lounge Bar 140, 164
Porirua City
 cleaners 41
 Cannons Creek 10, 40, 102, 123,
  146, 181
 Corinna School 180
 living wage network/meetings 102,
  104, 105
 Living Wage Porirua 110, 123–24,
  132, 139, 140, 145–47, 155–56,
  179–81, 190–91, 192, 223–24
Porirua City Council 110, 124, 132,
  140, 145–47, 155–56, 181, 190–91,
  204–05, 223–24
Porirua Union and Community Health
  Service 102–03, 104, 105, 179, 208,
  224
posters/billboards 131, 201, **I–VIII**
Post (newspaper) 149
poverty
 Auckland Action Against Poverty
  26, 49, 65
 child poverty 10, 47, 50, 98, 110, 160

Hutt Valley 7
 New Zealand Poverty Measurement
  Project 46
 Porirua 113
 poverty pay/wages 13–15, 16, 18, 25,
  26, 27, 30, 98, 130, 163, 205, 225,
  226, 232
 working poor 8–10, 38, 49, 160, 168,
  182, 230
 see also inequality
Poverty Action Waikato 174
power
 community power 44, 63, 76, 86, 91,
  93, 111, 114, 131, 134–36, 206, 227
 union power 14, 48, 225, 227
Power, Simon 185
'Precarious Work and the Living Wage
  in Our Communities' (symposium)
  54, 56–59, **57–58**
Presbyterian Church
 interfaith unity 49
 Mayman, Margaret 28, 39, 40, 45, 68,
  70, 72, 83
 Pacific Islanders' Presbyterian Church
  (Cannons Creek) 40, 123, **146, 181**
 Pacific Islanders' Presbyterian Church
  (Newtown) 40, 81
 St Andrew's on The Terrace
  (Presbyterian church) 39–40, 50, 83
 St Stephen's (Presbyterian church) 27,
  33
Press (newspaper) 32–33, 75, 76, 159
Principal Partners Council (Living Wage
  Employers) 216–19
Printers Union 17
productivity 59, 62, 77, 100, 137, 171
protections, worker 13–14, 15, 22, 210,
  215–16, 232
protests/protest movements 16, 18, 139,
  186
Puaula, Maria **161**
Public Service Association Te Pūkenga
  Here Tikanga Mahi 45, 74, 76, 103,
  125, 148, **174**, 191, 199, 227

public support for living wage 97, 98, 114, 118, 144, 176, 210, 227

Radio New Zealand 56, 70, 142–43, 185
Rahman, Maliki 67
rallies/marches 33, 66, 98, 110, 114, 116, **117, 165, 229, II**
  see also protests/protest movements
Ram, Satya **183**
'Rapping Reverend' 27, **31**
Rashbrooke, Max 42, 70, 127–28
Recon Security 140
Reedy-Taare, Mei 162
refugees/refugee-background workers
  Christchurch 2019 mosque attacks 187–88
  collectivism 48
  forums 78
  Living Wage for Vic event 104
  Living Wage Hutt Valley 136
  minimum wage workers/jobs 50
  My Life To Live (exhibition) 197–99
  photo exhibition 11
  workers' stories 20, 158, 170, 175–76, 194, 198–99, 206, 219
  World Refugee Day 194, 198, 199
  see also migrant workers/groups
Reid, Robert 16, 45, 84, 103
Reihana, Charmaine 110, 132
relational approach 61, 96–97, 111, 227, 230
  see also partnership model; transactional approach
relationships between communities, faith groups and unions 22, 48–51, 61, 62, 83, 85–87, 96–97, 111–12, 187, 225, 227–28
religion *see* churches; faith groups
rent levels, housing 7, 30, 46, 59
Resettlement Portraits, The (exhibition) 194
retail sector 60, 76, 189, 210, 211, 212, 227

right-wing lobby groups 85, 177
  New Zealand Initiative 177
  Taxpayers' Union 85–86, 100–101, 115, 130–31, 137, 177, 192
Robertson, Grant 102, 198, 220
Rock, Cissy 131
Rogue & Vagabond (bar) 169, 218–19, 220
Rose, Jim 85, 100–101
Rosenberg, Bill 82
Rotherham, Fiona 177
Rushton, Andrea 22–23, 25, 27–28, 37, 38–39
Ryall, John
  activism 15, 16, 22
  alliance building 230
  'Campaigning for a Living Wage in 2012' 23
  education/background 15–16
  election forums 162
  Greater Wellington Regional Council (GWRC) 149
  governance board 103
  Halt All Racist Tours (HART) 16, 18
  Hotel and Hospital Workers Union 16
  legal cases 16–17
  Littman, Deborah (living wage relationship) 20
  Living Wage Hutt Valley 121, **135**, 155, 156, 179, **223**
  Living Wage Movement Aotearoa NZ launch 28–29, **29**
  living wage movement, genesis of 13, 22–24, 220
  Local Government Act 2002 166
  London, visit to 19–20, 21–22
  Service and Food Workers Union (SFWU) 15–17, 18, 22–23, **29**, 100
  Taxpayers' Union 101
  Wellington City Council living wage 73, 77, 100
  Wellington living wage network 39–40
Ryan, Katherine 56

Salient (student newspaper) 16, 193
Salih, Suleman 194, **196, 198**
Sanele, Lalopua 81
Sanford (seafood company) 173, 182
Sanson, Marion 153, 159
Scherrer, Felicia 200, 218
Scott, Brian 61, 115
Seashore Cabaret (café) 190, **191**
security guards
   contractors/contracted workers 128–29, 130, 136, 138, 140–41, 160, 166, 213–14, **213, 214–15**
   E tū (union) 8, 205–06, 213–14, **214–15**, 219
   Fair Pay Agreements Act 2022 232
   Living Wage Week 206–07
   Ministry of Social Development (MSD) 166, 213–14, **213, 214–15**, 219
   My Life To Live (exhibition) **197**
   Parliament, New Zealand **167**, 213–14, **213, 214–15**
   pay rates 141, 164, 233
   Wellington City Council 128–29, 130, 136–37, 140–41
   workers' stories 136, 160, 164, 194, 233
   working hours 164
   see also individuals
Selwyn Supporters Coalition 121–23, **122**
Selwyn Village 121–23
Sepuloni, Carmel 213
Service and Food Workers Union (SFWU)
   amalgamations 8, 14, 75, 124
   campaigns/causes 15, 22–23, 24, 25–26, 27, 100, 108, 121, 206, 225
   Campbell Live (TV programme) 10, 11, 30–32, 223–24
   conferences 53
   contractors/contracting 15
   detractors, living wage movement 62
   forum organising 80
   job security 15
   legal cases 16–17
   living wage detractors/opposition 62
   Living Wage Movement, support of 38–39, 53, 153, 225
   McIntyre, Lyndy 8, 18, 67
   parking wardens 91, 99–100
   pay rates/wage levels 15, 28
   research, poverty 46
   see also E tū (union); Newman, Annie; Ryall, John; Service Workers Union of Aotearoa; Tunoho, Muriel
Service Workers Union of Aotearoa 14–15
   see also Service and Food Workers Union (SFWU)
Simone, Ann 154
Simpson Grierson (law firm) 155
single mothers 30–32, 132, 158, 206, 233
Sinoti, Mareta **9**, 10, **174**, 223–24
'sleepover case' (SFWU) 16–17
Social Justice Council 45
South Africa *see* Halt All Racist Tours (HART)
South Sudanese Dancers **135**
Spotless (cleaning company) 59, 140, 154, 170
St Andrew's on The Terrace (Presbyterian church) 39–40, 50, 83
St Anne's Catholic Church (Manurewa) 160, **161**, 182
St Matthew-in-the-City (Anglican church) 38, 131–32, **131, 142, 201, 209**, III
St Peter's on Willis (Anglican Church) 70, 80, 81, 141, 162, **163, 201, 202, 203**
St Stephen's (Presbyterian church) 27, 33
Stallinger, Tony 136, 156, 172, 179
Standing, Guy 54, **57**
Stapleton, Carl **183**
Stats NZ 46, 95, **235**

Stokes Valley 7, 8, 206
stories, workers'
  Campbell Live (TV programme) 10, 11, 30–32, 223–24
  cleaners 8–10, **9**, 42, 68–70, 75–76, 80, 132, **142**, 158, 179, 193, 194, 219, 222
  customer service operator 155
  gardener 53
  hospitality worker 198–99
  library workers 70, 170
  London Citizens Workers Centre 19–20
  My Life To Live (exhibition) 194–99, **195–96, 197, 198**
  parking wardens 101, 124, 175
  refugees/refugee-background workers 20, 158, 170, 175–76, 194, 198–99, 206, 219
  school workers 171, 233
  security guards 136, 160, 164, 194, 233
Strickson-Pua, Mua 27, **31**
strikes *see* industrial action
Stuart, Pat 114
student groups/associations 45, 49, 80, 84, 103
Stuff (media company) 140, 190, 199–200
submissions 68, 97, 112, 114, 136, 140, 155, 179, 189, 190
Sullivan, Chris 63–64
Sunday Star-Times (newspaper) 60
supermarkets/supermarket workers 189, 210, 211, 212, 227
Sustainable Business Network 206
Sutorius, Tony 181
Sutton, Leigh 172, 192

Taimalelagi, Sonny 49, 168
Taituave, Faepepele 133, 144–45
Tāmaki Makaurau *see* Auckland (Tāmaki Makaurau)
Tan, Lee 82
Tana, Mike 132, 145–46, 147, 179, 180–81, 190–91, 204, 205
Taniela, Esau **69**
Tanu, Toreka 179, 204
taxation 16, 85
Taxpayers' Union 85–86, 100–101, 115, 130–31, 137, 177, 192
Taylor, Yvette 80, 88, 91, 98, 99, 121, 213
Te Karere (Māori television programme) 118
Te Muka Rau Charitable Trust 111
Te Ohu Whakawhanaunga (community alliance) 182–83, 212, 230, 233–34
Te Pāti Māori (Māori Party) 160, 162, 163, 214
Te Whanganui a Tara *see* Wellington (Te Whanganui a Tara)
Teariki, Stella 102, 103, 105, 139, 146, 155, 191, 204
TELCO *see* East London Communities Organisation (TELCO)
Teppett, Ross 208
Tertiary Education Union – Te Hautū Kahurangi 27, 48, 66, 102, 108, 109, 134, 169, **201**, 221, 227
  see also Victoria University of Wellington Te Herenga Waka
Thames Publications *see* Pivotal (previously Pivotal Thames, Thames Publications)
Think Tank Charitable Trust 111
Timaru 164, 189
timeline 236–39
Toa, Angela 41, 42, 90
Tofilau, Ola 40
Tongan Youth Trust 159–60
Tonzu (food manufacturers) 56, **217**
trademark/branding, Living Wage Employers' 65, 66, 76, 226
trade unions *see* unions, trade
training courses, living wage 73, 88–90, 103, 118, 159–60, 181

transactional approach 61, 89, 96–97, 186, 227, 230
  see also partnership model; relational approach
Transport and General Workers Union 20
Treasury New Zealand 61–62, 111
Tric Malcolm **69**, 88, 150
Trlin, Josh 224, 225
Trotter, Chris 32–33
Tūaropaki Trust 118
Tunoho, Muriel
  activism 18, 22
  Ardern, Jacinda 207, 216
  background 18–19
  collective employment agreements 50–51
  community action/activism 18–19, 21
  Covid-19 pandemic 224
  E tū national conference 216
  forum, local body election 204
  Industrial Areas Foundation (IAF) training 118
  Living Wage Hutt Valley **135**, 145, 192, **223**
  Living Wage Movement Aotearoa NZ branding 25
  living wage rate announcement **58**
  London, visit to 19–20
  Wellington living wage network 39–40

Unasa, Uesifili 27, 28, 33, 39, 47, **58**
Unga, Teisa 212, 224
unionism
  activism 22, 23, 36
  community relationships 38–39, 61
  compulsory unionism 23, 44, 108
  Employment Contracts Act 1991, effects of 14–15, 74–75, 108–09, 225
  impact of Living Wage Movement 61, 96–97, 186, 226–27, 230
  living wage detractors/opposition 62
  membership levels 13, 14, 36, 225
  organising model 14, 22, 26, 62, 48, 86
  power/lack of power 14, 48, 225, 227
  relational approach 61, 96–97, 111, 227, 230
  relationships between communities, faith groups and unions 22, 48–51, 61, 62, 83, 85–87, 96–97, 111–12, 187, 225, 227–28
  servicing model 14
  transactional approach 61, 89, 96–97, 186, 227, 230
  union organisers 19, 24, 62, 80, 110, 114, 125, 134, 158, 161, 210
  voluntary unionism 13
unions, trade
  Association of University Staff of New Zealand 44
  Community Services Union 18–19
  Engineering, Printing and Manufacturing Union (EPMU) 74, 75, 76, 103, 124
  Finance, Industrial (Textile and Wood) Retail, Stores and Transport Union 44, 45, 97, 185–87, 212, 227
  Finance Sector Union (Finsec) 43, 44, 114, 186
  Hotel and Hospital Workers Union 16, 17, 23, 110
  New Zealand Clerical Workers Union 75
  New Zealand Council of Trade Unions Te Kauae Kaimah (NZCTU) **28**, 45, 82–83, 186, 226
  New Zealand Nurses Organisation 113, 174, 204
  Public Service Association Te Pūkenga Here Tikanga Mahi 45, 74, 76, 103, 125, 148, **174**, 191, 199, 227
  Service Workers Union of Aotearoa 14–15

INDEX

Tertiary Education Union – Te Hautū Kahurangi 27, 48, 66, 102, 108, 109, 134, 169, **201**, 221, 227
Transport and General Workers Union 20
UNISON (public sector union) 19–20, 35
  see also E tū (union); Service and Food Workers Union (SFWU)
UNISON (public sector union) 19–20, 35
Unitarian Church 45
United Kingdom *see* Great Britain
United Neighborhoods Organization 87
United States of America (USA)
  living wage campaigns/movements 36
  New York visit by Annie Newman 36
  United Neighborhoods Organization 87
  see also Industrial Areas Foundation (IAF)

Vector (power company) 164, 218
Vernon, Blair 177, 198, 216–18, **217**
Victoria University of Wellington Students' Association (VUWSA) 45, 49, 80, 84, 103
Victoria University of Wellington Te Herenga Waka
  Campus Care 222
  cleaners 7, 108, 124, 151, 158, 193–94, **195**, 206, 219, 221–23
  forums 118, 193, 222
  Living Wage Day 157–58, **157**, 193, 222, **VII**
  Living Wage for Vic 102, 103, 104, 108, 109, 118, 124, 132, 134, 187, 193, 221–23
  Omer, Ibrahim 90, 219
  Ryall, John 16
  Salient (student newspaper) 16, 193

student volunteer army 208–10
Tertiary Education Union – Te Hautū Kahurangi 109, 169
Vincente-Angeles, Jo 212
voluntary unionism 13
volunteers/volunteering 64–65, 111, 208–10

Wade-Brown, Celia
  background/early life 43
  living wage for council workers 41, 42–43, 44, 66–67, 68, 70–71, 81, 89, 98, 114, 126, 129, 173, 176
  Living Wage Wellington launch 41, 42–43
  mayoral elections 125, 144
wage levels *see* pay rates/wage levels
Wagstaff, Richard 134, 226
Waitangi Day 110
Waldegrave, Charles 46–47, 55, 56, **57**, 61, 82, 94, 95, 169, 170–71, 210, 226
Waldren, Gwilym 169, 219
Walker, Wendy 146–47, 191, 225
Wallace, Ray 145, 157, 170–72, 178–79, 190, 192, 204
Ward-Lealand, Jennifer 95
Warehouse, The (retail business) 76–77
We Shall Not Be Moved (protest song) 42
Wellington Cathedral of St Paul 102, 112–13, 160, 161, 199
Wellington Chamber of Commerce 67, 72, 73–74, 85, 115, 125, 130–31, 137, 138–39, 147, 177
Wellington City Council
  cleaners 153–54, 169, **196**
  contracted workers 73–74, 97–98, 99–100, 114–16, 127, 129, 144, 154, 178
  Lavery, Kevin 73–74, 82, 127, 128, 130, 136, 137, 138, 175, 177
  living wage accreditation 118, 168, 174–75, **175**, 176, 200–201

273

living wage for council workers (campaign) 41, 42–43, 44, 66–68, **69**, 70–72, 73–74, 97–98
living wage for council workers (implementation/delay) 73–74, 77, 85, 91, 93, 97, 113–16, 125–31, 140, 147, 153–54, 170, 173, 174, 201
living wage rate announcement 95–96
long-term plans 91, 98, 111, 112, 113–16, 118
My Life To Live (exhibition) 197
parking wardens 91, 97–98, 99–100, 105, 124, 154, 175
security guards 128–29, 130, 136–37, 140–41
see also Foster, Andrew; Lester, Justin; Wade-Brown, Celia
Wellington (Te Whanganui a Tara)
Aro Valley 17
Greater Wellington Regional Council (GWRC) 148–50, **229**
living wage city campaign 67, 68, 72, 97, 147, 189, 203, 208
Newtown 40, 81, 103, 113, 134, 168, 170, 187, 207–08, **209**
Wesley Methodist Church 40, 41, 50, 70, 116, **117**, 143, **201**
see also Hutt Valley; Porirua City; Living Wage Wellington; Parliament, New Zealand; Victoria University of Wellington Te Herenga Waka
Wendt, Alan **69**, 90
Wesley Methodist Church 40, 41, 50, 70, 116, **117**, 143, **201**
Western Springs College 200
West Fest for a Living Wage 99

Westpac 185, 206, 218
Whaitiri, Meka 166
Whānau Day 93, 99, 113, **IV**
Whanganui 103, 153, 187
White, Jolyon 74, **75**, 83, 84, 88, 103
Wilford, Nicki 124
Wilkins, Norman 90, 114, 134, **135**
Williams, Jordan 85, 115, 192
Williams, Lyn 103
Williams, Vera **69**
Wilson, Dorothy **135**
Wilson, Matt 190
Wilson, Ross 190
Winther, Robyn **135**
Wiri Licensing Trust 218
women's rights/equal pay 17, 23, 50, 78, 94, 232
Wood, Michael 164
working hours
cleaners 8, 10, 30, 41–42, 154, 175–76, 222
minimum-wage workers 28, 219
parking wardens 100, 175
security guards 164
single mothers 30, 158
World Refugee Day 194, 198, 199
'Worth It' (campaign) 227
Wrigley, Jo 174
Wyeth, Barbara 28, 29, **79**

Young Christian Students 15–16
Young, Nicola 80, 125
Yukich, Diana 64–65, 77, 82, 84, 93, 94, 98–99, 107–08, 111, 131, 142, 216

Zealandia (wildlife sanctuary) 189–90
Zhuang, Shirley 83–84
Zwaan, Rick 49, **69**, 88, 90, 103

Published by Otago University Press
Te Whare Tā o Te Wānanga o Ōtākou
533 Castle Street
Dunedin, New Zealand
university.press@otago.ac.nz
www.oup.nz

First published 2024
Copyright © Lyndy McIntyre

The moral rights of the author have been asserted.

ISBN 978-1-99-004875-3

A catalogue record for this book is available from the National Library of New Zealand. This book is copyright. Except for the purpose of fair review, no part may be stored or transmitted in any form or by any means, electronic or mechanical, including recording or storage in any information retrieval system, without permission in writing from the publishers. No reproduction may be made, whether by photocopying or by any other means, unless a licence has been obtained from the publisher.

Front cover: Palutea Talofolo came to Aotearoa from Tonga for a better life, 'but a better life needs a living wage'. A cleaner employed by a multi-national contractor, Palu is pictured at the national launch of the Living Wage Movement at St Stephen's Church hall in Ponsonby, Auckland, 23 May 2012. Photo: Simon Oosterman Beckers.

Editor: Imogen Coxhead

Author photo: Mark Coote

Printed in Aotearoa New Zealand by Pivotal